BLAIR'S WARS

Inside Yeltsin's Russia
Robin Cook: The Biography

BLAIR'S WARS

JOHN KAMPFNER

FREE PRESS

First published in Great Britain by The Free Press in 2003
An imprint of Simon & Schuster UK Ltd
A Viacom company

1 3 5 7 9 10 8 6 4 2

Simon & Schuster UK Ltd
Africa House
64–78 Kingsway
London WC2B 6AH

Simon & Schuster Australia
Sydney

www.simonsays.co.uk

A CIP catalogue for this book is available
from the British Library.

ISBN: 0-7432-4829-5

Typeset by M Rules
Printed and bound in Great Britain by
The Bath Press, Bath

To Lucy, Alex and Constance

CONTENTS

PREFACE

It is some feat to go to war five times in six years. That statistic impelled me to write this book. No British Prime Minister and few world leaders come close, and none of these five wars could be defined through the traditional concepts of national interest or repelling an invader. So what is it about Tony Blair that has given him such a taste for the battlefield?

This is the story of a man who came to office in 1997 knowing precious little about foreign affairs, who within a year had defined a new mission for Britain overseas. The idea of humanitarian intervention was developed as he went along. It came awry when confronted by the new realities after the terrorist attacks of 11 September 2001, and by George W. Bush's strategic doctrine of pre-emption and primacy for the United States. As Blair struggled to maintain his authority on the global stage, as his approach unravelled, the mismatch between his ends and his means became ever more stark. This is the story of a man who had convinced himself that his powers of persuasion could overcome all problems and defy all logic – only to see those powers ebb away.

Blair's Wars traces the evolution of the relationship between the Prime Minister and war in three sections. Part I looks at his approach to foreign affairs in opposition and then in Downing Street, taking in his first military conflict, the air strikes against Saddam Hussein in 1998; the Kosovo war a year later and the despatch of British troops to Sierra Leone in 2000.

The second part takes in Blair's response to the rise of the neo-conservatives in the US, the events of September 11, the war in Afghanistan, and the early diplomatic manoeuvres against Iraq, culminating in the passing of Resolution 1441 by the United Nations Security Council. It was during this period that Britain and the US agreed on war. It was during this period that British and American intelligence pointed up the threat posed by Saddam's weapons of mass destruction – a threat they would later struggle to sustain. How much did Blair really know? How accurate was the story he told?

Part III tells the dramatic story of the road to war. It gives an insider's account of the failures in British diplomacy and the tensions at the heart of government. It reveals the extent of the concern in much of Whitehall at the speed with which Blair dismissed the efforts of UN weapons inspectors and embraced the strategy of the White House. After the war, as the reconstruction of Iraq faltered and as evidence of WMD proved elusive, it shows how an increasingly fraught government machine battled to vindicate its approach.

Blair's Wars is the culmination of more than sixty interviews conducted over six months with more than forty people. These include senior ministers, senior advisers and senior civil servants across government – from Downing Street to the Foreign Office to other Whitehall departments and security agencies. These officials were all players in the five military conflicts and the processes that led up to them. Most are still serving in their posts, some are not. My enquiries also led me to senior figures in the US, France, Germany, Russia, the Middle East, the UN and Nato.

The rules of engagement throughout were 'strict background': no attribution that could identify the source. All those who spoke to me know who they are, but I hope they do not know whose company they keep. I am very grateful to them all for speaking to me so candidly on sensitive subjects in obviously difficult circumstances, especially given the events that transpired over the summer of 2003. My publisher and I took the view that, since note numbers in the text would often lead only to references to 'private conversations', we would not encumber the narrative with source notes on each page. All open-source material derives from speeches, newspaper interviews and the like.

When I began the task in January 2003, my intention was to fill a gap in the bibliography of Blair studies – foreign policy. Neither I nor my interlocutors had any idea at the time how sensitive the subject would over the course of the year become. For all the acrimony around the Iraq war, I have sought in this book to play it straight, to tell it as it is, rather than as either the government or its opponents would want it told. As the news story on Iraq developed on a day-to-day basis, I sought to include the salient points, not to follow it slavishly. This is a book as much about the motivation of Tony Blair as his actions.

My thanks go to all those interviewees who gave me their time – sometimes for several hours in one session – and to friends and colleagues who helped fill in the background or pointed me in particular directions.

At the *New Statesman* I received considerable support, notably from Peter Wilby, the Editor; Cristina Odone, the Deputy Editor; and Geoffrey Robinson MP, the owner. Dougal Stenson was always on-hand to provide back-up. For six months I have been lucky to have such an assiduous and talented researcher as Abbie Fielding-Smith.

I am particularly grateful to my agent, Bruce Hunter at David Higham Associates, for encouraging me in the venture and for linking me with Simon & Schuster. I would like to thank Tim Judah for giving me invaluable help on Kosovo and Sierra Leone. I am indebted to several former special advisers who provided insights, including David Mepham, now at the IPPR, Bernard Gray, Andrew Hood and David Clark. The same goes for Professor Lawrence Freedman at King's College, London; Professor Timothy Garton Ash at St Antony's College, Oxford; and Charles Grant and Heather Grabbe at the Centre for European Reform.

Throughout the past six months two close friends and confidants have given me much of their time. Steve Richards at the *Independent on Sunday* and Jonathan Steele at the *Guardian* read through various drafts, providing telling insights and advice page by page. I am forever in their debt. At Simon & Schuster my editor, Andrew Gordon, showed calm when nothing appeared for months, and more calm when it all appeared at the last moment. Working with him has been a pleasure and an inspiration. The publicity side has been managed superbly by Hannah Corbett.

For about three months I turned into the kind of person I vowed never to become – an absent father. For their forbearance and love, I would like to dedicate this book to my wife Lucy Ash, and to our two daughters, Alex and Constance.

JOHN KAMPFNER
August 2003

PART I

HUMANITARIAN WARRIOR

1

TRAVELLING LIGHT

'I AM A BRITISH PATRIOT AND I AM PROUD TO BE A BRITISH patriot. I love my country. I will always put the interests of my country first. The Britain in my vision is not Britain turning its back on the world – narrow, shy, uncertain. It is a Britain confident of its place in the world, sure of itself, able to negotiate with the world and provide leadership in the world.'

Tony Blair had got into his stride. With each page of his speech his delivery became more assured. This was what he believed in. The Conservative government, he said, was guilty of 'presiding over the largest reduction in our military capability since the war'. John Major's 'negative' vision had damaged transatlantic ties. His years in power were synonymous with national decline, weakness and uncertainty over Britain's place in the world. New Labour would not make the same mistake. 'Century upon century it has been the destiny of Britain to lead other nations,' the Prime Minister-in-waiting proclaimed to his handpicked audience. 'That should not be a destiny that is part of our history. It should be part of our future. We are a leader of nations or nothing.'

Bridgewater Hall, Manchester, 21 April 1997. This was Blair's only speech on foreign policy in the General Election campaign. Labour's pledge cards had been issued. The messages on public services, on the economy and on Europe had been carefully crafted. Governments across the world were now curious to know what this new visionary had to say about problems further afield. Their ambassadors to the Court of St James travelled eagerly to the northwest even at the risk of appearing as extras in another New Labour public relations triumph. It had been hard for Blair's aides to convince him to engage in foreign policy – he saw it as a distraction from what he called the real issues of the campaign.

The speech he delivered in Manchester that day bore little resemblance to the Labour manifesto he had launched two weeks earlier, in which the party pledged to be a force for good in the world. There was no mention of controlling the arms trade, let alone of setting up a defence diversification agency to shift weapons production to goods for civilian use. Third World poverty was skated over. Blair's right-hand man, Jonathan Powell, a diplomat wooed back from the British Embassy in Washington, had asked party officials for contributions to the speech. Labour's foreign policy commission was entrusted with setting out an agenda for the next five years. Its officials sent Powell a draft emphasising the importance of development and humanitarianism. He rejected it. Robin Cook, shadow Foreign Secretary and head of the commission, was aghast when he read the final version. The only success they had was to convince Blair, minutes before he was due to give the speech, to excise a line written by Powell which proclaimed: 'I am proud of the British Empire.'

Blair was not shy about Britain's past military glories. He was particularly pleased with one Labour party election broadcast, which featured a British bulldog. This was just the message he wanted to project. But the image-makers faced a technical problem, or rather a problem of taste: the dog's testicles occupied too much of the screen, and had to be airbrushed out.

Four months before the election Blair had had another

showdown with Cook. The two had been waiting in an anteroom just off the main hall of Labour's media centre in Millbank Tower. They were preparing the presentation of the policy commission's report, 'Britain and the World'. Peter Mandelson was also there, hovering. The two close friends discussed whether it was necessary to raise the issue of Trident – opposition to Britain's nuclear deterrent had been one of the left's talismanic issues of the 1980s. Blair and Mandelson agreed that one journalist would be encouraged to raise the question during the press conference. Cook objected, arguing that this would detract from the more positive proposals contained in a report that had taken years to compile. 'That is what I'm going to do,' Blair told him tersely. Sure enough, in question number three, Blair was asked if he was prepared to launch a nuclear strike. 'Yes,' he replied. The next day's headlines were 'I WILL PRESS THE BUTTON – BLAIR'. There was barely a mention of Labour's other foreign policy commitments. Mission accomplished.

Ever since becoming party leader in 1994, Blair had sought to 'close down' foreign policy as a contentious issue. Labour had form. It was still seen in many voters' eyes as the unilateralist party that was 'weak on defence'. Blair wanted to move on, to stress that any government under him would be tough. It would fight when needed.

The pillars of Labour's 1980s internationalism – unilateral nuclear disarmament, hostility to American foreign policy and withdrawal from the European Community – meant nothing to Blair. It wasn't that he was actively pushing a different line at party meetings; he just didn't engage in these issues at all. One friend who remembered Blair and his wife Cherie at the Hackney South Labour Party recalls: 'We talked an awful lot of politics in those days, but I can't remember him talking about foreign affairs at all.'

Blair's first real experience of the popular mood had come in May 1982, when he was selected as Labour's candidate in a by-election in the staunchly Conservative seat of Beaconsfield in Buckinghamshire. As Blair hit the stump, British troops were landing in the Falklands to force out the Argentine invaders. Blair showed early signs of 'Third Way-ism', supporting the dispatch of the task force, but adding: 'At the same time I want a negotiated settlement and I believe that given the starkness of the military option we need to compromise on certain things. I don't think that ultimately the wishes of the Falkland islanders must determine our position.' For that he was harangued in papers like the *Daily Telegraph* as just another dangerously anti-patriotic left-winger. This, after all, was a former member of CND who at Fettes public school had opted to do community work rather than join the Combined Cadet Force.

On other foreign policy issues Blair fastidiously toed the party line as set out by his leader, Michael Foot. 'We'll negotiate withdrawal from the EEC, which has drained our natural resources and destroyed jobs,' he said in his personal manifesto. The young candidate knew he was never going to win in a constituency like this. But even so, the reception at the doorstep shocked him. This would be a seminal experience. Blair commented to a friend that he had been 'turned over', that he had been forced to realise that 'wars seem to make Prime Ministers popular'. Labour were beaten into third place. Its share of the vote collapsed, and Blair lost his deposit. But he believed he had been taught a valuable lesson. Significantly, it had come in foreign policy.

A year later, Blair was selected for the safe seat of Sedgefield in County Durham. Curiously for a privately educated, London-based lawyer, he felt more at home in this predominantly working-class cluster of small towns and former mining villages. The people there seemed to have concerns more in tune with his. 'The experience of being a north-east MP turned him into the politician he became,' says a friend active with him at the time. 'He was never very interested in the passions of the post-'68 London crowd. He was driven by the feeling that the language of the Labour Party then had nothing to do with working people. The only thing that mattered to him was getting the party elected.' The talk in the pubs, clubs and local party committee meetings was not of Britain's

nuclear deterrent, the collapse of Communism or the fate of the
Middle East.

As Labour – first under Neil Kinnock and then John Smith –
divested itself of the old shibboleths of unilateralism and hostility to
Europe, Blair grew a little more confident in talking about foreign
affairs. But on all the big international issues of the late 1980s and
early and mid-1990s he played it safe. His comments on arms sales
and human rights did not extend beyond generalities.

Many of his colleagues, however, had taken up these causes.
The gassing of Kurds at Halabja in March 1988 by Saddam Hussein's
forces exercised a large number of Labour MPs. Eight parliamentary
motions were tabled condemning it. If Blair had joined his colleagues, he would have been in the company of the likes of George
Robertson, Paul Murphy, Ian McCartney, Mo Mowlam, Chris Smith
and Harriet Harman, all of whom were later to serve in his Cabinet.
Other motions condemned the British and American governments
for supplying Saddam with chemical weapons. One called for the
immediate termination of all financial aid to the Iraqi government,
including a £340 million export credit guarantee signed a month
after Halabja.

One signatory was Ann Clwyd. From the late 1980s onwards
she became an ardent advocate of the Kurdish cause. Her attempts
to highlight their suffering at the hands of Saddam were distinctly
unfashionable. In April 1995 she was sacked as shadow Spokes-
woman for Overseas Development for going to Turkey and
northern Iraq without permission, and missing an important
Commons vote on Europe. She was the first person Blair dismissed
as party leader.

The extent of the Conservative government's complicity in
arming Saddam from the start of Iraq's war with Iran in 1980 until
the end of that decade only really came to light during the dog-days
of the Major regime. Alan Clark, the former trade minister, admitted during the trial of the Matrix Churchill executives accused of
breaking the arms embargo against Iraq that the government had

secretly relaxed the rules and should have known all along that the equipment was not intended for peaceful purposes. Major responded to the uproar by setting up a public inquiry led by Sir Richard Scott, a judge of the Court of Appeal. The hearings began in 1993. They made for gripping theatre, with Tory ministers subjected to fierce cross-questioning. Robin Cook, who was in charge of the operation for Labour, attended the sessions most days. He pared the issue down to a simple charge: 'Britain armed Saddam Hussein. Ministers engineered a cover-up and were prepared to let three men go to jail for doing no more than what ministers had agreed they should do.'

When Scott finally published his report in February 1996, Cook was given just two hours to read it before speaking in the Commons debate. He then demolished the Conservatives. Blair thanked Cook for his parliamentary *tour de force*. He was grateful for a performance that had nearly brought down John Major's government. He dwelt less on the principle at stake – the duplicitous behaviour of British and American governments that had armed Saddam before, during and after his gassing of civilians.

When Blair swept into Downing Street on 2 May 1997, past the carefully choreographed lines of well-wishers, he was taking charge of Britain's role in the world with less foreign policy knowledge or experience than almost any incoming Prime Minister since the Second World War. He had not served on any parliamentary committee on foreign affairs and, prior to his Manchester address, was not known to have made a single significant speech on global issues. He spoke serviceable French – an achievement in itself for Britain's linguistically challenged parliamentarians – and had a typical British middle-class knowledge of France and Italy. But overall he was not particularly well-travelled. In his decade in parliament before becoming party leader he had not signed a single parliamentary motion on the Kurds, the first Gulf War in 1991 or the disintegration of Yugoslavia. He had travelled light.

Much of his inner circle knew – and cared – as little as he did about 'foreign'. Alastair Campbell, his head of communications, brought with him a tabloid view of political priorities that rarely ventured away from domestic issues. Anji Hunter, Blair's friend and gatekeeper whom he had known since school, saw as part of her role the need to convey the prevailing view from the Home Counties. Since Blair's election as party leader both Campbell and Hunter had been focused on one goal alone: making Labour credible, electable and unthreatening to Middle England. It was the job of Jonathan Powell, the new chief of staff, to deal with foreign affairs. He had clear views of his own and Blair saw no need to question them. For all those around Blair, the bottom line was defence. When Blair was working on a draft of a new Clause Four for the Labour Party, Mandelson saw that there was no reference to defence. He is said to have scribbled on one version: 'Won't TB fight wars?'

Powell first met Blair when he was tasked to show him and Gordon Brown around Washington, and to introduce them to key figures on Capitol Hill. They instantly warmed to each other and early in 1995 Blair asked him to join his team. By this point Powell had acquired close contacts inside the new Democratic administration. One of the traditional tasks of the First Secretary at the embassy is to follow the campaign trails of the main candidates during US elections. In the 1992 contest, Powell spent considerable time with Bill Clinton's camp as well as that of the Republican incumbent, George Bush senior. Powell described to friends the Clinton operation as 'awesome'. In his small room at the House of Commons, next to Blair's, he proudly displayed memorabilia from the Clinton campaign – posters, coffee mugs, signed photographs.

These were heady days. Blair too was fascinated by the Clinton phenomenon, the marriage of centre-left politics with electoral success, by the idea of triangulation – identifying the two traditional conflicting views of an argument and placing oneself in the middle of them. Fresh from the humiliation of Neil Kinnock's second General Election defeat in April 1992, Philip Gould, Blair's behind-

the-scenes strategist, spent time in the US learning the arts of the
Clinton campaign.

As leader of the opposition, Blair was required as a matter of
etiquette to meet foreign dignitaries if they requested it. Senior party
figures at the time recall how he would agree to do so, but how his
mind was rarely on the ensuing conversations. On one occasion
Blair was talking to a delegation from South-East Asia but forgot
exactly where they were from. His visitors did most of the talking,
and for the first fifteen minutes he chipped in with the occasional 'In
your country . . .' He avoided any embarrassment with a consum-
mate piece of improvisation. It taught him a lesson about the
importance of detail.

With the Major government in its death throes, Powell organised a series of discreet meetings to talk Blair through the finer
points of diplomacy and to go through the global hot-spots one by
one. Several gatherings were held over coffee in the front room of
the Blairs' house in Islington. In each, around half a dozen eminent
former diplomats and academics were invited to give their views.
The only condition was strict secrecy. Among the great and the good
were Sir David Hannay, former ambassador to the United Nations;
Sir Robin Renwick, former ambassador to Washington; Sir Rodric
Braithwaite, once our man in Moscow, who also spent time as
Major's adviser at Number 10; Sir Michael Butler; Sir Nicholas
Henderson; Raymond Seitz, who had just stood down as the
US ambassador to London; Timothy Garton Ash, fellow of St
Antony's College, Oxford; and Lawrence Freedman, Professor of
War Studies at King's College, London. This was the orthodox view
of the mandarins. Blair, given his inexperience, was in no position to
challenge it.

One of the participants recalls: 'The thing that attracted me
about Blair was his intelligence and willingness to listen. The thing
that alarmed me was his almost complete lack of knowledge of
detail.' Another says: 'Blair was educating himself. He was listening.
He gave no impression of having a foreign policy philosophy worked

out. His aim was to ensure that foreign affairs didn't become an election issue.'

Once in Downing Street, Blair was careful to stick to prevailing orthodoxies. The Foreign Office had had decades of experience in moulding ministers to its image. But an entire generation of diplomats had never worked with a Labour government. Still, they were eager to move on and to help the new Prime Minister establish a more central role for Britain in Europe. They knew that such was the scale of the election victory, such was his novelty value and such was Blair's charisma that he would instantly command the attention of other world leaders.

Blair was happy to rely on a close-knit team of advisers in Downing Street – all seconded from the Foreign and Commonwealth Office (FCO). The mandarins were eager to impress their thoughts upon him. One of their central concerns was to restore the so-called 'special relationship' with Washington. British concern at nurturing good relations with the US had been an obsession in Downing Street since Winston Churchill first started writing long letters to Franklin Roosevelt in 1940. The relationship had endured several cyclical downturns, most famously Anthony Eden's falling-out with Dwight Eisenhower over Suez and Harold Wilson's refusal of Lyndon Johnson's request to send British troops to Vietnam.

Then came Major and Clinton. They had never hit it off since revelations that the then Prime Minister had sent people to Washington to help the Republican campaign in 1992. In July 1994, on one of his first visits to Europe as President, Clinton stood alongside Chancellor Helmut Kohl at the Brandenburg Gate and made it clear the US now looked to the new united Germany as the pivot of a new united Europe. Echoing John F. Kennedy thirty years earlier, Clinton declared: '*Nichts wird uns aufhalten. Alles ist möglich. Berlin ist frei*' ('Nothing will stop us. Everything is possible. Berlin is free'). In London, the Foreign Office was alarmed. But with a Conservative government in turmoil over Europe, there was little the diplomats could do. Relations deteriorated further as Clinton and Major clashed frequently and furiously over Bosnia and Northern Ireland.

The FCO was keen that Blair and Clinton rejuvenate the Anglo-American relationship. They were preaching to the converted. The two had met several times before Blair's election victory, but their first meeting in Downing Street, on 29 May 1997, set the tone for the two men in office. Clinton was the first US President to be invited to address the British Cabinet since Richard Nixon in 1969. Alone, the pair discussed Ulster, the withdrawal of Nato peacekeepers from Bosnia and the imminent handover of Hong Kong. But they also spent time comparing notes on their domestic agendas, discussing election strategies and just 'shooting the breeze'. Inside the building they were called the 'kindred spirits'. Outside, as sunny skies shone down on the garden of 10 Downing Street, they had the perfect backdrop for their first press conference together. Clinton knew how to press the right buttons. He spoke of the 'unspeakably beautiful British spring'. He paid homage to his host and said he would like to learn how to acquire for himself a 179-seat majority. He joked that Blair wasn't his clone. 'I'm sick of it, because he's seven years younger than I am and has no grey hair.' He then went into serious mode. Recalling the 'unique partnership' between the US and UK, he said: 'Over the last fifty years our unbreakable alliance has helped to bring unparalleled peace and prosperity and security. It's an alliance based on shared values and common aspirations.'

Clinton had another message for Blair that the Prime Minister was happy to hear. British influence in Washington would in future depend largely on British influence across Europe. Henry Kissinger's comment that he could not consult Europe because 'Europe has no phone number' would now have to be rectified. But it went further than that. Prime Minister and President also had a domestic agenda they wanted to share with the rest of the world: the Third Way, or 'progressive politics', 'modernisation', 'progressive internationalism' – it came with many labels as they tried to put flesh on the broad idea of remaking centre-left politics. Their Third Way roadshow would take like-minded politicians and thinkers to Washington, Florence, Berlin and New York.

Blair's own European odyssey as Prime Minister began on 6 June in the southern Swedish port of Malmö, at the Congress of European Socialists. Blair told them the institutions they were constructing were 'impossibly remote' from the people. He asked rhetorically: 'Am I satisfied with Europe? Frankly, no.' 'Modernise or die,' he told them starkly. Blair's willingness to sermonise, so soon after joining the elite club of European leaders, ruffled the feathers of his more experienced counterparts, notably Lionel Jospin of France, who had also only just been elected but whose views on social democracy were lodged very firmly in the traditional continental European mould. Blair was confident that others in the room would eventually come round to his view. His hopes were invested most in Gerhard Schröder, the leader of the German Social Democrats, who was also seen as a 'moderniser' ready to bring his party back in from the wilderness.

Blair's behaviour that day was put down to exuberance. But it left a mark. European leaders and diplomats would later recall it as the first sign of a British Prime Minister given to hubris, of a man who wanted to use the political stage as a pulpit and who was convinced that he possessed extraordinary powers of persuasion.

In those first months of summer in 1997 Blair was indulged like a prodigal son. The sight of a Prime Minister just trying to get along with other European leaders was remarkable in itself. Blair's first EU outing was at the Amsterdam summit in June. Two photo opportunities with accompanying prepared soundbites were engineered for him. The traditional 'family photograph' of the leaders of the fifteen, on a canal bridge, ensured that he was centre-stage. Then the mayor of the city gave each of them shiny new seven-speed bicycles. After a warning not to get caught in the tram tracks, Blair made the fastest start, and sped ahead. The Prime Minister, who had earlier called for a 'change in gear' to bring Europe closer to its citizens, was among the first to cross the finishing line – together with the Dutch and Austrian leaders. Some of the more portly members of the club, such as Germany's Chancellor Helmut Kohl, declined the invitation to mount their bikes. The headlines in British newspapers read: 'BLAIR LEADS FROM THE FRONT'. Amsterdam gave Blair his first taste of the big stage, and he relished it.

Unless it was a big set-piece event, however, it was difficult for Powell to get foreign policy dates in Blair's diary. Every foreign bid had to go into the 'mix' – even visiting prime ministers. 'During our meetings Alastair would impersonate a quiz-show host and go "bzzz" every time Jonathan mentioned something foreign, and suggest they move on,' says one member of the team. 'It wasn't seen as a priority. It wasn't one of our key pledges. But Jonathan persevered.'

A similar pattern emerged in Blair's Cabinet meetings. The weekly Thursday gatherings were short and to the point. Rarely did they venture away from the domestic agenda. When they did, they would begin with brief presentations from either Cook or from George Robertson, the Defence Secretary, followed by a few cursory and polite questions and a reminder from Blair for everyone around the table to adhere to 'the line'. Members of the Cabinet cannot recall in-depth discussions about Europe, the Middle East, Saddam or the Balkans – anything at all, in fact. 'At no stage over those first four years did we have a single Cabinet discussion about the principles, or conduct, of foreign policy,' recalls one Cabinet member at the time. 'There was nothing about the justification or otherwise of going to war in any of our wars, nothing about the role of the United Nations, nothing about the special relationship with the US.'

Across the road from Downing Street, in the grandeur of the Foreign Office, Robin Cook was pursuing a foreign policy of his own. It began on 12 May with a fanfare, his mission statement, in which he promised to put human rights at the top of his agenda. He described his main aims as 'making the UK a leading player in Europe; strengthening the Commonwealth and securing reform for a more effective UN'. There was no mention of relations with the United States. Britain, Cook proclaimed, would 'once again be a force for good in the world'. He called for a new ethical dimension to foreign policy. As they spun the speech to journalists, Cook's aides shortened that term to an 'ethical foreign policy'.

The statement had been cleared with Downing Street, but not the spin. When Powell heard what they were doing, he shouted to his colleagues in Number 10, 'What a load of crap!' Blair was prepared to give Cook some latitude, but as soon as the Foreign Secretary tried to guide policy towards a leftist interpretation of human rights and antipathy towards arms sales, Blair was advised by his two senior aides, Powell and John Holmes, his principal private secretary, to rein him in. Blair agreed. This was not a strategy he was comfortable with.

In opposition, Cook had pledged that a Labour government would 'not license the export of arms to any regime that will use them for internal oppression or external aggression'. One specific problem loomed straight away in office – the sale to Indonesia of sixteen Hawk training aircraft, armoured cars and water-cannons signed in 1996 by the outgoing Tory government. By the time of the election the Indonesian air force had already taken delivery of a previous consignment of forty Hawks made by BAE Systems, Britain's largest weapons manufacturer. The UK had become the largest supplier of arms to the Indonesian dictatorship of President Suharto, despite its illegal occupation of and its human rights abuses in East Timor and elsewhere. The legal advice the new government received was unclear, but Britain was under pressure to honour the deal. Blair and Cook agreed that it should go ahead, but the timing was designed to coincide with the announcement of a new set of criteria for arms sales in general.

From his first day in office Blair was eager not to antagonise British arms companies, and BAE Systems in particular, which

developed extremely close relationships with senior figures in
Downing Street. Its Chairman, Dick Evans, was one of a very small
group of outsiders whose requests to see Blair were always granted.
Blair saw the whole issue as a policy diversion. 'It was a rod for our
back,' says one key adviser. 'We were asking ourselves to be judged by
impossible standards.' Blair was unhappy with the final draft of
Cook's new arms criteria. Holmes went through it with officials
from Cook's private office line by line for four hours, ordering them
to tone down various clauses. When Cook and Blair met on 25 July,
the last working day before the announcement, it was largely a one-
way conversation. Blair inevitably prevailed, but two months later
the issue and the acrimony resurfaced. At the end of September, on
the eve of the party conference, Cook told the *Guardian* he had
blocked two contracts to supply Indonesia with sniper rifles and
armoured troop-carriers worth up to £1 million. Downing Street
knew nothing about it and Blair was furious: this was just the sort of
gesture politics he could not abide. Powell let it be known he was
'extremely pissed off'. Holmes fired off official memoranda to the
Foreign Office demanding to see all documents relating to the
decision.

On 11 November Blair gave the first definitive statement of
his priorities – as opposed to Cook's. The Lord Mayor's banquet is
traditionally an occasion for foreign policy pronouncements.
Almost all the press focus at the time was on what Blair would say
about the Euro, after he and Gordon Brown, the Chancellor of the
Exchequer, had sent out damaging mixed messages on the single
currency. When he came to the broader international scene, Blair
trod a traditional foreign office line. His words would not have sat
uncomfortably with Margaret Thatcher. He urged people to stop
wringing their hands over Britain's imperial past and use the valuable connections it had provided in terms of the Commonwealth
and the English language. 'When Britain and America work together
on the international scene there is little we cannot achieve,' he said.
'Our aim should be to deepen our relationship with the US at all

levels. We are the bridge between the US and Europe – let us use it. By virtue of our geography, our history and the strengths of our people, Britain is a global player. We need strong defence . . . It is an instrument of influence . . . We must not reduce our capability to exercise a role on the international stage.'

What he was lacking in terms of experience and detailed knowledge, Blair was compensating for in ambition. He saw the John Major era, of distancing itself from many of the world's problems, as an aberration in British history. As Blair asserted to the distinguished guests at the Guildhall, post-colonial Britain still had a global role. To maintain it, he would rely on the two traditional pillars of the armed forces and the 'special relationship' with the US. The man who had travelled light into Downing Street was determined to show that he – a Labour Prime Minister – could, and would, do wars. If Winston Churchill and Margaret Thatcher could do them, so could he.

2

Fox in the Desert

ON 27 FEBRUARY 1991, SEVEN MONTHS AFTER THE IRAQI invasion, General 'Stormin" Norman Schwarzkopf of the US Army liberated Kuwait. President George Bush senior announced a cease-fire.

A six-week aerial bombardment had seen 85,000 tonnes of allied bombs dropped on Iraqi positions. A combined land, air and sea assault had overwhelmed the Iraqi army within a hundred hours. Iraq's armed forces, the fourth largest in the world, had been reduced to a wreck. UN estimates for Iraqi military casualties ranged from 50,000 to 120,000. Up to 15,000 civilians were killed in the fighting and at least twice that number died in uprisings and other violence that followed the end of the war. By contrast, the allies had lost fewer than 400 soldiers.

Operation Desert Storm had been a resounding success. As victory was declared, Bush met his War Cabinet in the Oval Office. The men around the table included General Colin Powell, Chairman of the Joint Chiefs of Staff, and Dick Cheney, Secretary of Defense. Another present was Paul Wolfowitz, Under-Secretary for Policy at the Pentagon. They agreed that their objectives had been met.

Schwarzkopf also agreed. There was never any doubt in Bush's mind that the war had to end. US and allied troops had completed their mission and would soon be demobilised. The decision was taken not to go into Iraq itself and topple Saddam Hussein – a decision many of them would later sorely regret.

American hopes of engineering the downfall of the Iraqi leader by other means came to nothing. Within weeks of the end of the war, uprisings by the Kurdish minority in the north and by Shias in the south, encouraged by the US, had been brutally put down by Saddam's forces. The allies hurriedly declared safe havens for the Kurds, to be policed by a 'no-fly zone'. The same was later declared for the Shias. American and British planes would enforce them.

The UN enshrined the terms of the victory on 3 April. It built in an added requirement. Under Resolution 687, economic sanctions would be imposed on Iraq until it could prove that it had got rid of its chemical weapons, such as those used in Halabja, and until it had shown that it did not possess a biological arsenal and was not developing its own nuclear capability. The UN gave Saddam fifteen days to hand over the information, which would then be verified by a team of inspectors – the UN Special Commission to Oversee the Destruction of Iraq's Weapons of Mass Destruction (Unscom). The template for more than a decade of tension, hostility and military conflict with Iraq had been established.

Everything had changed on 2 August 1990, the day Saddam sent his forces south to annexe Kuwait. The international community had responded quickly. The UN Security Council passed Resolution 678, permitting member states to 'use all necessary means' to repel the Iraqi invasion – the standard formula for authorising war. The only country to join Cuba was the impoverished Middle Eastern state of Yemen. After its delegate registered his dissent, a senior American diplomat was instructed to tell him, 'That was the most expensive "No" vote you ever cast.' He meant what he said: America immediately cut off more than $70 million in foreign aid to Yemen.

But for the most part, this was American diplomacy at its most effective. Bush and his Secretary of State, James Baker, began the determined but laborious task of assembling an international coalition to fight Saddam. As they built up new alliances and revived old ones, they tried to use the Gulf crisis to craft an entirely new security order for the Middle East. In one sweep, the White House announced it would forget Egypt's massive $7 billion military debt. That sent a powerful message across the region – co-operation pays. Baker later admitted how he had dealt with the Security Council 'in an intricate process of cajoling, extracting, threatening, and occasionally buying votes'.

It worked. Until the invasion of Kuwait, Iraq, Egypt, Jordan and Yemen were united in an economic coalition. Syria had been isolated from much of the Arab world by its support for the government in Tehran during the Iran–Iraq war. Syria became an unlikely new member of the American family. The US looked to Kuwait, Saudi Arabia, Japan, Germany and other states to help finance the military operation. The UN set Saddam a deadline of 15 January 1991 to withdraw. By the time it had passed, Bush had assembled an impressive coalition of twenty-nine countries. Operation Desert Storm was launched with significant international backing.

In the UK, John Major, who had developed a good relationship with Bush, was foursquare behind the US. Britain, as was expected, had sent by far the largest military contingent of all America's allies. The Labour opposition was once again split. The official line was full support. At the party conference of October 1990, delegates had voted seven to one to send in troops, a majority reinforced by the trade union block vote. 'Our forces are engaged in pursuing a legitimate objective and should enjoy full support across the political spectrum,' Neil Kinnock declared. 'Dictators don't withdraw. They have to be defeated.' The Labour leader was well aware after the Falklands experience of the dangers of any sense of equivocation whenever 'our boys' were sent in to battle. But Kinnock's attempts at presenting a united front were undermined in the constituencies and on the parliamentary benches. Clare Short resigned from the shadow team in protest at the war. Two days before Desert Storm was launched, fifty-five Labour MPs voted against.

Throughout the 1990s Iraq was an economic and diplomatic pariah. Tensions would ebb and flow in the no-fly zones. The UN would meet sporadically to review sanctions, with all sides aware, but reluctant to admit, that the embargo was increasingly porous. At the same time, it was causing considerable human suffering – a suffering the British and Americans insisted was the fault of the Iraqi dictator. In 1995, the UN allowed a partial resumption of Iraq's oil exports to buy food and medicine, the so-called 'oil for food' programme. In September 1996, when Major and Clinton ordered air strikes against Saddam in retaliation for Iraqi attacks on Kurdish areas in the north, Blair ordered the shadow Cabinet to support them. He was convinced that Labour had learned the hard way not to oppose military action, that parties seen as 'soft' on defence were punished at the polling station, whatever the merits of the conflict in question.

Once in government, Blair received Foreign Office and intelligence briefings arguing that the policy on Iraq was not working. Public attention was beginning to focus on the suffering of Iraqi civilians, thousands of whom had died from food shortages and a lack of basic medical care. The moral case was being lost. Blair was coming under mild pressure from some Labour MPs – all pressure then was mild – to deal with the humanitarian consequences of sanctions. At the same time the embargo was so leaky that flights were landing at Baghdad airport in direct contravention of UN resolutions. Meanwhile, the French, Russians and other governments were agitating for a resumption of normal trade, while the UN inspectors were being blatantly defied.

Richard Butler, an Australian who had taken over from Rolf Ekeus as the head of the inspections team in July 1997, issued his first report in October of that year. He concluded that Saddam was continuing to hide information on biological arms and withholding some data on chemical weapons. His subsequent reports would accuse the Iraqis of playing cat and mouse, of not allowing his specialists to mount the surprise visits they had been authorised to carry out by the UN.

Blair was clear in his mind that Saddam could not be allowed to get in the inspectors' way. 'It is absolutely essential that he backs down on this, that he be made to back down,' he told MPs. 'If he does not we will simply face this problem, perhaps in a far worse form, in a few years' time.' Those remarks turned out to be prophetic. Blair asked one of the Foreign Office's rising stars, Robert Cooper, for a position paper on weapons of mass destruction (WMD). The Joint Intelligence Committee (JIC), the body that co-ordinates the work of the three main intelligence services – the foreign intelligence agency, SIS; MI5, which handles domestic threats; and GCHQ, the government's listening station – was presenting Blair with increasingly gloomy assessments of the threat posed by Saddam's regime.

Those assessments prompted Blair to confide to Paddy Ashdown, the Liberal Democrat leader, that November: 'I have seen some of the stuff on this. It really is pretty scary. He is very close to some appalling weapons of mass destruction. I don't understand why the French and others don't understand this. We cannot let him get away with it. The world thinks this is just gamesmanship. But it's deadly serious.'

Blair was determined to win the trust of what he called 'the professionals', Britain's military and security chiefs, whom he assumed would be instinctively suspicious of a Labour government. What began as a confidence-building exercise turned into something much more profound. He would talk to his closest aides about his 'huge respect for these guys'. He would privately contrast their expertise with 'amateur' politicians. He got on well with the Chairman of the JIC, Peter Ricketts, but their dealings were correct, nothing more. His relationship with his top military man, however, was extraordinary. General Sir Charles Guthrie became, in Blair's early years, a figure he could depend on. Bluff and charismatic, Guthrie felt similarly respectful of his Prime Minister. He also knew how to work him. It was Guthrie who persuaded him to override the Treasury and provide the first real-terms increase in defence spending since 1985. It was Guthrie who persuaded Blair that the Strategic Defence Review should focus on more flexible and responsive armed forces, capable of moving units quickly to overseas trouble-spots. Much-feared cuts to front-line troops were not made. It was Guthrie who allayed the reservations Blair had early on about using force.

The new US Secretary of State, Madeleine Albright, signalled a hardening of the policy of containment against Iraq. Sanctions would never be lifted, she declared, while Saddam remained in power. Over the years the Americans and British had kept to a three-pronged strategy. They had sought to inspire mutinies and assassination attempts against Saddam, without success. They had relied on economic sanctions and international isolation to keep him in check. When Saddam's defiance of the international community became especially brazen, they deployed air power to 'put him back in his box'.

In Washington a new school of thought was coalescing, mainly in academic circles. The neoconservatives, as they came to be known, saw in the Clinton administration a fundamental abrogation of America's global responsibilities, particularly in the Middle East. One of their leading lights was Paul Wolfowitz, whose experience in the Pentagon at the end of Desert Storm was a defining moment. He was horrified when the US stood by as Saddam's helicopter gunships mowed down the Shias. 'Some might say – and I think I would sympathise with this view – that perhaps if we had delayed the ceasefire by a few more days, we might have got rid of him,' he later told a Congressional hearing.

In 1992, in the last days of the Bush senior administration, Wolfowitz had presided over the writing of a new defence plan to 'set the nation's direction for the next century'. It was a radical departure from anything seen before in official Washington circles. It was based on two principles – US primacy and pre-emptive power. It argued that with demise of the USSR, the US should ensure that no other superpower emerge; that other nations – Germany and Japan were two named – should be discouraged 'from challenging our leadership'; and that the US would be 'postured to act independently when collective action cannot be orchestrated'. The document said the US 'may be faced with the question of whether to take military steps to prevent the development or use of weapons of mass destruction', in other words pre-emptive strikes. It cited hypothetical scenarios of wars for which the military should be prepared. One of them was Iraq. Another was North Korea. It suggested that alliances should be 'ad hoc assemblies, often not lasting beyond the crisis being confronted'.

When a draft was leaked to the *New York Times*, the Pentagon was forced on to the back foot, calling it a 'low-level' document and professing that Cheney had not seen it. That claim was put into perspective when Cheney and Wolfowitz released a final version of the blueprint hours before Bush left the White House.

In the Clinton years, Wolfowitz used his perch at the Johns Hopkins School of Advanced International Studies as a test-bed for a new conservative world vision. By 1997, as Clinton's second term became mired in controversy, he and like-minded souls formalised themselves into a group called Project for the New American Century. Its members would later become a veritable who's who of George W. Bush's administration: Elliott Abrams, Richard Perle, Douglas Feith and . . . Donald Rumsfeld.

Theirs was a curious combination of optimism and pessimism. Their ideology had it that the world was a dangerous place, that civilisation was hanging by a thread. At the same time the US was endowed by Providence with the power to make the world better if only it would take the risks of leadership – if only it were sufficiently 'forward-leaning'. They spoke of 'full-spectrum dominance' and of a world in which each nation's relationship with the US would be the most important. The US writ would run everywhere, supported by a ring of American bases. 'After Baghdad, Beijing' ran one boast. They saw especially in the Middle East a web of corrupt dictators, whose people would, if given the chance, embrace a Jeffersonian view of democracy. Iraq was top of the list. They saw in Israel the role model for the region.

The ideological standard-bearer was William Kristol's *Weekly Standard* magazine. In December 1997, as the Iraqis continued to frustrate Unscom, Kristol devoted one edition to a 'Saddam must go – a how-to guide'. Wolfowitz co-authored one of the articles in which he pondered whether Clinton's most important foreign policy legacy would be to have let 'this tyrant get stronger'. A month later, on the eve of Clinton's State of the Union speech, Wolfowitz drew up an open letter to the President on Iraq. The eighteen signatories included Rumsfeld and Perle, who went on to become Chairman of the Defense Policy Board at the Pentagon. 'We are writing to you because we are convinced that current American policy towards Iraq is not succeeding, and that we may soon face a threat in the Middle East more serious than any we have known since the end of the Cold War,' he wrote. 'We urge you to seize that opportunity, to enunciate a new strategy that would secure the interests of the US and our friends and allies around the world. That strategy should aim, above all, at the removal of Saddam Hussein's regime from power.' The letter concluded: 'American policy cannot continue to be crippled by a misguided insistence on unanimity in the UN Security Council.'

One man, an Iraqi, played a pivotal role in the neoconservatives' campaign. Ahmed Chalabi, a Shia Muslim born in 1945 to a wealthy banking family, left his home country in 1956. He lived mainly in the US and London, establishing an exile group called the Iraqi National Congress. In the mid-1990s he tried to organise an uprising in Kurdish-controlled northern Iraq. The venture ended in failure, with hundreds of deaths. Soon after, the INC was routed from northern Iraq. A number of party officials were executed and others – including Chalabi – fled. He became a seasoned lobbyist on the Washington circuit, and his vocal opposition to Saddam made him a favourite son of the Republican right. Wolfowitz urged Clinton to recognise a provisional government headed by the INC under Chalabi.

Clinton refused. His aides in the White House saw the 'neo-cons' as a voluble but largely peripheral lobby group that needed to be humoured. 'They were not a force to be reckoned with,' recalls one senior administration figure. 'The National Security team would invite them in from time to time. We saw them as a problem that had to be managed.'

But from early 1998, the President was fighting for his political life. Iraq was one area where he had no intention of taking on an increasingly assertive and hostile Congress. Clinton was coming under pressure to launch a new round of air strikes. Blair was worried. He did not want to go into his first military venture lightly. He called the President several times to suggest that he give the process more time. Clinton's determination to move against Saddam coincided with the start of revelations about his liaison with Monica Lewinsky. What began in January as a piece of Internet muckraking would within weeks entangle the forty-second US President in one of the most damaging scandals of modern times. As Blair made his first official visit to Washington on 4 February, Clinton was desperately trying to fend off a media frenzy. Blair took a strategic decision. He gave his host a bear hug, describing him as 'someone I can rely upon, a man I am proud to call not just a colleague but a friend'.

Two weeks later, the UN Secretary-General, Kofi Annan, went to Baghdad in a last-ditch attempt to convince Saddam that any further failure to comply with UN resolutions would lead to military reprisals. After a three-hour meeting with the Iraqi leader, he received that assurance, and Clinton and Blair were both relieved that he had. But Clinton was now locked into a strategy. Having threatened attacks before Annan's visit, he would have no choice if Saddam's assurances proved worthless. Relations between the Iraqi government and the UN inspectors did not improve. Richard Butler became involved in open confrontation with Saddam's regime. Time and again his team of inspectors was prevented from entering sus- pected weapons sites – in front of television cameras. Saddam accused Unscom of using their UN status as cover for spying on his government. (Later, the Clinton administration admitted that the US had indeed received intelligence information about Iraq from the inspectors.) The fear in Washington and London was that the inspectors were becoming part of the problem and were not finding Saddam's stores of chemical and biological weapons. Blair, Clinton and Jacques Chirac, the French President, held a series of three-way telephone calls to try to find a way round the impasse. At home, however, Clinton's authority was collapsing. Impeachment pro- ceedings were looming.

On 7 August, terrorists struck US embassies in Kenya and Tanzania. Some 224 people were killed in the biggest attacks yet on US targets overseas. US intelligence quickly pointed the finger at a shadowy terrorist group, al-Qaeda, which had been operating in small cells and targeting American sites around the world. Al-Qaeda had been operating from bases in Sudan, with support from the Taleban regime in Afghanistan. On 19 August, Clinton authorised military strikes on Kabul and Khartoum. He announced to the American people:

> The United States launched an attack this morning on one of the most active terrorist bases in the world. It is located in Afghanistan and operated by groups affiliated with Osama bin Laden, a network not sponsored by any state, but as dangerous as any we face. We also struck a chemical weapons-related facility in Sudan. Our target was the terrorists' base of operation and infrastructure. Our objective was to damage their capacity to strike at Americans and other innocent people.

If only it had been so surgical. One story that did the rounds at the Foreign Office in London was of a tragicomic blunder. The CIA had been under pressure to identify a target. They tried to track down one of their main operatives, who had better information than most. According to British diplomats, the man happened on the day in question to be on a golf course. They called him and asked him to get to a secure phone, but didn't tell him why. He said he would once he had finished his round.

The target they hit was the al-Shifa pharmaceuticals factory. Five missiles demolished the plant, where Washington said VX nerve gas was being produced with technical assistance from Baghdad. It turned out that the factory made nothing more sinister than veterinary antibiotics. Its identity had been based on extremely suspect intelligence. 'They never did tell us exactly what happened and why,' says one UK defence official. 'There was an embarrassing silence when we heard the news. As we had supported them, we couldn't backtrack.'

Blair was virtually alone in defending the action and rejecting accusations that Clinton had ordered the attacks as a distraction from the unfolding Lewinsky saga. Two days before the US air strikes the former White House intern had begun her testimony before a Washington grand jury and Clinton had made his televised confession of his 'inappropriate relationship' with her. One member of Blair's inner circle reflects on the dilemma they faced: 'Everyone knew that what Clinton was doing was wrong – bombing that plant – but we also knew that supporting him was right.' Privately, Blair was becoming increasingly alarmed at Clinton's character flaws. He was not particularly moralistic – 'That's Bill for you,' he would tell his aides. He was more concerned about whether Clinton could survive the crisis.

The air strikes on Kabul and Khartoum provided a brief interlude from the ongoing concern about Saddam and his weapons programme – and from Clinton's personal travails. Under pressure from Congress, on 31 October the President signed the Iraq

Liberation Act, which provided for up to $100 million in weapons, 'defence services' and military training to opposition groups who were 'opposed to the Saddam Hussein regime [and] committed to democratic values' – principally, the INC. When Senate majority leader Trent Lott introduced the bill, he said: 'It is time to openly state that our policy goal is the removal of Saddam Hussein's regime from power.' Yet only a week earlier, Marine Corps General Anthony Zinni, the US commanding officer in the region, had said: 'I don't think this has been thought out. A Saddam in place and contained is better than promoting something that causes Iraq to explode, implode, fragment into pieces, cause turmoil.'

Clinton was goaded throughout the autumn of 1998. As the Iraqis ran rings around the UN weapons inspectors, Wolfowitz told a Congressional Committee the White House did not have the sense of purpose to 'liberate ourselves, our friends and allies in the region, and the Iraqi people themselves from the menace of Saddam Hussein'.

At the end of October, Saddam again withdrew co-operation from Unscom. Blair was coming round to the view that some form of military action against Iraq was inevitable. While he had gone out of his way to expunge any suggestions that his government would ever be 'soft' on rogue leaders or unwilling to commit troops, he was still nervous about the response of the public – and more particularly the Labour Party – to such action. He and Campbell accepted the need to prepare opinion. They came up with the idea of a briefing note, setting out both the dangers posed and the obstructions faced. The three-page document, entitled 'Iraq's Weapons of Mass Destruction', was presented to MPs on 12 November 1998. Containing photographs of presidential palaces and other suspected sites, it was a curious mixture of understatement and exaggeration. In a less-than-striking example of research it said: 'Chemical weapons casualties from the Iran–Iraq war number more than 20,000.' The more accurate figure, freely available, was over 50,000. It said Iraq could build a crude air-delivered nuclear device 'in about five years', acknowledging that this would only happen if it were 'to procure the necessary materials abroad'. It said Iraq was only weeks away from making biological weapons and might still have Scud missiles.

It was rough and ready, the facts might not be all they seemed, but the rhetoric was strong. This was the first example of the New Labour communications machine turning its hand to military conflict. The war-made-simple dossier was deemed a success. It would be revived as and when required.

The US and Britain were going it alone. Chirac had made clear his opposition to any attack. The UN was deeply concerned, arguing for negotiations to resume to get the inspectors back. The chances of a Security Council resolution authorising it were remote. Robin Cook suggested to Blair that any action might otherwise be deemed illegal. Blair, after receiving advice from elsewhere, insisted Resolution 687, which had ended the Gulf War, was all the justification he needed. In any case, he had little time for such nitpicking.

Clinton and Blair gave the green light. Some 250 targets were agreed for what they expected would be around six days of bombing. Western personnel, including the Unscom contingent, were withdrawn. The plan was to dispatch Tomahawk cruise missiles on Saturday 15 November. On the evening before, Annan had faxed Saddam's foreign ministry urging the Iraqis to 'resume immediate co-operation' with Unscom. At lunchtime, London time, with some of the planes airborne, Defence Secretary George Robertson received a call from William Cohen, his US opposite number, saying the Americans were about to turn them back. The Iraqis had sent a letter to Annan, agreeing greater compliance. The US wanted to see what was in it. Robertson was alarmed and contacted Blair immediately. They got back in touch with the Americans, telling them to ignore the letter. It was almost certainly meaningless, and once the US government and the UN engaged with Saddam on those terms then they would face an indefinite delay. It was too late. The planes were sent back to base. In New York at 8:30 A.M. the letter was delivered to Annan's house, but he had gone out shopping. There was a scramble to track him down. They did, and for four frantic hours the letter was analysed. Blair's hunch was right. The promises were vague. The Americans acknowledged they didn't believe a word of it, and suggested they should restart the attack the next day.

At that point, the British view changed. Blair and Robertson spent that Saturday night on the phone to Clinton and Cohen, arguing that having aborted the mission and given diplomacy one last chance, they would lose credibility by resuming the attack less than twenty-four hours later. An exasperated Blair told Clinton that he could use RAF Tornados, that the British would publicly support the strikes, but that privately he felt the timing was wrong. At 2 A.M. London time, despite considerable pressure from the Pentagon, Clinton agreed to wait. Butler and his team returned, but within a week they were complaining again of obstruction.

The timing was acute. Ramadan was approaching and Clinton and Blair had long before agreed that they did not want to infringe on Islamic sensibilities by bombing during the holy month. They had to get it over and done with. 'We were going to have real difficulty squeezing in enough bombing time before the start of Ramadan,' recalls one senior official at the time. 'We all became instant experts, trying to work out when a certain Imam in Riyadh would catch sight of the new moon.' Guthrie tried to make light of it all. For Blair, his was a reassuring mix of toughness and imperviousness to problems. When asked by his secretary if he should cancel a tennis game because of the impending air strikes, he was overheard saying: 'Can't let that squirt Saddam get in the way.'

On 10 December the Pentagon shipped three Patriot antimissile batteries to Israel, a harbinger of things to come. Two days later, on an official visit to Jerusalem, Clinton talked by secure video link to Cohen, giving him the authorisation to 'prepare to execute' an attack three days later. The inspectors were again withdrawn. On 15 December, on the flight back to Washington on Air Force One,

Clinton had the draft wording of a report that Butler was due to finalise later that day, listing the many areas where Saddam was not co-operating. It had not been presented to Annan or the Security Council. That report found its way back to Blair. The public needed to be alerted. One senior figure in the Foreign Office remembers proudly how he passed it to the BBC. 'We got it to the top of the *Today* programme. Suddenly the whole board started lighting up. Within hours we'd managed to create expectations and a justification for the military action that followed.'

Clinton directed Cohen to sign the combat order on 16 December. On the same morning American newspapers carried banner headlines announcing that the President was sure to be impeached by the House of Representatives the following day. It was just past 8 P.M. in London when the first Tomahawk missile was fired. Blair was informed of his first taste of military combat. He and Cherie were at home, in the upstairs flat in Downing Street, having dinner with their close friend, Barry Cox, a television executive. They were all supposed to have gone to the theatre that night, but Cox and his wife were informed cryptically a few hours earlier by the Prime Minister's office that this 'wouldn't be possible'. Could they come round instead? As they began their meal, first John Holmes and then Campbell rushed upstairs with the news. They all tried to relieve the tension by cracking jokes. British Tornados began bombing at just before 10 P.M. Blair immediately went over to the Commons to make a statement. On his return, he rejoined the group. From time to time other aides would come in with updates. Blair was distinctly nervous. He remained so until he was told that the first British Tornado pilots had returned home safely. Cook, meanwhile, was hosting the Foreign Office Christmas party that night and did not let slip that dramatic events were about to take place. When aides confirmed that the air strikes had begun, he slipped away.

Britain was the only ally to join the US in military action, setting it at odds with almost all its European partners. Germany's

Gerhard Schröder managed some lukewarm support, but Italy was ambivalent and France positively hostile. Even Kuwait, which had been invaded by Iraq in 1990, refused to support the strikes. For many in America and many governments abroad, the parallels with the recent satirical movie, *Wag the Dog*, were too close for comfort. In the Hollywood version a war in Albania was fabricated to deflect attention from a presidential sex scandal. Was the timing of Operation Desert Fox purely a coincidence? This came to be known as 'Monica's war'.

In spite of the criticism and the international isolation, Blair had few doubts about the need to support Clinton. As one Cabinet minister at the time put it: 'Supporting the Americans is part of Tony's DNA.' Parliament was allowed to discuss the crisis only after the bombing had begun, and it was not given a meaningful vote. The government's objective, Blair told MPs, was clear: 'To degrade [Saddam's] capability to build and use weapons of mass destruction. To diminish the military threat he poses to his neighbours.' He said 30,000 chemical weapons warheads and 4,000 tonnes of precursor chemicals remained unaccounted for. He also told them how successful the inspectors had been since 1991. 'Our quarrel is not with the Iraqi people. It is with him and the evil regime he represents. There is no realistic alternative to military force. We are taking military action with real regret, but also with real determination. We have exhausted all other avenues. We act because we must.'

Three days later, hours before Ramadan was declared, Blair and Clinton simultaneously announced the end of the bombing. Some 650 sorties had been launched. Some 250 targets had been selected and hit – with professed 'pinpoint accuracy'. What, though, had actually been achieved? The object of the exercise was to destroy WMD facilities and to deter the Iraqi regime from flouting international law. The main targets hit were barracks, ministries, airfields and drones. However, the military assessments conducted later provided little evidence that these facilities were part of Saddam's chemical and biological weapons programme. 'Our idea was that if the inspectors couldn't find the stuff, we would bomb it out of existence,' recalls one senior official. 'Trouble is, if they couldn't find it on the ground, nor could we from the air, either because we didn't know where it was or because it wasn't there.'

And what if the weapons really weren't there? What if over seven years the UN inspectors had actually done a good job, and had either found what there was to find or forced the Iraqis to dismantle or disperse their biological and chemical arsenal? These questions were dismissed out of hand, but even then – five years before Blair's final reckoning with Saddam – some in Whitehall were wondering how three days of supposed pinpoint air strikes had not been able to disable his WMD. At this point, the intelligence was better than it had ever been – and was much better than it would later turn out to be.

Beyond a display of power and punishment, what had the operation achieved? Foreign Office diplomats explained to Blair that once the bombing was over, Saddam would almost certainly not allow the UN back. Then what? If the aim was to degrade Saddam's military structures, would that, the diplomats wondered, be achieved more effectively without an international presence inside the country?

The inspectors were not, as Blair would later maintain, thrown out by Saddam. They were withdrawn by the UN for their own safety on the eve of the bombing. It would take four years for them to return, and then only briefly.

Desert Fox was important for Clinton. One aim was to get Richard Butler and his men out of Iraq. Television footage of the UN team being given the runaround had not played well back home. It also did the President good to show his detractors that he had the stomach for military engagement – albeit a brief aerial one. And then there was the Lewinsky scandal. For a few days, as the formal impeachment process began in the House of Representatives, Clinton had some competing, better news.

Blair's first taste of military adventure pales into insignificance with the four wars that were to follow. It was off the front pages within days. But it was a crucial test of his resolve and his determination to show that this Labour Prime Minister would not shrink from using force.

Blair was determined to prove the point. Straight after his Christmas holiday, on 9 January 1999, he flew to Kuwait to thank the RAF pilots who had carried out the bombings. At the base, he was invited to sit in the cockpit of a Tornado jet. He hesitated long enough for accompanying journalists to bet on whether he would climb aboard. They were mindful of the pictures of Margaret Thatcher in a tank after the Falklands. Even Alastair Campbell did not expect him to do it. But he did.

3

MOST MORAL OF WARS?

KOSOVO, BLAIR'S SECOND WAR, TRANSFORMED THE WORLD'S view of him and transformed his view of the world. It played a decisive role in changing his attitude to conflict and his relationship with the United States.

Blair was not even leader of his party when the conflagration began. The dismantling of Yugoslavia and the war in Bosnia that followed marked the end of the old era, when the major powers still felt constrained by Cold War demarcations and spheres of influence. The Foreign Office under the patrician Conservative school of Douglas Hurd had taken an imperious approach, regarding all sides as as bad as each other and doing everything it could not to get involved. One senior diplomat who worked closely with both John Major and Tony Blair describes the Bosnia period as one of the most inglorious in recent British diplomatic history. 'We were absolutely trapped. We were in the worst of all possible worlds. We had been sent in to do a humanitarian job, but the mission had changed. But there was no will in government to change with it. The only choice was to either pull out or to go in and fight a war.'

David Manning was Britain's lead civil servant on the 'Contact

Group' in which the US, UK, France, Germany and Russia came together to try to find a solution to the Bosnian crisis. Italy joined later. After Manning became Blair's right-hand man in 2001, he would recount his experiences in the Balkans. He met Milošević twice on his own, and remembered him as an impressively sinister interlocutor. He would provide a copious lunch, but would sit there, just smoking and staring across the table in a not-so-subtle but effective form of political intimidation. Manning helped convince Blair – not that he needed much convincing – that diplomacy in those situations without the credible threat of force was worthless. All threats had to contain the phrase 'or else . . .' to carry any weight.

Once in government, Blair read up his Bosnian history. He had shown little interest in opposition, but he wanted to make up for lost time. He looked through UN reports, especially on the massacre in Srebrenica in July 1995, which denounced the approach of the international community as 'amoral equivalency'. The UN arms embargo, which Britain refused time and again to lift, did little more than freeze in place the military balance within the former Yugoslavia, giving Serbian nationalists military carte blanche. The UN also chastised itself and the big powers for relying on peace-keeping and humanitarian assistance to solve a problem 'which cried out for a political–military solution'. In their rhetoric British ministers had likened ethnic cleansing to Nazi atrocities. They accepted the scale of the crisis, but they refused to act upon it. From the very beginning of the break-up of Yugoslavia in 1991, the British refused a French idea of a force to protect Croatia. The next year they rejected the idea of a no-fly zone to protect non-Serbs in Bosnia. Between 1993 and 1995 Britain was the most ardent opponent of the US strategy of 'lift and strike' – lifting the embargo on arms supplies to the Bosnian government, and using massive air strikes against Bosnian Serb positions to even out the odds on the ground. Hurd dug in his heels and implied that Britain would veto it in the Security Council. Bizarrely, through this period the Clinton administration often found itself closer to the French stance than the British.

On 21 November 1995, after three and a half years of war in which 200,000 people were killed and almost 2 million were made homeless, Clinton brokered a peace settlement. The General Framework Agreement was negotiated and initialled at a US airbase in Dayton, Ohio, after the leaders of the warring factions had effectively been held there until they could reach a compromise. Bosnia would remain a single state, but would be divided into two almost equal parts: a Muslim–Croat federation and a Serb Republic. Eventually the international community had been galvanised into action, but relations had been badly soured. American diplomats described the British position as 'hyper-realist' – in other words lacking any form of principle.

Relations between Clinton and Major were at rock bottom. By the time of the 1997 General Election, Blair did not have much to prove to the Americans. 'We couldn't imagine how things could be worse than they were,' commented one US official.

When Milošević returned home from Paris after signing the deal there in December 1995 he was hailed as a hero and peacemaker. Most of the sanctions were suspended. For a year or so he went quiet, but when his authority came under threat from opposition groups in local elections in November 1996 he reverted to type. He defrauded them of victory, sought to drag the army and Special Forces on to the streets of Belgrade to intimidate the protesters and – in an appeal to his less educated, mainly rural support base – he played the nationalist card. At the same time the Kosovo Liberation Army was beginning to procure weapons and to organise. The international community treated the KLA with considerable suspicion. It operated almost in secret and had no visible political apparatus. With both sides talking up the prospect of full-scale war, the major powers reconstituted the Contact Group.

Blair concluded that Bosnia had constituted primarily a failure of nerve – one, he insisted to his advisers, that must not be repeated in Kosovo. He confined himself to the broad outline, leaving the detail to the Foreign Office, which was adamant that diplomacy had to run its course.

As the fighting intensified, Cook went to Belgrade to confront Milošević. He demanded the withdrawal of Serbian special police units and the start of a dialogue about Kosovo autonomy between Belgrade and the leaders of the ethnic Albanians, who formed the majority in Kosovo itself. At the very moment the talks were taking place, Milošević made a mockery of him and the West by ordering new raids. Serb forces went to the village of Prekaz in February 1998 where they hunted down, besieged and killed a KLA leader, Adem Jashari, along with more than fifty family and clan members hiding with him.

The Contact Group agreed a limited restoration of sanctions against the Serbs. It had little effect. In June Nato defence ministers ordered military chiefs to prepare a range of options, should the use of force ever become necessary. That prospect, however, seemed politically remote.

At the beginning of the summer, Serb forces appeared to fall back. But when KLA commanders took the initiative, trying to seize a mine and a small town, the Serbs mounted a counter-offensive. The police, and increasingly the army, swept through the central Drenica region and other KLA-held areas. Villages and crops were burned. Tens of thousands of people went into hiding in the hills.

The threats were half-hearted. One defence official recalls: 'We flew planes over the area in June to show how tough we are.' They flew over Macedonia and Albania. They did not enter Serbian airspace. The operation was dubbed 'the Balkan air show'. Meanwhile, the US sought out leaders of the KLA for a meeting at the end of July. The British soon followed. By early August, the UN estimated that 200,000 Kosovo Albanians had been displaced and were living out in the open. As the bitter Balkan winter approached, aid agencies warned of a humanitarian catastrophe. The pathetic images were beamed home on the TV news. The pressure to intervene grew.

The question for Blair, as for the other Western leaders, was whether they could use force against a sovereign country that had not attacked any of them, without a Security Council mandate. On the face of it, this was an armed uprising and an internal affair. Kosovo was an integral part of Yugoslavia. The Russians had made it clear to the Americans, British and French that they would not allow a UN resolution to be passed condemning the Serbs. For President Yeltsin this was a combination of solidarity with fellow Slavs, of watching his back against the many hardliners still in prominent positions, and of preventing a precedent from being set that would have repercussions for Russia's military campaigns in Chechnya and other outlying regions. Yeltsin made it clear that, if need be, he would veto any resolution, but suggested he would rather not be taken to the brink.

As the wrangling continued, two atrocities took place. There was fierce fighting around the village of Gornje Obrinje, in which at least fourteen Serb policemen died. Then came the retaliation. Twenty-one members of a single family were gunned down. Serb special forces fanned out into the forests killing fourteen more people, five of whom were children between the ages of eighteen months and nine years old. On the same day, a few miles away, Serb police rounded up a group of several thousand civilians who had fled shelling in Golubovac. Fourteen men were selected, physically abused and executed. The numbers were small compared to massacres that took place during the Bosnian and Croatian conflicts, but it was the memory of the West's weak response in the mid-1990s that helped galvanise public opinion – and governments.

Until the summer of 1998 Kosovo had not exercised the rank and file or the parliamentary party. 'We realised there was a problem, but domestically it was still below the radar,' recalls one minister. When a young MP, Ben Bradshaw, raised the issue in March at Prime Minister's Questions, there was little reaction among his colleagues. He asked Blair if he agreed that the situation in Kosovo 'could become the worst thing that Europe has seen since 1945'.

Blair agreed it was 'grave', but hedged his bets. 'I have no doubt that if there is substantial conflict there, or indeed in Bosnia, it will have an impact on us and on the whole of Europe as well as on that part of the world.'

Blair was content to leave the running on Kosovo to Cook. Foreign Office lawyers insisted there was no case in international law to use force. But pressure was growing. Schröder told Clinton that, reluctantly, he would support a limited campaign of air strikes. On 8 October, at a cramped VIP lounge at Heathrow, Cook convened a meeting of his Nato counterparts with Igor Ivanov, the Russian foreign minister. The Russians had long made it clear they would not formally agree, through the UN or any other international forum, to an attack on their fellows, but Ivanov hinted that militarily they would not stand in the way.

That was crucial. It was taken as a green light. Madeleine Albright, the US Secretary of State, declared that Nato now had 'the legitimacy to stop a catastrophe'. The alliance approved an 'activation order' authorising preparations for a limited bombing campaign. Cook and Blair dismissed the FCO lawyers' concerns. They argued that, with the EU and Nato backing it, the war might not be technically legal but it had all the international legitimacy it needed.

On 12 October Milošević struck a deal with the chief US negotiator, Richard Holbrooke. The Serb presence would be drawn down to its pre-war levels and political negotiations would begin. Unarmed international observers would be sent in. For Clinton this was a blessed relief. He had other international crises to deal with. More importantly, he was in the midst of the Lewinsky drama. Midterm elections were approaching and talk of war was a vote-loser.

Part of Clinton's reluctance stemmed from the realisation that it would be Americans who would be risking their lives in any war, not the Europeans in whose back yard it would be fought. Europe had over 3,000 combat aircraft and nearly 2 million men in uniform but was still unable or unwilling to muster effective combat operations. The US administration believed that at best the Europeans provided 'soft power' – such as peacekeeping.

Blair wanted to prove to the US that Europe could deliver more. For that reason he was comfortable with plans to expand and strengthen Europe's defence capabilities, as long as any strengthening of the EU was not seen as undermining the traditional alliance, Nato, which was struggling to prove its worth after the end of the Cold War. On 4 December, the British and the French signed a deal hailed as marking a new era in defence co-operation. Under the St Malo agreement, both countries pledged to begin planning and executing a combined response to crises, to share intelligence, planning, transport, even media handling. The French were required not to present themselves as rivals to the US. In return, the British would emphasise to Washington the important role France and Europe would play.

Hopes that the pause in fighting in Kosovo would lead to progress rapidly faded. International observers were increasingly being drawn into negotiating hostage and prisoner releases and local ceasefires. The KLA was re-arming. US intelligence was warning that the Kosovans were looking for a pretext to resume fighting and to draw Nato in. They did not have to wait long. Albright was the most outspoken advocate of a tough line against Milošević among the members of the 'Principals Committee', the US administration's top foreign policy advisers. As the frustration began to get the better of her, she complained: 'We're just gerbils running on a wheel.'

The turning point came on 8 January 1999. In a well-planned ambush, the KLA killed three Serbian policemen. Two days later they killed another. Serbian Special Forces gathered. Early on 15 January, fighting broke out around the village of Racak. The KLA retreated and the Serb police entered the village. According to accounts sent to Western governments, the Serbs took away as many men and boys as they could find, gunned them down by firing squad and left their bodies to pile up. The final death toll was forty-five.

In Washington, Paris and London, the governments began a

frantic round of meetings. Albright, whom the French nicknamed
'Madame Bomber', tried to build a consensus that any diplomatic
moves had to be backed by the threat of force. Cook was more cautious: 'If we are to take military action, military action must be in
support of a clear political demand and a clear political process.
Neither side is going to win this war,' he said. Under joint British and
French chairmanship, the Serbs and Albanians were summoned for
one last attempt at peace. It was agreed that Cook and Hubert
Vedrine, his French counterpart, would chair talks in the serene
setting of the eighteenth-century hunting lodge and summer presidential residence at Rambouillet. The negotiations began on 6
February. They were due to last a fortnight. The Kosovans were split.
The Serbs did not engage. The session was extended by three days,
but it broke up without agreement. They tried again shortly afterwards in Paris, but this time the Serbs produced a counter-proposal
that didn't even mention the word 'Kosovo'. Cook and Vedrine suspected Albright had determined the outcome in advance and that
she had quietly encouraged the Kosovans to demand full independence in the hope that the Serbs would buckle.

Few in the Contact Group had imagined that Milošević would
risk the bombs and go for broke. On the other hand, Milošević saw
Nato as a paper tiger, and did not believe it would undertake more
than a token mission. He saw Operation Desert Fox in Iraq as a
precedent. The bombing then had lasted seventy hours. After that
the monitors had never gone back and for Saddam that had been a
victory of sorts. Milošević was not impressed by the idea of 'bombing lite'. He thought Nato unity would be shattered within a couple
of days and that, in any case, the Russians would rally to their cause.
By this point, Blair was adamant that the Russians' friendship with
the Serbs should not be allowed to prevent war. He had given up on
Yeltsin. The Russians' threat to veto had precluded any attempt to get
a UN Security Council resolution, but the British were confident
that was as far as Russian opposition would go.

When Holbrooke visited Milošević in Belgrade for the last

time on 22 March, he warned that the bombing would be 'swift, severe and sustained'. He got nowhere. On the following day Blair prepared MPs for impending military action: 'To walk away now would not merely destroy Nato's credibility. More importantly, it would be a breach of faith to thousands of innocent civilians whose only desire is to live in peace and took us at our word: to protect them from military suppression . . . We have no alternative to act and act we will.'

Bombing attacks began the following evening, 24 March, at 8 P.M. local time. Among the first targets in the Belgrade suburbs were a military–technical institute, a military academy, an airbase and a communications mast. Some forty targets, from a list of fifty-one, were identified. Serb intelligence – rumoured to be coming from within Nato – ensured that the sites had been cleared ahead of time. On the first night RAF Tornados failed to hit a single target.

The original plan was for the bombing to last seventy-two hours. Blair and Clinton were advised that Milošević would come to his senses and negotiate seriously, even on the terms presented at Rambouillet. In his broadcast to the nation on 26 March, Blair said: 'To those who say the aim of military strikes is not clear, I say it is crystal clear. It is to curb Slobodan Milošević's ability to wage war on an innocent civilian population.' Initially, TV viewers saw nothing but the high-tech imagery of aerial bombing. Within days, however, the scale of the refugee crisis became apparent. The Serb forces had used the start of Nato action as an excuse to accelerate their programme of ethnic cleansing. Hundreds of thousands of refugees began flooding out across the borders into Albania and Macedonia. These apocalyptic scenes changed the whole context of the intervention.

Still the allies were flying blind – militarily, as the Pentagon ensured that the air force stay above the cloud to protect their pilots – and politically. They knew they had to act, but nobody had an idea of the end game.

On one point Clinton and Blair were adamant. 'I do not intend to put our troops in Kosovo to fight a war,' the President told the US people in his televised address. That line was written by Sandy Berger, his National Security chief, who has since maintained that neither the US Congress nor several European nations would have sanctioned any form of military action unless its limits had been made clear. For all the rewriting of history that subsequently took place, for all the apportioning of blame, Blair had made a similar commitment in his parliamentary statement: 'We do not plan to use ground troops in order to fight our way into Kosovo. No one should underestimate the sheer scale of what is involved in that action. We would be talking about 100,000 ground troops, and possibly more.'

Night after night US jets and sea-launched cruise missiles struck targets across Serbia and Kosovo. No matter how many they hit, they seemed to be making virtually no progress. Far from breaking Milošević's will, he was rallying his people. Blair became frustrated. But at the same time, he underwent a conversion in his approach to the use of military force. Like Clinton and others of his post-war generation, he had been lulled into believing that high-tech weaponry from the air could do the job. He was beginning to think again.

The presentation of the war was going from bad to worse. For all the spin, it was dawning on the public that the allied air attacks were not degrading Milošević's military might. 'We were in the MoD bunker every morning,' one senior figure recalls. 'They would brief us very frankly about what had happened overnight. The columns always seemed to show minimum damage. We tried not to say as much in our briefings to the press.'

Matters came to a head with the bombing of a refugee convoy outside the town of Djakovica on 14 April. American F-16s, flying at an altitude of 15,000 feet over the main road to the town of Prizren, spotted what they took to be a column of military trucks. Instead of owning up to killing more than seventy poor, bedraggled Kosovans, Nato went quiet. For five days, its spokesman, Jamie Shea, tried to stall the media. His attempts at getting information from military commanders were being blocked. They told him that the battle-damage assessments had not been completed and he would have to wait. He told the generals that the world's media did not operate according to that timetable, especially in the new age of twenty-four-hour television. Shea was in an impossible position, but for more sophisticated media managers like Campbell radical action was required. For some time Blair and Campbell had been shocked by what they saw as the ineptitude of Nato's propaganda campaign.

Campbell rushed to Brussels. Within days the walls of two conference rooms on the ground floor of Nato headquarters had been knocked down to create a 'war room'. Press officers, predominantly from Downing Street and other Whitehall departments, but also from the White House and the Pentagon, were sent in. The Labour Party's tried and trusted media operation of spin, rebuttal, 'lines to take', media monitoring, the planting of good stories on trusted reporters and the denunciation of those who caused trouble – all these tricks were exported to the Western military alliance. Even after he had returned to London, Campbell oversaw twice-daily conference calls.

What did not seem to change was the bombing accuracy. To accommodate Nato's targeting problems, a new lexicon was created. Sites were said to have been 'struck', rather than 'destroyed'. They called it creative ambiguity.

The most politically difficult case of 'collateral damage' came with the bombing of the Chinese Embassy in Belgrade on 7 May. Blair had started the war attending endless meetings, asking a barrage of questions, trying to micromanage every detail. As it progressed, he became less insistent on approving each UK sortie. But, with frustration growing, both the Americans and the British became less punctilious. Was the embassy bombing a conspiracy, as some afterwards suggested it might be? It seems unlikely. One British defence official remembers being in the media operations room in Brussels at 2 A.M. when he was rung and told about the embassy blunder. He went over to the high-tech operations room of Wesley Clark at Saceur, the Supreme Allied Commander in Europe, where he found the military chief poring over a map on the floor, and agreeing they had been sold a duff target. The phlegmatic Guthrie took it in his stride, suggesting that the Brits might have done their spadework ahead of time. 'If it had been us, we would have had a chap tying up his shoelace outside that house in Belgrade and taking a good look at the brass plaque before we bombed it,' he told one official.

In spite of the war's slow progress and the public relations disasters, the Cabinet remained united. Clare Short, the International Development Secretary, was as robust as anyone in defending the military action, portraying it as an act of liberation, as intervention for a greater good. So convincing was her justification for the war, both to the Labour Party and to the country at large, that Blair and Campbell willingly offered her up for television and radio interviews. Several times Campbell called her after her performances to thank her. Kosovo, for all its problems, was the high point in liberal intervention, when Blair enjoyed the support of most of the party and country not just for the moral justification of war but the means by which it was being prosecuted. At meetings of the War Cabinet Robertson, Cook and Short gave regular presentations about the military, diplomatic and humanitarian aspects of the conflict. The discussions were brief and to the point. Blair would talk about remaining 'rock solid'. Time after time he told his colleagues, 'We will all have to hold our nerve.' Public opinion was beginning to waver, but support was still firm enough. Labour officials were marvelling that a party of the centre-left could, in the words of one strategist, have 'turned itself so effortlessly into a war-fighting party'.

Initially, Blair did not report to Cabinet his misgivings about Clinton's strategy. Towards the end of April, a month into the war, Blair had made up his mind that ground troops had to be used. Blair sent Cook on a mission to sound out Albright – the most likely supporter of a more robust approach. Over a drink at a Washington hotel, Cook set out the reasons and the timetable. He asked her to persuade Cohen. She said she would do what she could, but that as she was the only one in the US government who believed in the need for ground forces, she surmised the British would be better off doing the lobbying themselves. Cook reported this back. Albright had inadvertently set out an approach that Blair would follow – a British Prime Minister taking it upon himself to lobby the American President on behalf of certain American government departments.

Blair was rarely off the phone to Clinton during this period. Their friendship was, however, stretched to breaking point. Blair urged him to think of his 'historic legacy'. He was despondent at Clinton's inability to focus. 'I cannot deliver Congress,' Clinton told Blair in one conversation. 'People don't know where Yugoslavia is, don't ask me to deliver the impossible.' Things became more heated when at one point Clinton suggested a pause in the bombing if the Serbs began to withdraw. For his part, Clinton was getting increasingly angry at the way Blair's frustration was being spun. His people blamed the row on Campbell's 'hype' and Blair's 'God thing'. One complained: 'We didn't need Blair to tell us we had to win this thing. Their suggestion that they convinced us is fantasy land.' Some in Clinton's camp started mockingly referring to Blair as 'Winston'.

Blair made clear that without an American lead, Nato would never be able to build a consensus for ground operations. The President told him repeatedly that he could and would keep on bombing, but he would not risk American lives. He reminded Blair that for all his tough talk, they would be endangering many more American lives than British. Robertson and Cohen had a similar argument, face to face, when they met with their French, German and Italian counterparts. Cohen told him: 'You're just pushing for it because it's American guys who are going to be killed.' Robertson replied 'fifty thousand', meaning the number of British troops he was prepared to deploy. 'You haven't got that many,' Cohen retorted. 'Fifty thousand,' Robertson repeated.

The Americans – Cohen and National Security chief Sandy

Berger in particular – kept backing off. 'We were pulling our hair out,' recalls one member of Blair's team. The timing was becoming acute. Blair asked Guthrie how much leeway they had. He was told a decision would have to be taken by mid-June, so that troops could be deployed by mid-September, well in advance of winter. Blair then asked Guthrie about casualties. The answer came back that he should prepare for the eventuality of 'tens of thousands overall'. One member of the War Cabinet recalls: 'We all looked at each other in silence. Blair took a deep intake of breath and moved on.' During this difficult period, Guthrie spent time keeping up Blair's morale. He became a friend and confidant and moulded Blair's respect for the army. Blair told one insider that Kosovo could be his Suez. One official who saw him frequently at the time remarked: 'Tony is doing too much, he's overdoing it and he's overplaying his hand.'

Plans for troop deployments had been drawn up a year before. There were several scenarios. The one Blair was considering most was called Operation B-Minus, involving up to 60,000 British soldiers as 'heavy peacekeepers'. This would constitute the largest British force assembled since 1945.

With the transatlantic phone channel becoming acrimonious, Blair decided he needed some 'face time' at the White House. Fortuitously, he was due in Washington for the fiftieth anniversary of the founding of Nato. He asked John Sawers, his principal private secretary, to arrange as many meetings as he could with Clinton and his people. Before leaving on 21 April he told MPs publicly for the first time that ground troops were an option. He reminded them that Nato was preparing to send in forces to enforce a post-war settlement and that 'Milošević does not have a veto' on the timing of that deployment. The language was cautious, but Blair was preparing for what he hoped would be a fundamental change to war strategy.

On arrival in Washington, Blair went straight into talks to try to win administration officials around to a tougher approach. Cohen told him use of US forces was 'an almost impossible sell'.

Berger was the least amenable. Publicly, Blair denied he was trying to persuade the Americans to change course. After meeting with Congressmen, he said cryptically, 'We must have an international military force that goes in to allow these people to go home' – the implication being that they would be sent in only at the end of the war. But he did not say as much. The atmosphere between the two leaders was fraught. 'Blair went to Washington to lecture Bill,' one American official recalls. 'It was counter-productive. It was the last thing Clinton wanted. It's not the way to win him round.'

Blair had a long-standing engagement for a speech to the Economic Club of Chicago the following morning that he was very eager to fulfil. This was to provide him with a tailor-made opportunity to set out some of his broader foreign policy goals. With Iraq, and with Kosovo, he had demonstrated his instincts, but he had yet to fashion them into a coherent vision. He had made clear what he did not represent – the leftist genuflections towards disarmament to which Cook was predisposed. He knew roughly what he wanted to say. But, preoccupied as they were with the war itself, neither the Prime Minister nor anyone in his office had time to work it through. Blair had always made a point of seeking out contributions from beyond his inner circle, going back to those early coffee mornings at his Islington house. Jonathan Powell approached one of the participants at those meetings, Lawrence Freedman. The two had known each other for a long time, since Powell was in the planning staff at the Foreign Office.

Powell told him Downing Street was too busy to write the speech, what with all the fighting in Kosovo and all the arguments with Clinton. Would Freedman oblige?

The unwieldy mechanisms of global governance were failing to respond to the new challenges of the post-Cold War era. These were increasingly intra- rather than inter-state. Security was also seen as being bound with issues of political development and justice in a way that it never was before. Yet it was difficult to put this idea into practice effectively because of the traditional notions of state sovereignty and the inviolability of borders.

On the centre-left, in the UK, US, Europe and elsewhere, politicians and thinkers were coalescing around the idea of 'humanitarian intervention' – marrying military force with ethical and internationalist ends to protect civilians from particularly gross repression by their own governments or in the course of civil wars. Much of the most important work was being done by a group called the ICISS, the International Commission on Intervention and State Sovereignty. Led by a former Australian foreign minister, Gareth Evans, its aim was to try to reconcile the international community's responsibility to act in the face of massive violations of humanitarian norms while respecting sovereign rights. Kofi Annan also signalled in a number of speeches that classical doctrines would have to be re-thought. He accepted that the UN Charter would have to be interpreted in a more interventionist way.

This conundrum had vexed social theorists throughout the modern era. Freedman was given two days to wrap it up. Powell told him he wanted to hone a philosophy that Blair could call his own. The Prime Minister wanted to present specific benchmarks denoting when the international community should intervene in the internal affairs of a sovereign state. Freedman referred back to one unlikely source – Ronald Reagan's former Defense Secretary, Caspar Weinberger, who had back in November 1984 in the light of the failures of American intervention in Vietnam and Lebanon set out six points defining the use of combat forces.

It was a Friday afternoon. To get over writer's block, Freedman went for a walk around Dundonald Park near his house in Wimbledon, working out the benchmarks in his mind. Then they came to him. He rushed back to his house and bashed them out on his computer. He e-mailed his response to Powell and arranged to see him the following week. He assumed he was one of several people consulted and that his offering would be fed in along with others' material.

On the plane to the US, with the head of his Downing Street policy unit, David Miliband, by his side, Blair had a look at the draft of the speech. Often these flights provided the best thinking time for him. He would spend time staring out the window, oblivious to those around him, or scribbling with his fountain pen. Few people knew how to decipher his handwriting. Powell was one. The Prime Minister's secretarial support could always be relied upon to interpret his words meticulously and type them up into the required memoranda. Blair kept repeating to himself the words 'international community' and then shaking his head. At one point he yelped with delight, proclaiming, 'The doctrine of international community!' He had found a phrase he thought summed up his approach. Some in his entourage rolled their eyes. 'We knew it wasn't buzzy,' recalls one, 'but we understood what he was getting at.' In these situations, Blair has an iterative style. He tests all kinds of propositions to whoever is around him, going through points over and over again and inviting his confidants to push him with counter-assertions. Then he alights on his conclusion.

'We are witnessing the beginnings of a new doctrine of international community,' Blair proclaimed to his Chicago audience on 22 April. 'We are all internationalists now, whether we like it or not. We cannot refuse to participate in global markets if we want to prosper. We cannot turn our backs on conflicts and the violation of human rights within other countries if we want still to be secure.' Taking aim at the doubters inside the Pentagon and the State Department, who had learned from humiliations in Vietnam, Somalia and elsewhere to think first about exit strategy, Blair said: 'Success is the only exit strategy I am prepared to consider.'

Blair then set out his criteria for intervention. They were: are we sure of our case? Have we exhausted diplomatic options? Does the military assessment offer prudent and achievable goals? Are we prepared to be in this for the long term, including the task of rebuilding? And is our national interest truly engaged?

When Freedman read the speech, he was surprised to find that so much of what he had written had been used. Blair told his aides afterwards he thought it was punchy, and sent Freedman a hand-written letter of thanks. In the Foreign Office, however, the reaction was very different. There was consternation, especially among the legal team. At his morning meeting with senior officials, Sir John Kerr, the Permanent Secretary, asked if anyone had known about the new doctrine ahead of time. There were glum faces all around. Nobody had.

This had become part of a pattern, in which Blair and his people often did not bother to consult the organisation supposedly in charge of British diplomacy.

Kerr turned to the idea of intervention *à la carte* and remarked: 'Where does this end?' Still, they put a brave face on it and tried to translate the speech into a strategy document, relating it to international institutions. The civil servant in the policy planning staff entrusted with the task was Hugh Powell, son of the scion of foreign affairs, Sir Charles Powell, and nephew of Jonathan. After weeks of effort they gave up. Among traditional diplomats there was no little scepticism. Henry Kissinger, who was on a speaker's platform with Mandelson, told him the idea of intervention for altruistic reasons was 'irresponsible'.

On his return to Washington from Chicago, Blair had another private chat with Clinton at the Nato banquet that evening. He told his aides afterwards that he might be on to something. An exasperated Clinton hinted privately to him that he might after all be prepared to use ground troops. As Blair set off for London the next day he remarked to his team that he was not sure if Clinton had meant it.

As more and more Albanians continued to flee across the mountains out of Kosovo, Blair and Cook sent a small team to Skopje, capital of Macedonia, to see what more could be done on the ground. The embassy at the time was staffed by just two people and could not cope with the crisis. The Macedonian government, under international pressure, had allowed a refugee camp, Stankovic 1, to be built in the no-man's-land by its border post at Blace. First to deliver a sit-rep was Blair's dependable general, Charles Guthrie. David Manning followed soon after with Clare Short. Their reports back home were deeply shocking. They told Blair that the situation was desperate, that thousands of people were 'on the wrong side of the wire, in the mud, collapsed in vomit and faeces'. At one point, trains carrying up to 6,000 people expelled from Priština, the Kosovo capital, were arriving at Blace. The refugees, mostly women and children, said they had been separated from their menfolk. The total was reaching 200,000, crowded together in row upon row of tents in a filthy field, with not enough clean water to go round.

Blair decided he wanted to see for himself. As ever, he and his people sought to ensure that the pictures would tell the right story. Anji Hunter, his dependable adviser, was sent out to check the logistical details. That included picking the right backdrop for the television cameras. Blair and Cherie arrived at Stankovic on 3 May, with entourage and hordes of journalists in tow. One tent was selected close to the perimeter. The Blairs spent nine minutes inside talking to a family. Emerging from the tent, the Prime Minister then exhorted a crowd that had gathered: 'This is not a battle for Nato, this is not a battle for territory, this is a battle for humanity. It is a just cause.'

He continued in that vein, for an exclusively British audience, in a newspaper piece he had penned in his name. 'No matter how many times you see these scenes on TV, nothing prepares you for the stench, the all-pervading air of fear or the awful stories that pour out. They come from women who have been raped. From old men who have seen their daughters violated. From children who have seen their fathers dragged away and shot. From sisters who've lost brothers, and brothers who have lost sisters.' He concluded the piece in the *Sunday Mirror* by saying: 'Nato will prevail. The Butchers of Belgrade will be defeated.'

And yet, for all the emotional rhetoric, Blair ended his visit to Blace without making any specific commitment on the number of refugees Britain would now take. Relief agencies had criticised Britain for taking only two planeloads, 300 in all, compared to Germany, which was increasing its quota to 20,000.

That had been Blair's first experience of a refugee camp any-where in the world. It was the kind of problem aid agencies deal with all the time, often failing to convince governments of the plights of the refugees concerned. But this had shocked the British Prime Minister. This was the moment when he was converted from the principle of intervention to the commitment to intervention.

The next leg of his trip was an address to the Romanian par-liament. On the flight from Skopje to Bucharest, Blair started writing furiously. He was reworking the speech. He handed it to Manning, who had trouble deciphering his notes in the margins, and to Campbell. Manning gasped when he realised what it said. In an instant Blair was tearing up established policy. He was promising the Romanians and other former Communist countries British sup-port for early membership of Nato and the EU. The only way, Blair explained, of preventing further violence in countries such as these was to create a more 'inclusive vision of a post-Cold War Europe'. Manning told him: 'It's not policy. We can't rush it. They need to take time.' Blair responded: 'But is there any reason why not?' Manning said there wasn't. He would later have to answer for him-self to his furious bosses. At the Foreign Office there was consternation – senior officials complained that one did not change European policy just like that. This was an early example of Blairite geostrategy being made up on a whim.

Blair was adamant. He was increasingly turning to the certi-tudes of the Second World War, of his father's generation, for moral guidance – to the appeasement of the 1930s, to the pictures of the trains taking people to camps, to the reconstruction of the van-quished countries after 1945. He told the Romanian parliament: 'In 1945 Germany was still under Hitler. Within ten years it had re-established its democracy, rebuilt its cities, joined Nato and was in at the birth of what is now the European Union. Serbia can rejoin the world community too. But that prospect will only be a reality when corrupt dictatorship is cast out and real democracy returns to the former Republic of Yugoslavia.' This comprised his first rudimentary thinking on regime change. Countries that rid themselves of bad leaders would receive their reward.

Two weeks later, Blair visited a second refugee camp, this time at Elbasan in Albania. Just before he arrived, he changed into a red shirt and black trousers – the Kosovan national colours. When it came to presentation, no detail was overlooked. He spent longer there, followed by chants of 'Nato, Nato' and outstretched hands as he walked through the camp. He made his way into a tent, which Hunter had identified beforehand. There he met 72-year-old Miftar Mazrekha, who told him how he was robbed, forced to strip naked in front of his village by armed Serbs who hit him with rifle butts and kicked him because he did not undress quickly enough. 'They hit me again in the ribs,' he said through an interpreter, 'and asked me for Deutschmarks. I told them I didn't have many because I was a pensioner and I gave them all the 200 marks I had. They told me it wasn't enough.' He said the Serbs had rounded up all the young men. By nightfall, his wife Shyret said, they went in search of 'all the beautiful girls'.

Blair likened the packing of Kosovans into trains and trucks to the fate of Jews in the Holocaust. 'This is no longer just a military conflict. It is a battle between good and evil, between civilisation and barbarity,' he said. 'Our promise to you, to all of you, is that you should return in peace to the land that is yours.' As the scale of the human suffering became ever more apparent, so his language became more biblical.

On the day of the Elbasan visit, a son was born to an Albanian family in Glasgow, the first to be granted refugee status in the UK. They called him Tony.

These two trips put further strain on his relations with Clinton. In one long phone conversation, the President suggested that the Prime

Minister 'pull himself together' and halt the 'domestic grandstand-ing' that he said was threatening to tear Nato apart. One aide to Clinton suggested Blair was 'sprinkling too much adrenalin on his cornflakes'.

Blair saw it in completely different terms. What was the point of international institutions like Nato, he told his aides, if they didn't deliver victory when they needed to? Gradually people around Blair were becoming more confident that they were breaking down Clinton's resistance. The breakthrough came when the President finally said: 'All options are on the table.'

Fundamental to Blair's way of thinking was that diplomacy could work only when backed up by force. The only country that Milošević would listen to seriously was Russia. In the first weeks of the war President Yeltsin had appointed his old fixer Viktor Chernomyrdin, the former prime minister, as his special envoy. Chernomyrdin had always enjoyed cannily good relations with Washington. Even more helpfully, on a personal note he did not like Milošević. Yeltsin, his authority and health waning, had come under sustained pressure from hardliners in Moscow over the Nato action. He wanted it over and done with. To give him political cover and diplomatic reinforcements, Chernomyrdin agreed to the idea of an EU envoy, the Finnish President, Martti Ahtisaari. He was one of a small number of international statesmen who had acquired a new role as troubleshooter. He had worked with Lord Owen in trying to settle the previous crises in the former Yugoslavia. The third player in this intricate diplomatic web was Strobe Talbott, US Deputy Secretary of State, and an experienced Eastern European hand. The British were not part of the equation.

Over the next month the veteran politicians conducted a series of negotiations in Bonn, Helsinki and twice in Moscow. The Russian military was resistant, but a single call from Yeltsin to his former PM broke the deadlock. On 3 June they agreed that 'all' Serb forces should leave Kosovo.

They then flew straight to Belgrade where they told Milošević that only when a verifiable withdrawal had begun would the bombing stop. On 9 June the Serbs agreed and the bombing ceased the next day. Under UN Security Council Resolution 1244, Nato troops were to be deployed to Kosovo to oversee the return of the refugees.

Air power on its own had not broken Milošević. The combination of bombing, the threat of ground troops and, towards the end of the conflict, astute diplomacy had persuaded him that reluctant acquiescence was his best strategy. He did not see himself as vanquished, nor did his people, nor did the Russians.

Milošević accepted the deal believing that the Russians would pour in thousands of troops and carve out a sector for themselves in the predominantly Serbian north of Kosovo, which in the event of the province ever becoming independent could be retained by Serbia. Indeed, immediately after the Serbs' agreement, a Russian convoy shot out from Bosnia, sped down the motorway through Serbia to Kosovo and grabbed Priština airport. It was thanks in large part to the judgement of General Sir Mike Jackson, the British commanding officer, who ignored an order from Wesley Clark to take the Russians on that prevented a potentially major conflict.

A war that was supposed to last seventy-two hours had lasted seventy-eight days. A total of 720 aircraft flew almost 36,000 sorties. The number of civilian casualties was disputed, but the Serbian government put it at 2,000. Some 462 Serb soldiers and 114 special police were killed. Just two Allied pilots were lost when their Apache helicopter crashed in a training accident. For the Americans and the rest of Nato, this was as risk-averse a war as it was possible to fight.

Militarily, the war had been anything but a resounding success. At the end of the war, Nato claimed it had destroyed some 120 Serbian tanks, 220 armoured personnel carriers and 450 artillery and mortar pieces. According to a suppressed US Air Force report obtained later, the Western alliance had verifiably destroyed just 14 tanks, 19 APCs and 20 artillery pieces. Milošević had tricked them by hiding most of his best kit, some in hillside bunkers, some even in people's garages, and also by drawing fire on to meticulously constructed model tanks made out of wood and plastic sheeting.

The planning and intelligence sides had fared little better. On 24 March, at the outset, Nato had identified a total of 219 targets – enough for less than a week's bombing. Once they had done that, and they realised they were in for the long haul, they were making it up as they went along. Western intelligence estimated that the war might create 200,000 more refugees. Within a month there were some 850,000 outside Kosovo and 200,000 inside its borders.

The war Blair originally had in mind was not the war they ended up fighting. Whether the air strikes strengthened Milošević's resolve to complete his ethnic cleansing, or whether he would have done it anyway, the humanitarian catastrophe ensured after the first day that the original 'bombing lite' strategy was not sustainable. The Allies were sucked inexorably into a bigger battle. 'Our whole policy was saved by the refugees,' says one of Blair's closest colleagues. 'Milošević provided evidence to prove the case for bombing.'

In so doing, Slobodan Milošević changed Blair and everything he stood for.

The war in Kosovo provided a template for future actions by Blair, and for his attempts to justify them. Western European leaders – with Britain, France and Germany acting in unison – set out a number of reasons for using military action without the sanction of a UN Security Council resolution. They stressed the moral imperative and the guilt over the West's and the UN's failure to act over Srebrenica. They pointed to the glaring humanitarian crisis. And they cited geography. This was ethnic cleansing in the heart of Europe.

Blair had started to feel the strain of his self-appointed role as Atlantic bridge-builder. He was deeply troubled by the arguments he had had with Clinton. 'Bill had real problems with the military,' says an aide who saw them both close up. 'Tony has had the reverse problem. Using force is important to him. He believes the way to prevent the US from acting unilaterally or from divorcing itself from Europe is to show that he is able to fight and to cope with responsibilities.'

Blair confided to a close colleague that he was in a bind. He could not rely on the Americans to 'do the right thing', and yet at the same time the Europeans could not always be trusted. He concluded that Britain should see its role as trying to push the Americans all the time in the 'right direction'.

Whatever the ambiguities, Blair had broken new ground in Europe. When he visited Priština on 31 July, for his third trip to the region in less than three months, Kosovans hailed him as saviour. 'I am so proud to be here in Kosovo and proud to see you back in your homeland where you belong,' he told the crowd, as they chanted the now familiar 'Tony, Tony'. He told them, 'We fought in this conflict for a cause and that cause was justice. We fought for an end to ethnic cleansing. We fought for peace and security for all people in Kosovo.'

Public opinion elsewhere saw him as a man of determination and principle, if not of great historical or geographical perspective. At the EU and G8 summits he was fêted as a hero. 'We are succeeding in Kosovo because this was a moral cause which was backed by the great majority of our citizens,' Blair proclaimed. 'We now have a chance to build a new internationalism based on values and the rule of law.' The next task, he made clear, was to get rid of Milošević. 'We can then embark on a new moral crusade to rebuild the Balkans without him.' Crusade. He was entirely at ease with the word.

It would, however, take more than a year for Milošević to be toppled, and then by his own people. Eight months after that he was sent to The Hague to face the Yugoslav war crimes tribunal – the first head of state to be tried for war crimes and genocide. It was the people of Serbia who finally overthrew him, not the Western powers. But Blair would retrospectively cite that as one of his main reasons for going to war in the first place. He did not use the term directly. But this is what he meant – regime change.

Four years on from the war the status of Kosovo remains unresolved and reconstruction and reconciliation efforts have made little progress. Since the conflict has ended some 200,000 Serb refugees, driven from Kosovo by Albanians in the aftermath of the conflict, have been forgotten by the same people who invoked humanitarian principles to defend Albanians from ethnic cleansing.

The first war fought in the name of humanitarian intervention, a war that Blair and Clinton thought would last hours, left in its wake the tasks of reconstruction and reconciliation that years later remain elusive. But when Blair looked back at the benchmarks he set out in Chicago, he was confident that he had done the right thing. Britain's national interest was engaged, as this was Europe's back yard and a crucial test of the international community's resolve. The diplomatic options had, just about, been exhausted. The military tasks were prudent and achievable, in that they forced the Serb army out of Kosovo and enabled the return of the refugees. Britain, the EU and Nato did show themselves prepared to be in it for the long term . . . and he was most definitely convinced of the moral case.

4

WHITE MAN'S BURDEN

IN MARCH 1998, BILL CLINTON ISSUED AN APOLOGY. HE WAS
at the ramshackle airport of Kigali, capital of Rwanda. It was a lame
sort of apology, but the best he could muster. 'We come here today
partly in recognition of the fact that we in the United States and the
world community did not do as much as we could have and should
have done to try to limit what occurred.'

Not many world leaders could match that for understatement
and sheer gall. For months the world stood by as Hutu militias carried out an extermination programme on a par with Hitler and Pol
Pot. The French military arrived in force to 'keep order', but were
reluctant to intervene against a faction they had tended to support
in the past. The Americans and the British did not want to get
involved at all. Within 100 days in the summer of 1994 around
800,000 Tutsis and moderate Hutus were slaughtered. When the
militias fled to the area around Goma in neighbouring Zaire, they
took up to 2 million refugees with them. Many of them would die of
cholera and other diseases.

No crisis reflected more accurately Neville Chamberlain's
dictum: a far-away place about which we know little. At the time, the

US government owed half a billion dollars in UN dues and peace-keeping costs. It had tired of its obligation to foot a third of the bill to combat what had come to feel like an insatiable global appetite for mischief and an equally insatiable appetite by the international organisation to carry out missions in remote parts of the world.

Africa had always been bottom of the United States' list of priorities – except as a bulwark against Soviet advances during the early stages of the Cold War, when each superpower picked off and then rewarded individual African countries for coming into its sphere of influence. In 1993, in one of his first foreign policy decisions, Clinton did get involved in another failed state – Somalia. He despatched crack troops on a mission to capture warlords in the capital of Mogadishu. Some 18 US commandos and Rangers and around 500 Somalis died. Pictures of two US soldiers being dragged around the streets by Somali mobs sent shockwaves in Washington and around the world.

The Somali débâcle – later dramatised in the book and film *Black Hawk Down* – prompted Clinton to issue an order. He asked his National Security Council to put together a set of criteria for judging when intervention in foreign countries would be appropriate. Presidential Decision Directive PDD-25, published on 5 May 1994, during the height of the Rwandan crisis, listed no fewer than sixteen factors that policymakers needed to consider when deciding whether to support peacekeeping activities. The checklist was so comprehensive that one member of the House of Representatives said approvingly it satisfied the US desire for 'zero degree of involvement and zero degree of risk and zero degree of pain and confusion'.

American leaders have a deliberately circular relationship with public opinion. It is circular because public opinion is rarely if ever aroused by foreign crises, even genocidal ones, in the absence of political leadership, and yet at the same time American leaders continually cite the absence of public support as grounds for inaction.

The Major government had paid scant attention to Africa. Spending on international development remained pitifully low,

although the professionals in the Overseas Development Administration (ODA), as it was then called, usually did a good job in
spending what money they had wisely.

There was little indication early on that the Blair government
would be much different. Its front-bench spokesmen said little about
Rwanda, beyond the usual 'something must be done' rhetoric. When
in 1994 Clare Short denounced the Conservative government for
inaction in the crisis, operatives at Labour's Millbank headquarters
told her 'not to get involved in African conflicts'.

In its 1997 manifesto, Labour made two commitments affect-
ing the developing world. It committed itself to raising international
development spending to the UN average – although no target date
was mentioned. It also promised to give the issue a full government
department. In place of the ODA, which had been an adjunct of the
Foreign Office, a Department for International Development would
be set up under Clare Short. And yet, as the election approached,
Blair came under pressure from three sides to water down that
pledge. Robin Cook was not particularly happy to see the good-
news side of his future department hived off. The diplomats Blair
consulted on the eve of the election were wary of the idea. So was
Powell, schooled as he was in the traditional thinking of the FCO.
When the election came Blair had still not made up his mind. On
the following day, as he was formulating his first Cabinet, he finally
committed himself during his one-to-one chat with Short. Had he
reneged on that, which he might easily have done, she would not
have joined the government. That day was the first of many threats
she made to resign. The next came when Gordon Brown was final-
ising his first Comprehensive Spending Review. Short struggled to
get both Chancellor and Prime Minister to agree to a serious
increase in the overseas aid budget. The initial offer she regarded as
risible. She complained to Brown, who provided a bit more. Blair
rang her and told her to take it or leave it.

Short and Brown formed a close alliance over subsequent years
to promote debt relief and other development policies for Africa.

This became one of the Labour government's success stories. MPs and party activists despondent at other measures could cite development as one area where the government was trying to be radical. It was not to everyone's liking. Short and Brown were far less critical than many experts and non-governmental organisations would have wanted on the role of free trade. They saw its extension to poor countries as a good thing in itself and sometimes seemed blind to the malign affect it had, especially as the major economic blocs – the US and EU – continued with trade barriers while preventing imports from the Third World and flooding their markets with cheap goods. In his first year in office Blair paid scant notice. On his travels at international conferences he would hear praise for Short and the DfID. It was only then that he started taking an interest. Reflected glory concentrated the mind.

What concerns Blair did have about Africa did not translate into leftist dependency theory – the idea that the continent was underdeveloped due to the exploitative West. He took a more straightforward approach. He would work to protect and help African leaders he regarded as 'modernisers' who wanted to clean up corruption, open up their economies and work towards some form of democracy.

Within weeks of coming to office, one country provided an opportunity to put this theory into practice. The West African state of Sierra Leone gained independence in 1961. Founded in 1787 partly as a refuge for freed slaves, it had been one of Britain's most lucrative colonial redoubts. Trade flourished and civil society was relatively developed. Much of the forty-year period since independence was disfigured by a series of coups and counter-coups, with a succession of governments dependent upon or involved in the trade of diamonds. Over the past decade the vast diamond resources have caused incalculable damage to Sierra Leone as various military groups, notably the Revolutionary United Front (RUF), have fought for the spoils. The civil war saw nearly half the country's 4.5 million population displaced. At least 50,000 people died and tens of thousands more were victims of amputations and rape, mainly at the hands of the RUF, which controlled much of the country.

After a brief intervention by a South African private security company, Executive Outcomes, a lull in the fighting allowed elections to be held in March 1996. Those elections, which were funded largely by Britain and deemed by international observers to be free and fair, brought to power Ahmad Tejan Kabbah, a former UN official. After years of civil war the people had some cause for hope. Kabbah began negotiations with the RUF and its leader, Foday Sankoh. As part of those talks, he agreed that Executive Outcomes should leave. The RUF took advantage of the military vacuum by entering Freetown and ousting Kabbah in a coup in May 1997.

The UK and other industrialised nations were determined to do what they could to help Kabbah back to power. He had fled to Conakry, capital of neighbouring Guinea. The problem was that Kabbah would have to rely largely on the support of Nigeria, the regional superpower, to help him return. Nigeria itself had been expelled from the Commonwealth for abuse of human rights. It was a delicate balancing act for the Foreign Office. Blair was advised by the FCO that Kabbah was just his kind of moderniser. He committed himself in principle to bringing him back to power, and in a symbolic gesture of support he invited him as his personal guest to the Commonwealth conference in Edinburgh that October.

That was as far as Blair went. He had many more pressing issues on his mind and left the detail to Robin Cook – until, that is, the Foreign Secretary had fallen victim to a classic case of dodgy means being used for good ends. In an attempt to equip himself with a fighting force, Kabbah was trading arms for mining concessions – in effect mortgaging Sierra Leone's diamond resources – through a man called Rakesh Sakena, whom Cook would famously describe as 'an Indian businessman travelling on the passport of a dead Serb and awaiting extradition from Canada for alleged embezzlement from a bank in Thailand'. The arms were supplied by a firm called Sandline International, an associate of Executive Outcomes. It was the creation of Lieutenant-Colonel Tim Spicer, a former Guards officer who had served in Northern Ireland, the Gulf and the Falklands, to offer 'special forces rapid reaction' around the world – in other words, mercenaries.

On 28 April 1998, Cook's advisers told him that a fax had arrived from solicitors acting on behalf of Sandline. It informed the Foreign Secretary that Customs & Excise had launched an investigation into a shipment of arms to Sierra Leone in violation of a UN embargo. The company said it believed it had done nothing wrong because its plans had been approved by the Foreign Office. Cook would later insist this was the first he knew of any problem.

UN Resolution 1132 had been drawn up by the British and passed by the Security Council on 8 October 1997. It imposed sanctions against Sierra Leone, banning the supply of arms and petroleum products. The trouble was, the wording was ambiguous. It could be read as blocking arms sales not just to the RUF, but also to Kabbah and his legitimate government. The British High Commissioner saw it differently. An old Africa hand, Peter Penfold had returned to Sierra Leone in his mid-fifties. His close relations with Kabbah and his strong personal support for the ousted regime set him apart from the usual diplomat.

When Nigerian forces began a naval bombardment of Freetown to try to force the new military leaders to resign, Penfold became an instant folk hero by shepherding British and other nationals out of their burning hotel and to the safety of Conakry. From there Kabbah planned his return to power with the Nigerians and the British. He contacted Spicer shortly before Christmas. A month later, as he was preparing a shipment of arms to Kabbah, Spicer went to see Foreign Office officials. That shipment of cases of Bulgarian-made AK-47 rifles made it to Lungi airport on the outskirts of Freetown, only to be seized by the military junta.

Shortly after, in early March 1998, Nigerian forces deployed under a UN umbrella restored Kabbah to power. As he arrived in Freetown from Conakry he received a jubilant reception on the streets. Even though his grip on the country was tenuous, and even though it was the Nigerians who were maintaining a semblance of order, this was still an improvement on what had preceded it.

Yet within a month events in Sierra Leone would rock the British government. When the lawyers' fax that Cook had been alerted to found its way into the papers, the press had a field day. Ministers tied themselves up in knots, trying to explain away the violation or misreading of a UN resolution they had sponsored and written.

Blair could not believe what he was being told. He was furious that, weeks after the story had first appeared in the papers, Cook and his team could still not get themselves off the hook. To the Prime Minister the answer was simple. Whatever mistakes may have been made in the drafting of the resolution and in the distribution of messages around the Foreign Office, Britain had been right to support Sierra Leone's elected government. Kabbah was back in power, so what was the problem? The following Monday, 11 May, Blair performed one of his classic 'spontaneous' statements before the cameras. He happened to be visiting a London college, but he knew television reporters would ask his views about the Sandline furore. His words were carefully rehearsed. 'Don't let us forget that what was happening was that the UN and the UK were both trying to help the democratic regime restore its position from an illegal military coup. They were quite right in trying to do it,' Blair said. Penfold, he added, had done a 'superb job' working with Kabbah. 'That is the background and people can see that a lot of the hoo-ha is overblown.'

A subsequent inquiry into the affair by Sir Thomas Legg, a retired civil servant, exonerated ministers and suggested that civil servants in the Africa Department should have communicated better with the High Commissioner. Blair had gone so far out on a limb to back Penfold that it would have been awkward for Legg's report to go on to blame him. Cook's people, meanwhile, were angry that his staff in London should be criticised for doing what they were supposed to have done. For Blair this was a case of the Foreign Office being too absorbed in detail and failing to see the big moral picture. He would cite this example when dealing with future international crises. In a dig at Cook, Blair said: 'When people say "run an ethical foreign policy", I say Sierra Leone was an example of that, not an example of not doing it. It is up in the high ground.'

Blair portrayed it in terms of 'good guys' and 'bad guys'. He was largely, but not completely, right. The vast majority of the violence was carried out by the RUF. But the government's own Civil Defence Force, otherwise known as the Kamajors, was also responsible for acts of brutality. In any case, allegiances were confused. Some Sierra Leoneans were known as 'sobels', soldiers who were RUF collaborators – government forces by day, rebels by night.

In January 1999 the RUF made another incursion into Freetown, killing, mutilating and abducting thousands more people. They were once again forced to withdraw. Kabbah, meanwhile, was being put under pressure by Britain, the US and his neighbours to try another peace agreement with Sankoh, the RUF's leader. Six months later they signed a peace agreement in Lome, capital of Togo, in which the rebels were given seats in the government and a legal amnesty in return for peace. Bizarrely, Sankoh was given the title of vice-president and put in charge of strategic minerals, including diamonds. Some 6,000 UN peacekeepers were to be deployed to keep order. 'Unamsil' became the biggest UN peacekeeping operation at the time anywhere in the world. Human rights organisations criticised the inclusion of the RUF in the government, saying the rebels had used murder, rape and mutilation to gain a place at the negotiating table after nine years at war.

Within months, however, that deal too had unravelled. The UN contingent comprised troops mainly from sub-Saharan Africa, the Middle East and South Asia. They were under-resourced and had little experience of such operations. As the fighting intensified, the international force became unable to cope. It retreated into its compound and then came under attack. In February 2000 the UN Security Council adopted a resolution expanding Unamsil to 11,000.

In spite of the increasing numbers, RUF forces managed in May to take 500 of the foreign soldiers hostage. In London, that was a trigger for action.

Acting on military intelligence that Freetown was about to be taken again, Geoff Hoon, the new Defence Secretary, and Cook persuaded Blair that British troops should be sent in. On 7 May they took the decision to scramble a 'spearhead battalion' of about 700 troops, ostensibly to evacuate foreign nationals from Freetown. But at the Ministry of Defence and Foreign Office nobody was clear what the remit actually was.

The first contingent of soldiers was deployed in and around Freetown. Their job was to keep order while UN reinforcements arrived, and then to leave. General Guthrie flew in with the troops to oversee the operation. The mission was viewed in Downing Street and at the MoD as a test of Britain's post-Cold War capabilities, of its military prowess in a potential combat situation on the ground. The troops were to be backed up by aircraft, additional helicopters and a task force of British warships carrying 800 Royal Marine commandoes ready off the coast.

The first task, securing the airport, was achieved by a battalion of paratroopers who went in on their own, knowing that air support and an amphibious group organised around the helicopter carrier HMS *Ocean* were still some days' sailing away. If things had gone wrong, those reinforcements would have been badly needed. The UN hostages were released in stages. With British troops providing security in the capital and logistical support to the beleaguered UN operation, Kabbah's army was for the first time able to force the rebels back out of the capital.

Blair came under pressure from the Conservatives and parts of the media to withdraw. Two phrases did the rounds: 'mission creep' and 'overstretch'. In his enthusiasm to be seen to be doing something, Blair was running the risk of committing British troops to an intractable conflict of indeterminate length. Given Britain's military deployments in Northern Ireland, Bosnia, Kosovo and elsewhere, it

was said that the army simply could not sustain a long and dangerous intervention in Africa.

Nobody said as much, but this was Britain's colonial burden
returning. Blair tried to play it down. He told MPs the British forces
were there only to back up the UN. Hoon said they would not take
on a combat role, but they would stay in the area for a month while
Unamsil was reinforced. 'There is no question of the UK taking over
the UN mission or of being drawn into the civil war,' he said.

At ministerial meetings, the message was different. Hoon,
Cook and Short advised Blair that the situation was volatile, that
troops could not stand by and watch atrocities take place. Someone
had to keep order. 'It would be disgraceful to pull them out now,'
Short told Blair. His reply was succinct. 'Let them stay.' John Sawers,
Blair's principal private secretary, told a succession of ministerial
meetings that the instruction from the Prime Minister was to 'go for
the radical option'. Blair was confident that the cause outweighed the
criticisms and the dangers. There was little controversy abroad. The
British mission was backed by a number of UN resolutions, and
had overwhelming international consensus. The bilateral obligations were immense. The Labour government directed more money,
more aid per head of population and more political support to
Sierra Leone than to any other African country.

Ministers did not admit it, but the British remit had quietly
changed. Having been sent in to evacuate the expats and secure the
airport, the soldiers turned themselves into the only stabilising force
that existed in the country. They confronted the RUF in at least one
battle that left close to twenty rebels dead. The British success in
evicting the rebels from the Okra hills and clearing the once dangerous Masiaka route linking the capital to the provinces won the
British army accolades. UK troops also assisted in capturing Sankoh.
After that they began to help train and arm the Sierra Leone army.

On 25 August, however, disaster struck. Eleven soldiers from
the Royal Irish Regiment, along with their local military liaison,
were taken hostage. They were taken to a hide-out by a renegade

militia known as the West Side Boys. British forces launched an immediate search, but helicopter overflights failed to locate them. Five days later the militia, who were demanding the release from prison of their leader, set free five of the British soldiers in exchange for a satellite phone and medical supplies. As the negotiations continued, Blair and Hoon dispatched a force of 150 paratroopers. They were supported by twelve members of the SAS, although the government tried to keep that secret. This was Operation Barras.

At dawn on 10 September, the Paras descended from five helicopter gunships into a remote part of the jungle. They strafed the banks of the river where the rebels had set up camp. One of the Chinooks landed near the huts and the soldiers went in. The West Siders opened fire with a heavy machine gun before a second helicopter overwhelmed them. The highly risky but meticulously executed raid left twenty-five rebels dead. One British soldier was killed, but within twenty minutes the hostages were in a helicopter being whisked back to safety after their sixteen-day ordeal. The fighting continued for ten hours. However, as the men returned to Freetown, an argument began over the actions of the soldiers who had been kidnapped. The British said the men had driven out of the town to meet Jordanian troops serving with Unamsil. However, the UN commander said they had not informed him and had been deep inside enemy-held jungle when they were captured.

Still, as the men prepared to fly home and Britain prepared to scale down its operation in Sierra Leone, Blair had reason to be pleased. This was in effect a unilateral action, and unique for that, and had been carried out well. It had not registered that highly with the British public, but it was an important test case for his willingness to deploy troops and his commitment to fashion change in Africa. One minister passed on to Blair the congratulations of the Clinton administration. 'You guys have got a rapid reaction with a reach which nobody else has.' Blair remembered that with pride.

Three months later, in December 2000, Bill Clinton arrived in London for his swansong visit as President. The elections had been and gone. George W. Bush had controversially been declared the winner, defeating Al Gore. Clinton was now seeking to fashion a new role for himself as global elder statesman. A few months earlier, in August, he made his second official visit to Africa. None of his predecessors had shown anything like his interest in the continent. During his eight years at the White House he had sent all his most senior members on official visits. His voyage this time had taken him to Nigeria, Tanzania and Burundi.

Over dinner with Tony, Cherie and Hillary at Chequers, the outgoing president passed on two pieces of advice to his good friend. The first was: make Africa a bigger priority. That was not just morally right. Politically it would set Blair apart from the rest. The second was: 'Don't let your friendship with America wane, just because I'm gone.' Get as close as possible to Bush. On both counts, Blair did not need persuading.

It became axiomatic for Blair's friends to portray his commitment to Africa as profound and permanent. If so, where did it come from? His father, Leo, visited Sierra Leone's university several times in the 1960s as a law lecturer. But there is no evidence to suggest that this particularly influenced his son. At St John's College, Oxford, Blair made friends with several African students who went on to become involved in politics in their home continent. Prominent among them was Olara Otunnu, a Ugandan who was an overseas scholar at Oxford. Otunnu was briefly Uganda's foreign minister in the mid-1980s and was a candidate for Secretary-General of the UN. In Blair's first years in Downing Street, Otunnu, who had been appointed UN Special Representative for Children and Armed Conflict, came to see him whenever he was in London. Blair saw him as a model for a new generation of leaders, with a vision not influenced by legacies of colonialism or post-colonialism.

Africa went to the heart of Blair's core beliefs and his contradictions. It chimed with his religious beliefs. Back in 1993, before he became party leader, he wrote a Foreword to a collection of essays edited by John Smith entitled *Reclaiming the Ground: Christianity and Socialism*. 'Christianity is a very tough religion,' Blair wrote. 'It is judgemental. There is right and wrong. There is good and bad. We all know this, of course, but it has become fashionable to be uncomfortable about such language. But when we look at our world today and how much needs to be done, we should not hesitate to make such judgements. And then follow them with determined action. That would be Christian Socialism.' This was well before Blair had even begun to think about foreign policy. He made up for lack of detail with evangelical fervour.

As Prime Minister, Blair would find public discussion and deconstruction of his religious beliefs awkward. His interest in political philosophy was limited. His interest in religion and comparative religions was inexhaustible. From the summer of 1997 friends who visited him on holiday would notice copies of the Bible, the Koran and other religious works by his side. He liked to see himself as an intellectual ecumenist. He told one friend on holiday: 'The main religions are all about the same thing.' He abhorred the link between narrow nationalism and religion as personified by Slobodan Milošević. He was proud that Christian Europe had come to the aid of Muslim Kosovans.

The more involved he became in foreign affairs, the more Blair wrestled with his theological thinking. The communitarianism of the Scottish philosopher John Macmurray, to which he had been introduced by Peter Thomson, an Australian priest he met at Oxford, provided the broad outlines. Blair sought to apply Macmurray's premise – that only by pursuing the interest of the community as a whole do we help ourselves and those around us – to global problems.

On 30 June 2000 Blair made a trip to the small southern German town of Tübingen to give a speech on 'the values and the power of community'. His host was Hans Kung's Global Ethics Foundation. This was an unlikely event for a busy Prime Minister, but Blair saw Kung, a 72-year-old Swiss theologian who had fallen out with the Vatican, as a fellow radical explorer of values, ethics and community. In his speech, Blair spoke of the 'sole key to politics in the modern world – how to manage change'. He called for greater inter-faith dialogue and, returning to his theme of Chicago, said: 'I believe we will only succeed if we start to develop a doctrine of international community . . . a community based on the equal worth of all, on the foundation of mutual rights and mutual responsibilities.' He placed that doctrine in a line stemming from Dante's 'world law' to Erasmus' Council of Just Men.

Blair certainly did display a growing enthusiasm to tackle the seemingly intractable issues of debt and poverty that many other world leaders shied away from. But some around him, like Clare Short, who was actually responsible for the policy, wondered throughout about the sincerity of his commitment. Overall, Blair's approach to Africa was a jumbled mix of ambitious policy, passionate genuflexions and picture opportunities.

Blair would later develop these ideas with African and other international leaders into the New Partnership for Africa's Development (Nepad). Launched at the G8 summit in Genoa in July 2001, it was dubbed the 'Marshall Plan for Africa'. The idea was to link debt relief and development aid firmly to political and economic reform. It was a deal between Africa and the developed world in which the latter agreed to provide more aid for infrastructure projects, debt relief and education and to ease access for African goods to international markets. In return, Africa would accept the post-Cold War neo-liberal economic orthodoxies – in other words, globalisation – and commit itself to the principle of good governance. People around Blair say they never saw him more enthusiastic than when he was working on Nepad. He saw it as Britain using a role derived from its history to good effect. Africa demonstrated Blair's belief that he had powers to influence just about any country he engaged himself with. His was the antithesis of isolationism, and he wanted everyone to know.

Straight after Genoa, Blair arranged for a summit with six

reform-minded African leaders – from Nigeria, Ghana, Tanzania, Botswana, Senegal and Mozambique – at Chequers that September. When the events of September 11 took place, everyone around Blair assumed they would have to cancel the Africa gathering. Virtually all scheduled meetings had been removed from his diary. But he insisted that it go ahead as planned. He wanted to make a point. He told his team he wanted to show that the task of 'bringing the world together' had become all the more urgent.

The success of Nepad depended, however, on African leaders being tough on themselves and their neighbours. The refusal of South Africa's Thabo Mbeki to condemn President Robert Mugabe of Zimbabwe, as that country descended into vicious dictatorship, severely undermined Blair's broader Africa strategy. It left him deeply depressed. On one trip Blair found himself in the company of Clare Short. They talked for long periods together. They spoke about the principle of intervention. Blair confided in her that, 'If it were down to me, I'd do Zimbabwe as well' – that is, send troops.

For all Blair's professed commitment to Africa, nothing was done and very little said about the civil war in Congo, in which up to 3 million people had been killed, or killings in Liberia in which many hundreds died. Prime ministerial interest and outrage was consistently selective, as was the attention to human rights. Blair simply could not understand, for example, the howls of outrage in June 2002 over a £28 million contract to sell Tanzania an air traffic control system, again by BAE Systems, again backed by an export credit agreement underwritten by the British government. Even the World Bank called it a complete waste of money. At the height of the controversy, Blair turned to his advisers and said: 'What's the matter with these people?'

It was nearly three years after the despatch of British troops before Blair went back to Sierra Leone. At the start of a four-nation tour of Africa in February 2002, he used a speech to the Nigerian parliament to attack those who mocked his global ambition, his evangelising, his messianic tendencies. There was, he said, 'no leafy suburb far from the reach of bad things and bad people'. As for those who wondered about his involvement in Africa, he said: 'The cynics say, "Why should we succeed now when we have failed before?" But that is what they have said throughout human history. If we listened to them we would still be in the dark ages.'

It was only when Blair arrived at Freetown airport that, as he confided to one of his aides, he felt truly vindicated. After talking to the small British military contingent that had remained in the country, he was taken to a village nearby. 'We welcome your excellency the peacemaker, we love and respect you, trust and support you,' read a sign hanging from its ramshackle school. Blair told the cheering crowd of his unbending commitment. He spoke of creating a country worthy of its children. The women in the village told him stories of savagery meted out by the RUF. They then sang him a song. He told them he was convinced that 'a little could make a big difference'. They had, he added with utter seriousness, made him feel he was single-handedly responsible for their freedom.

5

UNLIKELY FRIENDS

WITH HIS BRIGHTLY COLOURED SOCKS AND A SELF-confidence effortlessly acquired at Lancing College and Peterhouse, Cambridge, Sir Christopher Meyer fits perfectly the American stereotype of an Establishment Brit.

As any civil servant should do, he made himself comfortable with Prime Ministers of all hues. He was charm personified when dead-batting a voracious press in the dying years of John Major's hapless rule. A twinkle in the eye from Downing Street's spin-doctor suggested that, yes, he was going through the motions, but that was his job. He cut and ran as soon as he could, saying that as the appointed ambassador to Germany he needed to brush up on his language, even though it was pretty good already. He needed distance from the *ancien régime* and had already been singled out by Blair as one of a small number of top Foreign Office mandarins New Labour could trust. Meyer had worked with Jonathan Powell, as his superior, and the two had got on well. Having barely unpacked his bags in Bonn, Meyer was given the plum job of Her Majesty's Ambassador to Washington.

Meyer arrived in the US in October 1997. Blair was at the

height of his honeymoon. Prime Minister and President were soul-
mates – leaders and proselytisers for their passionate but
indeterminate Third Way project. Meyer did not have to do too
much on that front. So he set about a longer-term task. He and the
rest of the embassy had established good links with Al Gore and his
team. The Vice-President would not make a charismatic successor,
but he was solid and uncontroversial. It was assumed by Jonathan
Powell that Gore would win. The Republican picture was less clear.
Meyer asked senior party figures who would be most likely to get
through the primaries and emerge as their candidate. Bush, they
said. Meyer assumed they were talking about Jeb, the governor of
Florida.

Surprised when he learned which brother they were referring
to, Meyer set off to meet the other Bush. He knew his way round the
Republicans. As deputy head of mission in the early 1990s, he had
made good contacts with the first Bush administration.

He first met Donald Rumsfeld in 1990. They were both part of
an outward-bound bonding trip to Arizona for diplomats, executives and opinion-formers. Rumsfeld was in the private sector,
making artificial sweeteners, a subject he loved talking about.
During their five-day trip they marched up the southern rim of the
Grand Canyon. They also went white-water rafting. Meyer recalls
how everyone fell into the water except Rumsfeld – he had pulled a
muscle in his back and insisted on being strapped into the canoe.

Meyer had also known Paul Wolfowitz in the 1990s. Both were
involved with the School of Advanced International Studies in
Washington, where Meyer did a doctorate in the mid-1960s.
Wolfowitz became dean there and the two met at several functions.

As for Condoleezza Rice, they did come across each other
during the first Gulf War, when she was a senior staffer at the
National Security Council. But their first meaningful conversation
came in the early summer of 1998, at a dinner hosted by a mutual
friend. They talked mostly about Russia, her speciality. Meyer was
struck by how vehemently she argued that the pillars of Cold War

détente, such as the ABM treaty, were now redundant. What was being contemplated, albeit still vaguely, was the dispensing of many of the tenets of international diplomacy with which the world had been familiar for decades.

Meyer's first impressions of George W. Bush were of an inarticulate and untutored conviction politician. Nevertheless, he concluded that he should not be underestimated. He passed this back to Powell. Another visit to Austin, via a courtesy call on Bush senior in Houston, followed the next year. By then people were pouring into the Texan capital to take a look, even though he had yet to declare his candidacy. A month after that trip, Meyer was followed by the then Tory leader William Hague, on a mission to the US to learn the secrets of 'compassionate conservativism'.

Meyer despatched the embassy's Political Secretary, Matthew Rycroft, to monitor the 2000 campaign. It was a job that Powell himself had done in 1992, in the Clinton ascendancy that had so allured him. Rycroft, who would later serve under David Manning in Downing Street, reported back that Gore and Bush would win their parties' nominations and that the election itself would be neck and neck. Meyer told Powell and Blair that they must take Bush seriously. This would take some recalibration. After all, the Texan governor had built his short but successful political career on sneering at the urbane, cosmopolitan liberalism that Blair and Clinton represented. Meyer told him not to repeat John Major's mistake of antagonising Clinton in the 1992 campaign. 'Whatever you think of Bush, no matter how much you might want Gore to win, keep it to yourselves,' Meyer said. The Blairites had already come to the same conclusion. New Labour and New Democrats had merged into one during the 1990s, sending platoons to each others' headquarters to help out in elections. Not this time. Out of political loyalty they wanted the Democratic candidate to win. But professionally, the more they saw of Gore's campaign, the more they despaired of it.

As Bush was assembling his team ahead of the showdown in November 2000, Meyer and Rice met privately several times to lay the ground. Downing Street had also done some homework of its own. Powell's own contacts were strong. Mandelson had met Rice at a conference in Aspen that year. He reported back to Blair that he had been impressed by her 'sharp, tidy mind'. Cook had already met Colin Powell, Bush's nominee as Secretary of State. However, a hoped-for visit to Europe by Bush between the primaries and the election, in which London would be the first port of call, was cancelled amid fears of negative headlines. Blair was disappointed. He had wanted to have some 'face time' before the voting.

He did have an intermediary. Bill Gammell had built up Cairn Energy into a significant oil drilling company. As an Edinburgh fund manager he invested in a fledgling firm by the name of Zapato Oil, set up by no less than George Bush senior in the 1950s. The two became good friends, so much so that they enjoyed a summer together at the Gammells' family farm in Perthshire. George W. was thirteen at the time. That was his first trip to Europe. The young Gammell, whom he would call 'Willy', was six. The two boys followed their fathers into the oil business. Their friendship continued as they met at drilling projects in Texas in the 1980s and they did business together for six years, with Gammell helping out his American friend when his company fell on hard times. Bush junior made several return visits to Scotland and in 1983 attended Gammell's wedding.

Gammell also happened to have known a young Tony Blair. They played in the basketball team together at their Edinburgh public school, Fettes. They renewed their friendship at a Labour Party fundraising dinner in 1994. Three years later, at the Commonwealth conference in Edinburgh in October 1997, Blair did his friend a favour of his own. He took time off from the diplomacy and opened Gammell's new headquarters in the city. For good measure, Blair took the Bangladeshi Prime Minister with him. Cairn had been developing Bangladesh's offshore natural gas fields. It was a joint venture, the consortium including the state-owned energy company – and Halliburton, headed by a certain Dick Cheney.

When Gammell saw the prospect of his two childhood buddies taking over at the helm of the world's only superpower and its junior partner, he was keen to help out. He described these friendships as 'a curious and extraordinary accident of fate. It is an accident of history that I was in the same house at school as Tony Blair, and that I also know George Bush. The two have not met.' He went to Downing Street to brief Blair about Bush, and would keep in constant touch with Anji Hunter. He told them that Bush was straightforward, and that in spite of the negative headlines they would be able to work with him. Gammell then went to the US to pass on exactly the same positive message to Bush's team.

Still, moderate European opinion did not like what it saw. The government-in-waiting in Washington was setting a wholly unfamiliar tone. Bush had admitted to Meyer that he didn't know much about foreign affairs. He was relying heavily on Rice and Wolfowitz. Those were the names on everyone's lips. Colin Powell, the acceptable face of the new administration, seemed but an afterthought.

The most intriguing new name was that of Rice. Raised in Birmingham, Alabama under the shadow of segregation, she often said that to get ahead she had to be 'twice as good'. After serving as Soviet affairs adviser on Bush senior's National Security Council, Rice returned to Stanford where she became its youngest, the first female and first non-white provost. A very meticulous person, a keen pianist, she became one of the most inscrutable and influential National Security Advisors and an unflappable gatekeeper in what would be a highly fractious administration.

Rice and Wolfowitz were at the head of a group of foreign policy advisers known affectionately as the Vulcans. Wolfowitz was the brains behind the project. The son of a mathematician, he had abandoned an academic career to pursue politics, taking a job with the Arms Control and Disarmament Agency during the dying days of the Reagan administration and then serving under his mentor, Cheney, in the Defense Department under Bush senior.

Rumsfeld was one of those young men who decided that

Washington would be his life. In 1962, at the age of twenty-nine, he won a Congressional seat in Chicago. His first campaign statement was to 'maintain a firm, no-back-down foreign policy based on the rightness of our position and backed by military strength'. Just before the Watergate scandal broke he quit his job as an economic adviser to President Nixon and became US Ambassador to Nato. This was a brief, but illuminating, experience for him. This was the height of the Cold War, of a divided Europe looking deferentially to America for its security. In 1975, Gerald Ford called Rumsfeld back to become the youngest ever US Secretary of Defense. In 2002 he would become the oldest man to hold the post.

The neoconservatives had in the mid-1990s identified George W. Bush as a potential vehicle for gaining power. Most of them were old-timers who knew their way around Washington. They provided an experience on which the inexperienced Republican nominee could rely. Rumsfeld was earmarked for defence, with Wolfowitz as his deputy. With them were other leading lights in the Project for the New American Century such as Douglas Feith, who became Under-Secretary for Defense responsible for policy, and Richard Perle. He had turned down the job of number three at the Pentagon to become head of the Defense Policy Board. Even though it had no official status, this group was given access to classified documents and the right to make recommendations direct to the White House.

The State Department, the traditional home of foreign policy, was aghast at the line-up. Colin Powell, Bush's choice as Secretary of State, also had to contend with a number three in John Bolton who belonged firmly in the neocon camp. Powell assumed that, given his contacts with the Pentagon as former Joint Chiefs of Staff, he could deal with its new clique of civilian bosses. One of the most outspoken members of the neoconservative group, Bolton famously stated in 1994: 'There is no such thing as the United Nations. There is only the international community, which can only be led by the only remaining superpower, which is the US.' He added: 'If the UN

Secretariat building in New York lost ten stories, it wouldn't make a bit of difference.'

On one point there was no disagreement within the Bush team. They gave themselves the acronym ABC – Anything But Clinton. In tone, in style and in substance they were to be altogether different from anything that had come before. Clinton was damaged goods. Gore knew that, and had distanced himself from the outgoing president during the election campaign. Blair also knew that. Even before the Florida recounts and the Supreme Court's verdict in favour of Bush, Downing Street had taken cover, studiously avoiding any comment that might prejudice relations.

Bush took the oath on 20 January 2001, politically crippled. If Gore had found the 500 votes needed to carry Florida, his margin would have been quite comfortable. Only three presidents had received fewer votes than their opponent, the last in the nineteenth century. The American media, not known for their scepticism or disrespect of their leaders, had a field day with Bush. Jay Leno, the chat-show host, called Bush–Cheney 'the Wizard of Oz ticket' – 'one needs a heart, the other needs a brain'. Bush replied that his critics 'misunderestimated' him. As for his knowledge of foreign affairs, he would be tainted by that interview in November 1999 in which he could not remember the name of the President of Pakistan or the Prime Minister of India.

What worried Blair, however, about the incoming administration was not ignorance – that, he was convinced, could be overcome – or overweaning ambition, as set out by Wolfowitz and the Project. Rather the reverse. The fear was of a stay-at-home President, withdrawing from peacekeeping and other international obligations on which Europe had so relied. During the campaign, Bush had struck a cautious note. 'If we're an arrogant nation, they'll resent us,' he said in his second televised debate with Gore. 'If we're a humble nation, but strong, they'll welcome us.' That was a promise to check hubris at the door, an effort to guard against the temptation to believe that because he would soon have awesome power at his fingertips, he could and should use it to achieve grandiose objectives.

On the eve of the inauguration, Rice also suggested a less interventionist role. 'American foreign policy cannot be all things to all people – or rather to all interest groups,' she said. Bush, she promised, would 'refocus the United States on the national interest and the pursuit of key priorities'. She listed five of them. Number five was 'to deal decisively with the threat of rogue regimes and hostile powers'.

'Our great fear of Bush during the campaign was of disengagement from the world, of a fortress America,' says one figure close to Blair. 'The idea that they would be too interventionist seemed crazy at the time.' On Iraq, Bush told one aide during the campaign: 'We have a festering problem.' But there was little indication that the standard approach of containment was changing – perhaps there would be more money for exile groups to challenge Saddam's hegemony from outside, but that was it. Across the world there was a feeling that the Americans were looking to disengage – from the former Yugoslavia, and from the Northern Ireland peace process, where the Bush team had told Jonathan Powell they had no intention of getting involved. At one meeting held to discuss strategy for the new administration, Blair turned to Mandelson and said: 'We've got to turn these people into internationalists.'

The most immediate task was to win influence in the tightly knit Bush camp. They knew it wasn't going to be easy. Meyer had agreed with Rice that Blair's inner circle should visit in January 2001, in the days leading up to the swearing-in of the new president. They all traipsed over, headed by Powell and Sawers, and were reassured by what they heard. Meyer had suggested to Rice that London should be Bush's first foreign venture, only to find that it would be Mexico. Was Bush showing that his priorities lay more with the North American Free Trade Agreement than with old Blighty? Rice tried to reassure Meyer that this would simply be an 'easy way in' for an inexperienced president in his first weeks of office.

Bush's trip to President Vicente Fox's ranch at San Cristobal on 16 February, dubbed the 'Cowboy Summit', left its mark on Downing Street. Blair's people were feverishly discussing dates with the new administration for his visit. They were determined to ensure that Bush's geostrategic recalibration did not go too far.

Yet even Colin Powell, whom they identified as the most Europe-friendly of the inner circle, served notice that the new America was looking elsewhere for its special relationships. During his Senate confirmation hearings, he talked in detail about his plans for the Pacific area, for Asia, the Middle East, Russia and China. There was barely a word about Europe. The only reference to Britain was in the context of a history lesson about how Washington won the Cold War despite the Greenham Common protesters. 'You have to understand that after the end of the Cold War Europe has much less strategic importance for us,' one British diplomat was told. That truth had been hidden throughout the 1990s because of co-operation over the Balkans.

To make matters worse, the first European leader to meet Bush was, of all people, Jacques Chirac. With France holding the rotating EU presidency, he just happened to be in Washington. The Brits were told by the Americans not to worry. The courtesy call lasted only ten minutes and was held in the French Embassy. The date for Blair's moment was set. He would visit Bush on 23 February at Camp David. It would be their first meeting, and in Downing Street they worked frantically to prepare it down to the last detail.

Their nerves were not helped by the opening handshake. On arrival in Washington, Blair was met by Cheney. The greeting was stiff and formal. Both men kept to their briefs. Blair remarked to his aides afterwards that he had found Cheney's right-hand man, Lewis 'Scooter' Libby, intimidating. That relationship with Cheney would remain frosty.

Courtesies over, the helicopter took him to Camp David. Blair was familiar with the place, the rural idyll of wooden lodges and pine trees mixing uneasily with the antennae of security guard posts.

The only unfamiliar sight was its new tenant. Bush smiled, welcomed him and took him in for lunch. Bush was already in his chinos. Blair quickly changed out of his suit. There were no preliminaries. 'Let's talk about the Middle East,' Bush said. He had been well briefed and knew that, for Blair, the Israeli–Palestinian conflict would be top of the agenda. Bush invited Colin Powell to make a presentation. Bush knew how to tickle his guest. He reminded him that he was the first world leader to be asked to his Maryland retreat. He then asked Blair to share his wisdom about world affairs, and about Russia's Vladimir Putin in particular, whom the Prime Minister had met several times.

The agenda, faxed through to Downing Street a few days earlier, had an issue typed out in bold. Iraq was to be a major spine of the discussion. The two spent an hour talking about it. Bush told Blair he wanted to warn Saddam he should not 'cross any line or test our will'. Bush had put down a marker that he saw Iraq as an issue that needed to be dealt with. They didn't talk specifics. But they did talk about tightening sanctions, which they accepted weren't working. That was as far as it went. Blair was careful not to be too chummy, but the two immediately felt relaxed in each other's company. Bush flattered Blair, referred constantly to his international experience, to his high approval ratings. He did not mention his close friendship with Clinton. That, for both men, was history. 'It wasn't quite that Tony had the upper hand, but he had established himself as the key international statesman,' says one British official. 'Blair had credentials. Bush gave the impression that he looked up at Tony. It was flattering.'

The private bonhomie did not translate into their public appearances. At their first news conference straight after their first discussion, the body language between the open-shirted Prime Minister and the President in his bomber jacket was awkward. They did their best. Blair announced that the special relationship was alive and kicking in the post-Clinton era. 'And we're going to keep it that way,' Bush interjected. He called Britain 'our strongest friend and closest ally'. He added: 'He put the charm offensive on me – and it worked.' He knew that when he telephoned Blair in the future 'there'll be a friend on the other end of the phone'. Bush was then asked what they had in common, replying falteringly that they shared the same taste in toothpaste. An embarrassed Blair, his face fixed in his ubiquitous Colgate smile, countered: 'They're going to wonder how you know that, George.' Bush had been lost for words. All the lodges at the retreat are supplied with the standard fare of toiletries seen in upmarket hotels. The toothpaste is supplied by Colgate. It was the first thing that had come into his head. The British were kicking themselves that they had not briefed the travelling press more fully on the bigger issues, leading that first meeting to be dubbed 'the toothpaste summit'.

After a mid-afternoon break they met at Laurel Cabin, Bush's private residence at the retreat, talking by the roaring fire. Blair flattered Bush by asking him to talk about his successes in political campaigning. Bush was in his element. Blair was captivated, listening intently. They then split, the 'principals' dining all together, with Bush and Blair going it alone next door. After dinner it was time to relax. They adjourned to one of the lodges, which houses a cinema. On show that night was *Meet the Parents*. They all settled on to sofas and chairs. Bush spent the whole film 'laughing like a drain', according to one person present. Blair chuckled a few times, politely. Rice fell asleep, slumped in her armchair. Meyer wondered whether laughing in unison with Bush might seem somewhat contrived, so he confined himself to the odd titter. As the credits rolled, a good time had been had by all, and the two teams bade farewell for the evening. Thanks to Robert De Niro and Ben Stiller, the ice had been broken and that special relationship was back on track.

The meeting had gone as well as anyone could have expected. Both men said what the other wanted to hear. So co-ordinated had the 'lines to take' been that the *Washington Post* proclaimed that Bush's endorsement of a European defence force could have been written by Downing Street.

Both sides were working from a long-established template. The Americans, at their most diplomatic, would ceaselessly seek to reassure the Brits that their word counted in Washington, that they were first among international equals. Reagan had done that with Thatcher. Bush senior did that with Major. Clinton did that with Blair. Theirs was a dress-down informality of the 1990s, a back-slapping friendship in which privately they would use fruity language to make their points. Blair and Bush were much more formal, much more courteous, much more old-fashioned. But the same rules applied. Blair had long before acquired the habit of private advice, public friendship.

Blair had learned over the years how to press American buttons. He did it early on with Clinton. Giving the toast at a White House dinner in 1998, he quoted the biblical remarks of Harry Hopkins, Roosevelt's emissary to Churchill, at a wartime dinner. 'Whither thou goest I will go, and whither thou lodgest I will lodge. Thy people shall be my people, and thy God my God.' Then Blair continued. 'And Hopkins paused, and then he said, "even to the end", and Churchill wept.' Clinton wept at those words too.

Churchill was even more in vogue with the new administration. Meyer had picked up from Karl Rove, Bush's chief political strategist, that the new president was a great admirer of the wartime Prime Minister. He dutifully reported this back to Powell in Downing Street, who made discreet enquiries with the curators of the government's art collection. They had a copy made of the final draft of the 1941 Atlantic Charter and of a manuscript of suggested amendments handwritten by Churchill. Shortly before the first summit Meyer handed it over to Rove, and the framed manuscripts were hung in Camp David. Not content with that, five months later, just before Bush's first visit as President to the UK, Meyer organised a small ceremony at the embassy, where he handed over an Epstein bust of Churchill. This was loaned to Bush for the duration of his presidency at the request of Blair – and has pride of place in the Oval Office. Rove also set up an irregular series of lectures at the White House. One person invited to speak was Martin Gilbert, Churchill's most prolific biographer.

It soon became apparent, however, that for all the personal bonhomie, for all the carefully choreographed diplomacy, Bush was dragging US policy on to new ground. Blair did his best to say kind things. In March, in a newspaper interview, he proudly proclaimed: 'I've been as pro-America a Prime Minister as is possible to have. There is not a single issue I can think of in which we haven't stood foursquare with America.' It was a new and unsettling experience for him. Between February and July 2001 the US managed to antagonise most of its erstwhile allies over its approach to defence, the environment, international law, disarmament, free trade and diplomacy.

Top of Bush's agenda was National Missile Defense, a multi-billion-dollar plan that would lead to the abandonment of the thirty-year-old Anti-Ballistic Missile Treaty that had underpinned the Cold War status quo. Rice had served notice from an early stage that NMD would be a priority – under Clinton the first tests of the system had been successful. For Blair, it posed a serious political dilemma. At some point he would have to approve the upgrading of the Fylingdales radar station in Yorkshire – all for a project and a president his Labour Party saw as anathema.

Even before he had been sworn in, Rumsfeld was lecturing his European counterparts at the annual Wehrkunde security conference in Munich on the 'moral imperative' of NMD. He and the other neocons were also deeply suspicious of plans for European defence co-ordination. The man who had put together the St Malo deal, George Robertson, was now Nato Secretary-General. His first meeting with Rumsfeld at the German conference was decidedly tetchy. The Scotsman's attempts at small talk collapsed and their discussion became more of an interrogation. Robertson confided in a colleague that Rumsfeld tended to talk to other defence ministers as if he were shouting at neighbours over the garden fence.

Bush promised that NMD would be accompanied by deep cuts in US strategic nuclear missiles. But he and those around him made it clear they wanted to downgrade the new, post-Communist and less threatening Russia as a policy priority. After all, its economy was no bigger than that of the Netherlands, they said. At the Wehrkunde Rumsfeld snubbed Sergei Ivanov, Putin's security chief.

The plans for China were different. One of Bush's priorities was to veer away from Europe and more towards the Asia–Pacific region. Beijing presented opportunities but also a serious threat to US hegemony. Two months into the life of the new administration, tensions with China almost turned to conflict. On 31 March 2001, a Chinese fighter pilot rammed an American surveillance plane in international airspace over the South China Sea. The Chinese jet was destroyed and its pilot killed. The American plane crash-landed on Hainan island, a popular tourist destination for affluent Chinese. The American crew was detained for eleven days. China extracted an apology and a $50,000 payment to return the plane.

Blair had been advised to expect a rough start to the adminis-tration, but few in Downing Street predicted the atmospherics around the policy announcements would be so tense. In 1997 the world had come together to agree cuts in greenhouse gas emissions, the main cause of climate change. The Kyoto Protocol was regarded as a major step forward, but in March, four months before delegates were due to meet in Bonn to toughen the agreement, Bush served notice that the US would not be joining them. That set a pattern.

As Blair's first term drew to a close, he was preoccupied with one of his worst domestic crises – foot and mouth. It forced him to delay the General Election planned for May and dented his government's treasured reputation for managerial efficiency. Where government departments and other public bodies failed, Blair turned to the one organisation whose professionalism he truly appreciated – the armed forces. On a visit to a regimental base in Darlington, he said the military had 'coped brilliantly' with an outbreak that had been 'roughly several times more difficult in logistics and practicality than the Gulf War or Kosovo'. The affection and respect he had acquired for the army became an important factor in his calculations about the use of force to achieve his ends.

Like many prime ministers before him, Blair was less in awe of his foreign service. Some of the British diplomats he came across, especially in the field, he did rate highly. But he was also exasperated by the pomposity of the FCO and its emphasis on process rather than result. He felt too many mandarins allowed detail to obscure the big picture. He saw the problem partly as generational. Blair and Jonathan Powell wanted to push to the fore individual diplomats they respected. The structures at the heart of government were not helping. Bush had more foreign policy experts in his sprawling National Security Council for one individual country than Blair had for the entire world. There might be hundreds across the road at the FCO, but that was not the same. They were not his people.

Long before the election, Blair had decided he wanted to use his second term to shake up his Downing Street apparatus. He wanted the centre of command reinforced in all areas, including foreign policy. He created two full-time advisers with their own teams. Sir Stephen Wall, formerly private secretary to John Major and British Ambassador to the EU, was brought in to run European affairs from London. David Manning, the FCO official in whom Blair had confided after his visit to the Kosovan refugee camps, was brought back after serving only a year as Ambassador to Nato and told to take charge of 'the rest of the world'. His job was important when it began. It did not take long before it became crucial.

A diminutive, super-bright owl of a man, Manning was assiduous, polite, but not oleaginous, and extremely modest. These traits provided cover for a mind that worked at ferocious speed. He was schooled in the traditional Nato view – that America is the pivot for the 'free world', that it must be constantly prodded to stay engaged and that in times of trouble diplomacy only has any effect when reinforced by the threat of force. He did not lapse into fashionable thinking. As number three at the British Embassy in Moscow, he witnessed the collapse of the Soviet Union, seeing in it a moral good but also a geostrategic danger. Drawing President Putin into the Western fold would figure high on his list of priorities.

Manning's involvement in the Balkans – first as head of the Foreign Office's eastern department and then Britain's top diplomat in the Contact Group – left him convinced of the ethical case for military intervention, with or without a UN resolution. In his conversations with friends he would express outrage at what the Serbs were doing. He never had any problems with the Kosovo war. In November 1995 he was given his first ambassadorial post – to Israel. That too left a mark. It also brought him more closely to Blair's attention. It was during conversations at the ambassador's official residence in Tel Aviv that the bond was formed. Blair and Manning had several long and intense conversations there about foreign policy. As Blair was thinking through the various options for his new foreign policy adviser, he turned for advice to several of his confidants. One of them was Michael Levy, who combined being head of Labour's high-value donor unit (the man who extracted large private donations for the party), and the Prime Minister's special envoy to the Middle East. Levy pushed for Manning, whom he called 'my boy'. Blair was persuaded. After his brief spell in Brussels Manning was recalled personally by Blair to be his right-hand man.

Interestingly, several of Manning's colleagues in Moscow in the early 1990s became key players in Blair's government. Sir Francis Richards, who had been one rung above him, became head of the government's eavesdropping centre at GCHQ. The most intriguing of this group was John Scarlett, MI6's station chief in Moscow, who was expelled when his cover was blown and he was accused of running a spy in the Russian defence ministry. Scarlett had spent his entire working life in MI6 and SIS. In June 2001, as the changes were being rung in the Foreign Office following Manning's appointment to the new post in Downing Street, the post of chairman of the Joint Intelligence Committee became vacant. This job – the link man between the Prime Minister and his three intelligence agencies – had always been filled by a Foreign Office official. However, with strong support from Powell and Manning, but against strong resistance from the top of the FCO, Blair chose Scarlett. None of those involved in that decision would realise how politically sensitive it would become. Downing Street was not to be countermanded, but the resentment lingered.

The changes were unprecedented in the civil service. They reinforced accusations against Blair of a presidential style of government. The Downing Street staff was still tiny compared to, say, the National Security team in Washington, or the offices of the President of France or German Chancellor. What the changes did signify was a reappraisal of the role of the Foreign Office. Blair wanted to make sure that all major decisions were taken by him and his entourage, and not across the road in King Charles Street.

As for Cook, after all the difficulties of the first year in his job – the rows over arms sales, the rubbishing of his ethical dimension by Downing Street, a botched visit to India, the Sandline affair in Sierra Leone and his very public divorce from his wife – he had settled into the job. Blair had particularly appreciated his work on Kosovo and in arduous EU meetings. Blair never tired of telling people that wherever he went in the world he received plaudits for Cook's negotiating skills. Cook had his sights set on becoming the longest-serving Labour Foreign Secretary. He was confident he would.

Two days before the General Election Levy met Blair for one of their regular chats. As he was leaving, he asked Blair about Cook. Blair told him not to worry, that he was very happy with his Foreign Secretary and that he had other more pressing reshuffle issues to deal with. Levy telephoned Cook to tell him so. Cook was relieved. He never quite knew where he stood. He was kept firmly away from the election campaign. At one point he told Blair's team that he wanted to make a speech on Europe. He gave Powell the draft, only to be asked to hold off. Each time he resubmitted it, they said the time was not right. Eventually he said he would do it as a newspaper article, then as an address to his own constituency in Livingston. Not yet, they said, not yet.

On the afternoon of 9 June 2001, the day after the election, Cook sauntered into Downing Street. Jack Straw followed soon after, taking with him briefing notes about what he imagined would be a new job involving transport and the environment. Straw had even been to check out his new office. Still, he was nervous. He waited in Anji Hunter's office, just off the corridor from Blair's. She gave him a hug and told him knowingly that he had nothing to worry about.

Cook had not received the same friendly wink. A few minutes later he realised why. He was dumbfounded when Blair told him he wanted to change things more radically than envisaged. Would he take the position of Leader of the House of Commons? Cook did not know what to say. He was ushered into a side room, past several other ministers waiting their turn, to think about it. He asked for more time and went out via the back door and around to his old office. There he called in his civil servants and special advisers and asked their advice. They too were astounded, although from earlier that day Sherard Cowper-Coles, Cook's principal private secretary, had noticed a slightly different tone when he talked to Downing Street. They advised him to take it, and bade farewell. Cook was not the only person to react furiously. Levy was livid. He felt he had been deceived, and called Blair to tell him as much.

The next morning a bewildered Straw arrived early for a briefing from Cook's old team of civil servants. He confessed that he would have to 'brush up' on world issues and confined his questions to the size of the official car and bodyguard contingent.

Blair had had a last-minute change of mind. One of those who influenced the decision was Sir Richard Wilson, the Cabinet Secretary. One of Wilson's jobs was to filter to the Prime Minister during their weekly Monday meeting the gossip from the civil service. The word from the Foreign Office, he told him, had always been that Cook was difficult to work with. Sir John Kerr, the Foreign

Office Permanent Secretary, had let it be known that if Blair wanted to change his Foreign Secretary he would be advised to do it at the election, rather than a couple of years in. Blair and Powell had also been picking up misgivings, ever so gentle, from the Bush administration. On election day at his constituency home in Sedgefield, Blair had talked through his latest plan with Hunter, Powell and Campbell.

Straw was going to have learn quickly. A number of international crises were brewing. In Macedonia a peace deal between the government and ethnic Albanian guerrillas was on the point of collapse. In Zimbabwe Robert Mugabe's policy of expropriating white farms was intensifying. Straw's touch in the first few months was anything but sure, and even the most acerbic critics of Cook would begin to wonder whether Blair had made the right decision.

Relations between the new Bush administration and the rest of the world were going from bad to worse. Having repudiated the Kyoto discussions in March, Bush expected the other major countries to follow when the talks reached their conclusion in Bonn. They did not, although some did extract concessions on the targets. After years of wrangling and two days and nights of non-stop negotiation, 178 nations agreed to the most comprehensive, legally binding environmental treaty the world had seen – except the United States. Its chief representative at the talks declared: 'The Bush administration takes the issue of climate change seriously and we will not abdicate our responsibilities.' Her speech was met with boos from fellow ministers and delegates.

Having torn up the nuclear treaty, the Americans then set about destroying efforts to tighten a global ban on germ warfare. Talks on a protocol to enforce the 1972 Biological Weapons Convention were abandoned in July after the US withdrew. Washington said the draft would be ineffective in stopping countries from developing biological weapons, but would endanger US security and expose the commercial secrets of its biotech industry to industrial espionage. The other participants saw it as just another example of American disdain for international agreements, on an issue it would just a few months later claim to be a threat to world peace.

That same month saw a separate set of arms control negotiations but a similar story. The US objected to plans to curb the illicit trade in small arms and light weapons. At its opening session, John Bolton, Under-Secretary of State responsible for international security, said the US refused to support language in the original draft that 'conflicts with the constitutional right of US citizens to bear arms and restricts governments from supplying weapons to sub-state actors, such as rebel groups defending themselves'. In one sentence he drove a coach and horses through hopes of dealing with the proliferation of conventional weapons. African delegations were despondent. The UN estimated that, of the 500 million small arms and light weapons in the world, around half were illegal, and many were being used indiscriminately in the poorest countries. Bolton, by contrast, said the 'vast majority' of arms transfers in the world were 'routine and not problematic'. In the end, they agreed a compromise – non-binding and voluntary measures to curb the trade. In other words, they came up with a deal that was no deal. In the Foreign Office there was scarcely concealed fury. 'If any weapons proliferation can cause death, it's this,' said one minister. 'The US has obstructed it at every turn.'

This was one of the first problems Straw had to face. In one meeting with officials he described Bolton as a 'nightmare', and used more florid language about him within his office. 'It became clear from very early on in the brainstorming meetings that Jack had that handling the Bush administration would be by far the hardest challenge we faced,' said one person present. In one meeting attended by Blair, a senior official remarked: 'The trouble with the special relationship is: what do we get back?' On another occasion, Sawers suggested to Blair that he 'hadn't cashed in his chips with Clinton', and should try to get his way as much as possible with Bush.

Blair told them he regarded this kind of talk as defeatist. They had to deal with the US administration as it was, and not complain. He and his people were preparing to host Bush at the start of his second trip to Europe as President. The first visit in June had exposed the yawning gulf and the innate suspicions between a multilateral continental Europe and a new administration still finding its feet but serving notice that it was changing the terms of engagement. Bush had started with talks at Nato. He then went on to Gothenburg for an EU–US summit dominated by the dispute about Kyoto. Outside, tens of thousands of anti-globalisation protesters had vented their fury at the approach of the new President. After Clinton's urbane cosmopolitanism, Bush took some getting used to.

The second trip was going to be as much of a diplomatic minefield. Bush gave the team travelling with him strict instructions not to negotiate on Kyoto or the plans to abandon the ABM treaty. 'On both issues I have made my positions clear,' Bush said. 'People shouldn't doubt where the United States stands.'

The easy part for Bush came first – Chequers. Blair assembled his team. Alastair Campbell, Anji Hunter, Jonathan Powell and John Sawers had a dual mission: to find out more about Bush and his people and to gain their confidence. Camp David had been a good start, but both sides were still treading carefully. The formal side of the talks ranged widely, from Northern Ireland to Macedonia, climate change, the world economy and NMD. No single subject dominated, but there were several problem areas. They agreed to differ on Kyoto. Bush talked at length about defending the US and its allies from 'rogue states'. Blair knew the most immediate consequence of that was the Fylingdales base, and that meant trouble with the Labour Party. One participant at the meeting recalls: 'We were intensely twitched by all of this, but we tried not to say so.'

The real work took place over an informal dinner. Blair made it clear to Bush and his entourage that, whatever the differences, he would go out of his way to ensure relationships were at least as strong as they had been under Clinton. Bush remembered that in far tougher times ahead. At their joint appearance before the press, Bush described his host as a political ally 'willing to think anew' about difficult issues such as missile defence. That kind of praise was a mixed blessing for Blair, but he said in public what he had earlier promised the President. 'When Europe and America stand together and approach problems in sensible and serious ways, and realise that what unites us is more important than what divides us, then the world is a better place. When we fall out . . . the only people rejoicing are the bad guys.' The language was deliberately black and white, tailor-made to the one-man audience Blair was addressing.

Both leaders flew separately to Genoa for the annual meeting of the G8. This was a first for Bush. After the violence of Gothenburg, the police were preparing for trouble. But the violence, with one demonstrator shot dead by police, exceeded the Italians' worst expectations. While Blair sought to paper over the cracks, both the German Chancellor Gerhard Schröder and France's President, Jacques Chirac, scarcely concealed their anger to Bush over his environmental policies.

Bush had still not shaken off the controversial manner of his election. His first venture abroad had reinforced Europe's suspicions of him. Blair had been determined from the outset to play Britain's traditional role of a bridge between the two continents. Bush had got on with him well, but once again over that summer, it was to places like Mexico that he was looking. He met President Vicente Fox for the fifth time that year. According to people around Bush at the time, the Prime Minister was over-reaching himself. 'The job description Blair wrote for himself is for a post the White House wasn't planning on filling entirely. That's not to say the British aren't invaluable, but Blair seemed to see a bigger role for himself than was being earmarked.'

For all their early friendship, Blair had made no impact on Bush on Kyoto or the other points of contention. But on one issue, Russia, he did. Ask anyone in the Foreign Office about its main

achievements over the past two decades, and high up on the list will
be its recommendation to Margaret Thatcher that she should heap
praise on Mikhail Gorbachev in the early 1980s even before he had
become Soviet leader. With Boris Yeltsin more often than not either
incapacitated or inebriated in the closing years of the 1990s, Blair
was eager to hear from his diplomats that there was waiting in the
wings a man he could do business with. In August 1999 Yeltsin
appointed his fifth Prime Minister in eighteen months. The new
man, Vladimir Putin, was virtually unknown to the outside world
and even to most Russians, but quickly consolidated his power base.
At the turn of the millennium Yeltsin announced his resignation and
the appointment of Putin as his successor, subject to elections.

That summer Blair was advised by Jonathan Powell that if he
moved fast with Putin, even before his confirmation as president, he
could acquire the status of most-favoured foreign statesman. Blair
did this. In the course of a remarkable year the two men met five
times. Their first encounter was in March 2000, just two weeks
before the presidential elections. Blair had received 'colossal' advice
from the Foreign Office not to give rise to the accusation that he was
interfering in Russia's internal affairs. Kerr, the Permanent Secretary,
sent him a personal minute saying the *bona fides* of a man who had
spent most of his career in the KGB had not been proven and that a
visit, which would be seen as an endorsement, was premature.

Blair ignored the note. Putin laid out the red carpet in his
hometown of St Petersburg. Their discussions, one on one plus
interpreter and then broadened out, took place in rooms inside the
Hermitage Gallery. That evening, with their wives and their
entourages, Putin took Blair to the Mariinsky Palace to a gala performance by the Kirov ballet of *War and Peace*. The British guests
burst into particularly loud applause when the Russian army
defeated Napoleon.

Putin returned the compliment by making the UK the first
port of call after his election. Blair's strategy was not endorsed by
other Western countries. Both Chirac and Schröder studiously kept

their distance. When Clinton visited Moscow in June 2000, the Russians were furious when he criticised creeping press curbs and took part in a phone-in on a radio station critical of the government. Blair took a far more accommodating line. He signalled to Putin that he had a green light to crack down on militants in Chechnya, while offering to try to persuade Clinton and the Europeans to restrain their criticism. 'We deliberately moderated our language on Chechnya, and we advised others to do the same,' says one Blair aide. This provoked recriminations with Berlin and Paris. Chirac and Schröder reminded Blair that he was supposed to be following an ethical foreign policy, that only a few months ago the man described as the 'Butcher of Grozny' had presided over some of the worst violence there. This argument would help sow the seeds of future mistrust.

As ever with Blair, the picture opportunity was planned to perfection. Putin, unversed in such techniques, was prepared to indulge him. In November of that year Blair arrived in Moscow on a fifteen-hour flying visit, the purpose of which nobody quite knew. One Russian newspaper described the two leaders as 'the odd couple'. Their mini-summit was short on substance, long on mutual admiration. It included a late-night visit to a mock German bierkeller. Russian journalists suspected this was the first time Putin had ventured into a restaurant since becoming president. Playing on Thatcher's remark of twenty years earlier, Putin said Blair was 'a man with whom it is a great pleasure to have business with'. Blair responded: 'I know people say there is a risk in being so close with Russia and President Putin, but I think this is something that is well worth doing.'

In his first meeting with Bush at Camp David three months later, Blair pressed the point. Bush had already made it clear that Russia would not feature highly in his priorities. Blair argued that Putin had tried in his first year to bring about more political and economic reform than Yeltsin had done in his last several years in office. He argued that Putin faced considerable resistance from hardliners and that all forms of criticism played into their hands. And he argued that virtually all known alternatives would be worse. The price of keeping quiet on Chechnya was worth paying. Ironically, it was the hostile reception Bush received on his first trip to Western Europe that made him more amenable to the charms of the East. After the mayhem of Gothenburg, and the frostiness of Messrs Chirac and Schröder, Bush would remark that he felt more comfortable in the small-town charm of Ljubljana, the capital of Slovenia, which hosted his first summit with Putin. 'I'd rather come to this part of Europe than the other,' he told his officials. He could have called it 'New Europe'.

After two hours of talks, Bush seemed to turn his own policy on its head. He called Putin a 'paragon', who was remarkable and trustworthy and 'loves his country'. He talked of Russia as a 'partner and ally' which in time could become 'a strong partner and a friend'. He then said: 'I looked the man in the eye. I found him to be very straightforward and trustworthy. We had a very good dialogue. I was able to get a sense of his soul.' What brought about this sudden and near mystical affection? Bush would later concede that religion played a crucial part. During that first meeting, Putin had shown him a crucifix that his mother had given him, which he at one point lost and then found again. 'I sensed that we had the cross in common,' Bush said. After that meeting, Bush did engage with Putin. That would not remove future points of discord – the Americans would a year later formally abandon the ABM treaty – but Blair and his people would cite that relationship as vindicating his policy of gentle influence on the American president. But it was more than that. Blair's accommodation with Putin spoke volumes for his priorities, for his determination to use pragmatism to achieve what he believed was a bigger purpose, and for his unremitting confidence in his own powers of persuasion.

Blair told his aides that world leaders were naturally prone to get along because they were part of a unique club. He called it a 'fellowship'. He would joke that they were all united by the fact that someone out there wanted their jobs. He instinctively looked in each of them for something he could relate to. If he found it, he would nurture it. He wanted to use this fellowship to create a global order of leaders with the same ends – modernisation, reform and democracy. At that point this encompassed the US and Europe and was beginning to include Russia. In time it would be extended, he hoped, to powers such as India and China.

Wherever he saw a leader that was new and different, he tried – on a very personal level – to befriend him. It could be Putin; it could be Jordan's new king Abdullah, Syria's new president Bashar al-Assad or even China's premier Zhu Rongji, who on the eve of a visit to London in April 1998 was described by Alastair Campbell as 'China's Gorbachev'. It was an epithet the Foreign Office had plagiarised from the Americans. To encourage these leaders, problems were, wherever possible, overlooked. For the Chinese that meant not making much of a fuss over Tibet. When it came to Putin the same applied to Chechnya. They should always be given the benefit of the doubt.

The more confident Blair became of his stature, the more he enjoyed his foreign forays. They provided a welcome distraction from his more humdrum occupations back home.

After an exhausting election campaign, Blair went off on holiday more relaxed than he had been for a long time. He had secured that historic second victory, a second landslide. He had seen off foot and mouth, he had set the tone for a workmanlike domestic agenda, with painstaking reform of the public services. Blair could look around him and see few rivals on the international stage. Co-habitation in Paris between a centre-right president, Jacques Chirac, and a centre-left Prime Minister, Lionel Jospin, was preventing France from asserting itself. In Germany, Gerhard Schröder's red–green coalition was stuttering towards the end of its first term. Economic growth in the Eurozone was weaker than in Britain.

Blair had taken with him to France and Italy his usual range of reading material. That year it included books on Middle Eastern history and politics, and various briefing notes from the Foreign Office and the Joint Intelligence Committee. One of the papers was on international terrorism, and Osama bin Laden's al-Qaeda organisation in particular. Blair had been exercised by the problems caused by 'failed states' and splinter groups, but, according to one official close to him, this was not seen as one of his most immediate problems. 'I cannot remember a single conversation with anyone, or memo from anyone, about al-Qaeda that merited the attention of the Secretary of State or the Prime Minister.'

On Sunday 9 September, the commander of the anti-Taleban forces in Afghanistan, Ahmed Shah Masood, was giving an interview in the northern province of Takhar to two Arabs posing as journalists. They detonated a bomb concealed in their video camera. Masood was killed in the attack. Details of the incident were murky, but on the Monday morning it was reported to Straw and then passed up to Blair. The Prime Minister took note, but he was concentrating on a speech he was due to make the next day to a fractious TUC conference on the public services – a matter of much greater urgency.

PART II

RESOLUTE WARRIOR

6

SCARS AND TRAUMAS

DOWNING STREET IS A TOUCH CRAMPED, SO WHEN IT CAME to finding office space for the new man in the new job, they had to make do with the old kitchen. David Manning started as Blair's foreign policy adviser on 3 September 2001. He spent his first week 'in the house' sorting himself out. He had a table and chair. His next task was to find himself cupboards, phones and a secretary.

At the Chequers summit in July, which Blair had invited him to, Manning had agreed with Condoleezza Rice, Bush's National Security Advisor, that he should make Washington his first port of call. On Sunday 9 September he flew out, staying at the official residence of Sir Christopher Meyer, the ambassador, preparing for a day of talks on Monday and then a flight home. Manning did the rounds, introducing himself properly, and Rice suggested that he have dinner that evening with her and her deputy. Very early the next day, Tuesday, 11 September 2001, Manning was driven to Washington's Ronald Reagan airport to catch a shuttle to New York. From there he was to be whisked on to a daytime flight back to London. The plane was delayed, and he knew it would now be touch and go to make his connection. Still, it was a glorious sunny morning. From his window seat on the shuttle, as the plane flew over Staten Island on its descent, Manning looked out and saw smoke coming from the World Trade Center. He had no idea what was going on.

When the plane landed at JFK the passengers were herded into a lounge and told to wait. There, on a giant television screen, he saw the plane going into the second tower. Everyone was ordered to evacuate the terminal. In the panic he managed to locate his luggage. He tried to phone Washington, New York, Downing Street and his wife Catherine, but all the lines were down. He decided the best option was to find a hotel and take stock. The queue for taxis stretched around the block. He teamed up with a young British couple. After two hours of waiting on the street, they found a taxi and asked the driver to take them to the nearest hotel. All the airport hotels were now full. They drove further out of town, not risking the trip into Manhattan. Manning was worried they would run out of money. They clubbed together all the notes and coins they had and told the driver how much they could afford. They ended up in the poor neighbourhood of Jamaica in Queens. Manning asked the receptionist for a room for the night. The man was astonished. This was a place, he said, where you hire rooms by the hour.

At least the TV worked. From his shabby bedroom, Manning watched the momentous events unfold. Late that evening London time he finally reached 'Switch', the ever-dependable switchboard operators at Downing Street. They did the rest. With no flights in or out of New York, it was arranged that very early the next morning Sir Jeremy Greenstock, the British Ambassador to the UN, would despatch his official Rolls-Royce to drive Manning to Washington. Manning was back in business. Working out of the embassy, he spent the next few days in and out of the National Security Council. In adversity he and Rice created a working relationship that would be pivotal.

Greenstock had just left his office across the road from UN head-quarters. He was going to a meeting with other heads of mission a few blocks away on 46th Street. His driver said that he heard on the radio that a plane had hit the World Trade Center, but that all indications were that it was an accident. They started their meeting. Ten minutes later a note came round, advising them that the second tower had been struck. Greenstock said out loud: 'It must be al-Qaeda.' The ambassadors hurried to a television set and watched the towers collapse. Colleagues who were in the main UN building were evacuated. Greenstock sent members of his staff to the British Consulate General to help deal with calls from relatives of potential victims phoning from home. His wife joined the emergency team.

Over in Washington at the ambassador's residence, Meyer was sitting on the terrace drinking coffee with John Major, his old boss. The former prime minister was making one of his frequent trips to the US on business. Meyer's social secretary hurried in, telling them both of the first plane crash. They went inside and, as they were watching television, they heard a thud. Meyer raced to the embassy while his wife went on to the roof of the residence, which stands on a hill, to see what had happened. They thought there might have been an explosion at the White House, at the State Department or on Capitol Hill. It turned out to be the Pentagon, across the Potomac river. Meyer ordered the embassy into emergency mode. Non-essential staff were sent home. Meyer tried to find out if any of the several British military officers on exchange in the Pentagon had been injured. He then called Rice to see if the Americans needed any help. He phoned Jonathan Powell in London. He tried calling Manning, but couldn't get hold of him. To add to his worries he also had under his charge in Washington a delegation of British MPs and MEPs. Once they had all been accounted for, they were invited to stay at the residence.

    With airspace still closed they all had to stay in Washington until a special flight arrived that Thursday night, carrying the three heads of British intelligence, from MI5, SIS and GCHQ – Eliza Manningham-Buller (the deputy to Stephen Lander as head of domestic intelligence, but soon to take over from him), Sir Richard Dearlove and Sir Francis Richards. 'We had to get them there to find out what was going on,' one official who was involved recalls. 'The Americans were too busy to talk to us, so we had to get in to see them.' The next morning the same plane ferried Meyer's guests back to London: three spooks, the top adviser, a former prime minister and a miscellaneous bunch of politicians.

Blair had travelled to Brighton to address the TUC conference on the theme of the moment – the injection of private capital into public services. He was preparing for a bitter fight. At 1:48 P.M. he was sitting on a sofa in the Fitzherbert Suite of the Grand Hotel, giving his speech a last once-over. His was a split-level room. Down below, his spokesman, Godric Smith, was with Campbell and others in the entourage monitoring Sky TV to see what the commentators were predicting. Coverage of the conference was interrupted by news of a plane careering into the World Trade Center. The unflappable Smith went quietly upstairs to tell Blair. They assumed it was an accident and he resumed his reading. The Prime Minister's other official spokesman, Ulsterman Tom Kelly, was in Downing Street. He had also been watching and immediately phoned Smith. Blair was the only person not glued to the screen when the second plane crashed fifteen minutes later. Blair, Campbell and Smith left for the conference centre, clear in their minds that the speech could no longer be made. Visibly shaken, Blair told the delegates: 'There have been the most terrible, shocking events in the USA in the last hours. I am afraid we can only imagine the terror and carnage there and the many, many innocent people who would have lost their lives. The mass terrorism is the new evil in our world today.' He left the podium to applause.

Anji Hunter was waiting outside with his security detail. As they were driven to the station for the train back to London, everyone got on their phones. Blair's first calls were to Jonathan Powell; to David Blunkett, the new Home Secretary; to Straw and to Geoff

Hoon, the Defence Secretary. Hunter had an urgent private call to make. She had been preparing to announce her resignation from Number 10 and her controversial move to the oil company BP. This was quickly and discreetly postponed. In the interludes between phone calls, Blair was thinking aloud about the ramifications of the attacks. He told them all that whatever else happened, America should not feel isolated. Back in London, Powell was in charge, but he received unexpected assistance from his former colleague, John Sawers. He was on leave, on his way to becoming Ambassador to Cairo, and rushed in to his old office in his jeans to offer his services.

Everyone remembers what they were doing that day. Straw was focusing heavily on the crisis in Macedonia, preparing in his office for a 2 P.M. meeting with Hoon at the FCO to discuss the future of peacekeeping. One of Straw's officials recalls: 'As we were assembling we saw on TV that the first tower had been hit. We just stood there as the second one went down.' Straw turned to his spokesman, John Williams, and said: 'That's it. The world will never be the same again.' In his private office they frantically tried to get hold of their counterparts in Washington. That was proving extremely difficult. At the same time they needed to reassure people back home. As he was preparing to make a short statement before the media in the ambassadors' waiting room, Straw told his aides, 'The public are looking to people like Tony and me to show that the institutions of state have not collapsed. It's still there, in control.'

Gordon Brown was holding a meeting preparing for a forthcoming summit in Monterrey on international development. He had been increasingly frustrated about the difficulty in persuading the Bush administration to engage. That meeting had barely begun when one of his aides rushed in to tell them what had happened. Brown went straight back into his private office and, with his advisers, they stood hunched in front of the television set in the middle of the room.

Stephen Byers, the Transport Secretary, had been chairing a seminar on local government when an official from his private office interrupted and called him aside. In less than an hour Byers and Hoon had implemented a no-fly zone around central London and closed City airport. Hoon scrambled two fighter jets to enforce it. Within ten minutes of issuing the order, Byers saw from his office that the skies above him – part of the flight path into Heathrow – were empty. This was the clearest demonstration, he would tell colleagues later, of seeing a ministerial decision being put into practice.

On arrival back in Downing Street, Blair went straight into a meeting with the 'professionals' in his office, the 'den'. John Scarlett, the new head of the Joint Intelligence Committee, had, like Manning, only been in the job a week. He had rushed from his office on the second floor of the Cabinet Office, which is known as the 'closed area' and houses the JIC's eighty-strong staff. He went straight through the connecting door into Downing Street, where Stephen Lander, the head of MI5, was waiting for him. He was there to provide the Prime Minister with a security assessment for London. Sir Richard Wilson, the Cabinet Secretary, was also present, as were Campbell and Powell. 'This is grim,' said Blair by way of introduction. They did what they could to advise, but the details were extremely sketchy. Scarlett said without hesitation that it was the work of Bin Laden. He added there was also a tiny possibility that the attacks could have been carried out by Hizbollah or by an extreme right-wing American sect, such as the one that had planted the bomb in Oklahoma City in 1995. 'What does this all mean?' asked Blair, more than once. 'What are the implications?' Privately, they knew they were all in the dark, but nobody wanted to say as much.

The attacks in New York and Washington proved a devastating indictment of the intelligence capabilities of the CIA and FBI. It was clear immediately that questions would also be asked of the British security services. In fact, parliament's Intelligence and Security Committee would later report that the JIC had warned Blair in its weekly intelligence assessment given to him on 16 July that the al-Qaeda network – operating from its bases in Afghanistan and beyond – was in the 'final stages' of preparing a terrorist attack on the West. The heads of MI6, MI5 and GCHQ had said the most likely targets would be Americans or Israelis. But they added that UK interests were 'at risk, including from collateral damage in attacks on US targets'. They had qualified the information by saying the 'timings, targets and methods of attack' were not known. 'With hindsight, the scale of the threat and the vulnerability of Western states to terrorists with this degree of sophistication and a total disregard for their own lives was not understood,' the Committee said in its annual report, which laid out a number of frailties in the intelligence-gathering and sifting of the British security services. This was, it concluded, a failure of imagination.

Even on that day, 11 September, both Blair and his spy chiefs recalled that assessment and wondered if they could have chased up the leads more carefully. They knew that in future they would have to improve their responsiveness. Each and every piece of information would be talked up and followed through more assiduously. The nature of British intelligence changed at the Prime Minister's behest. The security services knew that they could not afford, as one senior official put it, to 'under-predict'. The failure by US and British agencies to appreciate the dangers posed by al-Qaeda sowed the seeds for the intelligence failures that would come later on Iraq.

The meeting in Blair's den did not last long. They reconvened straight away for their first session of 'Cobra', the government's emergency committee, which earns its name because of the meeting's location in Cabinet Office Briefing Room A. By the time it began at 5:30 P.M. Blair had already spoken to each minister individually. Brown was there, along with Straw, Hoon, Blunkett, Byers and Alan Milburn, the Health Secretary. Each brought one senior civil servant with him. Blair's team included Powell, Campbell and Hunter. Manning was still stranded in New York.

The room is spartan but functions well. Each team of two is

seated at a table. Each table has a laptop computer. Above them is a bank of television screens, carrying the various twenty-four-hour news channels. On another side of the room is a row of sound-proofed telephone booths. The meeting was brisk, about thirty minutes long, and focused. Blair made clear the first priority was domestic security. But he said he was trying hard to contact Bush, so far to no avail. 'They need allies to get through this,' he said. The brief presentations by the various security and intelligence agencies reinforced in Blair's mind his admiration for them. Blair was less in awe of the civil service. At that Cobra meeting, Wilson, the Cabinet Secretary, wondered out loud what the protocol should be for giving the order to shoot down any plane that violated the no-fly zone over London. Blair raised his eyebrows at the civil servant's attention to detail. They agreed it should be the new Chief of the Defence Staff, Admiral Sir Michael Boyce. The emergency machine worked well this time. The last time Cobra had been called into action had been during the fuel protests exactly a year before. The set-up had then been hopeless, and changes were made.

But even after that meeting they were none the wiser. 'I had the impression we were all there to fill the seats,' one official recalls. 'We were desperate to find someone who knew what was going on. We alighted on anyone who had insight into any particular detail, however small, as reassurance.' That official remembers walking out at the end of the Cobra meeting and turning to a Cabinet colleague: 'We've no idea what's going on, do we?' The ministers and officials returned to their departments, with immediate tasks to carry out. But beyond that, they knew little more than the public.

Blair wrote down – his words, not Campbell's – a quick statement for the press that he delivered outside the gates of Number 10. 'We've offered President Bush and the American people our solidarity, our profound sympathy, and our prayers . . . this is not a battle between the United States of America and terrorism, but between the free and democratic world and terrorism. We therefore here in Britain stand shoulder to shoulder with our American friends in this hour of tragedy, and we like them will not rest until this evil is driven from our world.'

That evening, however, Blair expressed his fears to his aides. Bush, he told them, did not seem in control of events. The President was being flown around the US in fear of his life. Cheney was temporarily in charge, something that put the fear of God into Downing Street. There was little they could do immediately but wait, and hope. They were all in shock. They spent much of the evening by their television screens watching events unfold, just like everyone else. 'That was the only way we knew what was going on,' recalls one official. They ordered a delivery of pizzas to sustain them. 'We didn't know what usefully we could be doing,' says another official. The inner team left for home around midnight. 'I went home, switched on the TV and expected American planes to start leaving their bases,' remembers one of them. 'We didn't know where they might strike, but we thought there would be some sort of almighty American retaliation. We didn't know what was going to happen.'

They were relieved when they got in early next day that no strike had yet been launched by the US. Overnight Greenstock had started working on a UN resolution, with his French counterpart, Jean-David Levitte, not just condemning the attacks on the Twin Towers and the Pentagon, but reaffirming the right of member states to respond to terrorism as they saw fit. This released the US from any obligations. Some countries felt uncomfortable about it, but this was not a time to haggle over wording.

Cobra met again at 8 A.M on the 12th. Then Blair started to work the phones. His first call was to Chirac, a man he considered a close ally and good friend. That was followed by conversations with Putin, Schröder and Guy Verhofstadt, the Prime Minister of Belgium, which held the six-month presidency of the EU. Hoon went straight off to Nato in Brussels. Straw was preparing for an emergency EU session. Cook announced an emergency session of parliament for that Friday.

At 12:30 P.M., 7:30 A.M. Washington time, and half an hour

after getting to work in the Oval Office, Bush made the first of what would be several crucial phone calls to Blair. The Prime Minister expressed shock and horror, relief that Bush was safe, and pledged his 'total support' for the US. He said he had assumed Bush was considering an immediate military response. Bush said he was thinking about it but was not going to 'pound sand with millions of dollars in weapons' to make himself feel good. Blair agreed, telling Bush he had to decide between rapid action and effective action. They agreed to move quickly on the diplomatic front, capitalising on the international outrage. Support from Nato and the UN would provide legal and political weight for a military response. Bush repeated that he did not want to fire missiles at irrelevant targets. He ended the conversation by telling Blair: 'We will make no distinction between the terrorists who committed these acts and those who harbour them.' With those words the war on terror had truly begun, and thirty-five years of policy in the Middle East had been over-turned.

At Blair's suggestion, Bush then phoned Putin. On the day of the terrorist attacks, Putin had cancelled a planned military exercise after the US had raised its defence alert to DefCon 3 – a gesture that impressed Bush. In their call Putin told him he had signed a decree calling for a moment of silence the next day, and the two agreed to work together.

This period marked the high point in Blair's diplomacy. He really did provide a bridge between an inexperienced US President and an international community both sympathetic to the Americans but eager to turn this adversity into a new beginning in the Middle East and beyond. Day after day Blair worked the phones and trav-elled, trying to put together not just a coalition for military action against the Taleban and al-Qaeda, but also a broader coalition to work with the US for a new world order. In adversity, in this time of crisis, Blair had found a mission, something that was taking him far away from his tedious domestic duties.

Manning's return at the end of the week was crucial. In two

days in Washington after what was quickly becoming known simply as '9/11', he had worked closely with Rice inside the NSC. He would play a pivotal role as Blair's right-hand man and interlocutor with the Americans. The more influential he became abroad, the more the Foreign Office and the rest of Whitehall deferred to him. Manning forged a new strategy for Blair in his dealings with Bush. He worked from the following dictum: 'At the best of times, Britain's influence on the US is limited. But the only way we exercise that influence is by attaching ourselves firmly to them and avoiding public criticism wherever possible.' This was to become the template for the military adventures to come.

The actions of the Bush administration in those early days seem almost designed to nullify the goodwill and sympathy even previously hostile states had extended. On 12 September, for the first time in its history, Nato invoked Article Five of its founding charter, its collective defence clause, declaring that the attacks on New York constituted an attack on all nineteen member states. Lord Robertson, the organisation's Secretary-General, whose idea it was, saw it as an act of great moment in US–European relations. Robertson had originally put the idea to Colin Powell, who had been on a visit to Peru on the fateful day. Encouraged by his response, he called a meeting of the North Atlantic Council, the policy-making body of Nato, for the following day. He tabled the motion at 4 P.M. They convened at 8 P.M. and were done by 9:20. It had taken less than an hour and a half for the previously unwieldy nineteen-nation alliance to do something it had never done before – to commit itself to fighting to defend the United States, rather than the US fighting to defend Europe. The Germans had even promised to rush through a tax increase to help pay for measures to improve global security. The American response – or lack of it – left Robertson and the whole Nato establishment flabbergasted. Not a single word of thanks was received. 'An immense reservoir of solidarity was wasted,' recalls one senior Nato official.

On 14 September, as he was preparing for his statement to

parliament, Blair took a second call from Bush. The Prime Minister had the day before sent a five-page memo to the President, outlining his thoughts. This proposed giving the Taleban regime in Afghanistan an ultimatum: hand over Bin Laden and his key lieutenants, shut down his terrorist training camps and allow in international inspectors. Bush would deliver the demands publicly seven days later in his historic address to Congress. Blair said shaping world opinion was critical and suggested a dossier of evidence linking Bin Laden to the attacks. Bush said he would think about that.

Undeterred, Blair ploughed on with his list of suggestions. He said a new start with Pakistan, the main ally of the fundamentalist state in Afghanistan, was vital, as was the need to improve relations with Iran – one of America's bitterest foes. He also emphasised restarting the Middle East peace process. The one recommendation Bush rejected was for a timetable. 'We focus on the first circle, then expand to the next circle and the next circle,' Bush told Blair. 'You've got to decide what you're going to do and then you've got to focus very single-mindedly on it,' Blair replied. Bush told him he agreed '100 per cent'.

A week after 9/11 Blair's thoughts crystallised. One of the main dilemmas he, Manning and Powell needed to solve was whether their target was specifically Bin Laden and the al-Qaeda network or whether it should include the Taleban as well. There was no question in their minds that the Taleban leader, Mullah Omar, had aided and abetted Bin Laden, giving him free rein to set up training camps across Afghanistan. It was clear that the Taleban supported al-Qaeda's aims. But could the Taleban be held directly responsible for the attacks on New York and Washington? Had it played a part in al-Qaeda's global operations? That was unlikely on both counts. Two factors clinched it for Blair. On a political level, they now had the ultimatum to the Taleban to fall back on. On a broader level, this was a hideous regime and if its removal were a by-product of an all-out invasion of Afghanistan – an invasion whose specific reason was to obliterate al-Qaeda – then so be it. And yet, with the British public fearful of a terrorist attack on London or other cities, Blair decided he could not set out the broader war aims. He made sure he and his ministers confined the public explanation to rooting out al-Qaeda. Talk of 'regime change' would come later.

Militarily, Afghanistan posed enormous risks, but it provided one important opportunity and foil for the Americans and the British. They had in the Northern Alliance a fighting force that had spent years in guerrilla warfare against the Taleban. Their methods were often brutal, but – if kept in check – they could provide the men on the ground. The strategy was to rely on heavy bombard-ment, supplemented by US and British Special Forces on the ground, working closely with the Northern Alliance. But this was a high-risk strategy. Afghanistan, the centre of the 'Great Game' of the nineteenth century, when Imperial Russia and the British Empire in India vied for influence, was now one of the most lawless countries in the world. The Soviet Union had learned to its cost the conse-quences of its invasion in 1979 and the installation of a puppet government. Its overthrow produced a political vacuum the Taleban was able to exploit. After that, Afghanistan returned to the dark ages.

Washington and London agreed to co-ordinate their military and counter-terrorist plans and their language. As Bush spoke of the 'first war of the twenty-first century', and of a 'war on terror', Blair said before attending church on the Sunday that 'we are at war with terrorism'. His diplomacy was gathering pace. Pakistan's military leader, General Pervez Musharraf, was crucial. On 18 September Blair made the first of several calls to him. Musharraf had been ostracised since overthrowing the elected government in a coup in October 1999. The ISI – Pakistan's security service, and effectively a state within a state – had nurtured and fostered the Taleban. Now it was being asked to destroy its own creation.

The following day Blair began that autumn's remarkable diplo-matic odyssey. His first of many journeys was to Berlin. From there he went on to Paris to see President Chirac. Next stop was New York. On board his flight, he had a fifteen-minute phone conversation with Iran's President Mohammed Khatami, which he described as 'remarkable'. Blair later told confidants this was one of his most exciting moments of that period. He was desperate to mend fences with Iran, to identify the reformers trying to open up the Islamic state and to pave the way for Tehran to join the coalition against al-Qaeda, and he felt in this initial conversation that he might have broken through to the Iranians. To set the mood, reporters on Blair's plane were told that the PM had brought a copy of the Koran with him on the trip.

Blair believed that out of the traumatic events some good could emerge. The war on terror provided an opportunity to reshape alliances in the Middle East. That approach had been adopted by Bush senior before and after Iraq's invasion in 1990. Blair knew that Bush junior had set himself against involvement in the region, having seen the pitfalls that Clinton had encountered. Blair told his advisers he had no idea if he would succeed in convincing him, but he would try.

Blair had only a few hours in New York. He and Cherie were whisked first to Ground Zero, where they were met by Bill Clinton and his wife Hillary, now a Senator for the state. He then attended a memorial for British victims at the Anglican St Thomas Church on Fifth Avenue. In a very English scene, the line of mourners snaked down the steps of the church, their black umbrellas doing little to shelter them from the horizontal rain. Blair had wanted to pay homage to the firefighters who had died, but his visit to the Central Fire Department was called off for lack of time. Cherie would later go with the Clintons. Both the horror of what he saw and the appreciation by ordinary people of his staunch support moved Blair. He had proved himself a master of the moment in a way Bush had singularly failed to. The *Washington Post* rated Blair alongside New York Mayor Rudolph Giuliani as 'the only other political figure who broke through the world's stunned disbelief'.

Late that afternoon Blair arrived in a Washington still bewildered by events. He had a quick supper with Bush in the Blue Room of the White House to discuss the preparations for war in Afghanistan. He was one of the guests of honour at Bush's emergency speech to Congress. As he, Laura Bush and Giuliani walked along the balcony to their VIP seats, they received thunderous applause. 'Every nation, in every region, now has a decision to make. Either you are with us, or you are with the terrorists. From this day forward, any nation that continues to harbour or support terrorism will be regarded by the United States as a hostile regime,' Bush declared. He then talked of Blair, looked up at him, and in his best Texan drawl said: 'Thank you for comin', friend.' Those two standing ovations that evening left an indelible mark on Blair. He struggled hard to keep a sombre face, to not let the emotions get to him. But this was a seminal moment. This was what being a British Prime Minister was all about. He felt vindicated in his strategy for linking Britain's fate and fortunes with those of its staunch ally, the US. The American public's love affair with him had been established long before. It had sometimes irked Clinton. Blair's ratings continue to exceed those of Bush. In early November, the Senate would pass a resolution expressing the 'most heartfelt appreciation to the UK for its unwavering solidarity and leadership as an ally of the United States'.

On his way back, at the end of a 9,000-mile trip, Blair stopped off at an emergency summit of EU leaders in Brussels. It was announced that Straw would make the first visit to Iran by a British Foreign Secretary since the 1979 Islamic revolution. Blair briefed his European counterparts about Bush's plans. They were eager to hear from him – the resentment that would later come to the fore about Blair's role had not yet surfaced. But the more Bush deferred to him, the more US public opinion lauded him, the less Blair felt the need to consult. Between 11 September and the end of the month, he convened his full Cabinet only once. His inner circle was all that mattered. Even Cobra met only three times. Downing Street said Blair was 'seeing people when necessary'.

The Labour Party conference went ahead as planned, but normal business was abandoned. The lack of delivery on health and education had been put to one side. Blair used his keynote speeches to try to set the tone for the coming political year. He was not shy of using hyperbole – from his '1,000 days for a 1,000 years' in 1996, to his battle against the 'forces of conservatism' in 2000, his speeches would be hailed as inspirational by Fleet Street's finest only to unravel shortly after. International affairs were rarely prominent, but this year Blair wanted to set out a grand vision. He began by putting Britain on a war footing:

> This is a battle with only one outcome – our victory, not theirs. Be in no doubt, Bin Laden and his people organised this atrocity. The Taleban aid and abet him. He will not desist from further acts of terror. They will not stop helping him. Yes, we should try to understand the causes of terrorism, but let there be no moral ambiguity about this, nothing could ever justify the events of 11 September, and it is to turn justice on its head to pretend it could.

He had this message to the Afghan people. 'The conflict will not be the end. We will not walk away, as the outside world has done so many times before.' He had this for Bush and the American people: 'We were with you at the first – we will stay with you to the last.'

Determination to stand shoulder to shoulder with the US in rooting out terrorism was one side of the coin. Blair understood the antipathy many in the Labour Party felt towards Bush – an antipathy that was cast aside when the Twin Towers were struck, but was reawakened by his gun-slinging 'wanted: dead or alive' declarations straight after. Blair knew that he needed to offer something more than American power and American retribution. He spoke of globalisation and said he understood people's fears. He spoke of poverty and debt, proclaiming in one of his most powerful oratorical flourishes: 'The state of Africa is a scar on the conscience of the world. But if the world as a community focused on it, we could heal it. And if we don't, it will become deeper and angrier.' He had rehearsed that line in a newspaper interview well before 11 September, when he spoke of the 'moral dimension' to poverty, 'which is why I've devoted some time to Africa, which I think is a blot on the conscience of the world'.

The peroration was one of the most powerful of his premiership. He promised to tackle problems from 'the slums of Gaza to the mountains of Afghanistan. This is a moment to seize. The kaleidoscope has been shaken. The pieces are in flux. Soon they will settle again. Before they do, let us reorder this world around us.'

Blair's team had always been a little miffed that his Chicago speech back in April 1999 had not had the impact they had wanted. In news terms it had been subsumed by the war in Kosovo and the arguments he was having at the time with Clinton over ground troops. His conference speech in 2001 allowed him to revisit and develop many of those early themes. More work had been done by policy-makers and academics around the idea of 'liberal intervention'. The speech was quintessential Blair. Although it had gone through the usual drafting process, much of it was his copyright. He was happy with the Gladstonian comparisons. He was content for his message to be described as a Manichaean definition of good and evil.

Some of those around him were nervous about all the talk of bridge-building and righting wrongs. The speech did mark in Blair's mind a final rejection of the sovereignty and national-interest tenets of foreign policy that had marked the Cold War years. One of its doyens, Henry Kissinger, said he was impressed but felt 'a little uneasy' about the inference that this was a good moment to solve every problem in the world.

The comparison Blair and his people were most comfortable with was President Woodrow Wilson who, as he sent his forces into the First World War, dedicated America to making the world safe for democracy, 'to spend her blood and her might for the principles that gave her birth. We have no selfish ends to serve. We desire no dominion. We are but one of the champions of the rights of mankind.' But what of a more recent comparison, one much closer to home – Robin Cook's mission statement back in 1997 that was so disparaged by Blair and his people at the time? Blair had belatedly found an ethical dimension of his own. The detail was different in places, but the idea was not.

The coalition Blair and Bush were seeking to assemble was remarkable. Russia and Pakistan were the biggest scalps, but even some of the more hostile Middle Eastern states were keeping their fears to themselves. Domestically, Blair was facing resistance from some Labour MPs, but they tended to be the usual suspects. Public opinion was solid, but in need of reassurance. Blair knew that he had to answer the criticism that an attack on Afghanistan, far from lessening the threat of terrorism, might increase it.

Campbell reminded Blair of the suggestion he had made to Bush on 12 September of a dossier against Bin Laden and al-Qaeda. They agreed to try again. When Manning put the idea to Rice, the Americans this time accepted. 'The Americans were oddly reluctant to produce the dossier,' recalls one senior security service official. 'They did not feel the need, but they were quite happy for us to do it. But we felt we needed to make the case.'

Blair knew this was new territory. A briefing paper had been prepared for MPs just before Operation Desert Fox in 1998, but this was designed as much for the public. For several days John Scarlett and his thirty-strong assessment staff at the Joint Intelligence Committee worked on a draft of the document. It was derived largely from open-source material, but did contain some intelligence material that had been cleared by SIS. The twenty-one-page dossier, entitled 'Responsibility for the Terrorist Atrocities in the United States', formed a central plank of the government's case to MPs in an emergency session of parliament on 4 October. Blair, citing the document, told the Commons he had 'absolutely no doubt' that Bin Laden was responsible for 9/11. Reading the report, he said: 'No other organisation has both the motivation and the capability to carry out attacks like those of September 11 – only the al-Qaeda network under Osama bin Laden.'

The report was notable as much for what it excluded as what it included. Another audience was America's Muslim allies, so the use the terrorists had made of places like Saudi Arabia, Pakistan, Yemen, the United Arab Emirates and Egypt was glossed over. In a number of foreign capitals they were not impressed. Aides to President Chirac suggested to British diplomats that Blair was 'straining a little bit too hard' to do the Americans' work for them. Still, the dossier was seen at the time as relatively uncontroversial. Bin Laden's own video missives amounted to admissions. Campbell was convinced that public dossiers provided important assistance in his perennial battle to overcome what he saw as media 'cynicism'. By now he and Scarlett were working well together. Originally Scarlett was required to request meetings with Blair through Manning, but it was not long before he would go into the Prime Minister's office on his own and see him on his own. The relationship did not, however, have the easy banter that Blair enjoyed with Campbell and Powell.

Fresh from making the case for the prosecution of military action against Bin Laden, Blair departed on his next tour. First stop was Moscow and Putin's *dacha*. Since the days of Ronald Reagan and Mikhail Gorbachev, the walk in the woods had become a useful place for a relaxed one-on-one conversation with the Russian premier – with interpreter if necessary, but without aides or note-takers. Blair got the answer he needed. As he strolled with his Labrador through the pine trees, Putin made it clear that he would support an attack on Afghanistan. He went further. He said he had no objections in principle to the US using former Soviet bases in Central Asia for military action against Afghanistan.

The two then had dinner, followed by a three-way phone call with Bush. Putin knew that Donald Rumsfeld was on his way to

Uzbekistan to try to secure a deal. He knew that these former republics would want to use the American presence as a means of distancing themselves further from Moscow. He also knew that hardliners would attack him for not trying to suppress this resistance. And yet in spite of all of that, Putin would allow the US over the following weeks to move into Uzbekistan, Tajikistan and Kyrgyzstan.

Blair was convinced that Russia should earn some kind of reward. Since his Kosovo experiences he had wanted to tie the former Communist states of Eastern Europe more closely into the Western European structures of Nato and the EU. In May 2002 Blair would achieve his goal with the establishment of the Nato–Russia Council, a talking shop, but important nonetheless for giving Moscow a voice in the alliance's decisions. He convinced Bush to override the stiff resistance of the neocons. At one point Blair asked Manning to write a paper to the President setting out the arguments for Russia's inclusion. That was rubbished by Rumsfeld and not supported by Cheney. In the end Condoleezza Rice came down on Blair's side. Even then Rumsfeld didn't stop trying to sabotage the plan. He would send orders to the US Ambassador to Nato trying to countermand it, prompting a philosophical Blair to tell one of his aides: 'It's a struggle dealing with the Americans. It always has been.' Blair was at the time happy to view the thaw in relations with Russia as the area where he had been most influential with Bush.

Putin would later see his role in a less positive light. Betrayal might be too strong a word, but the Russians insist that Blair assured them that after their help with 9/11 and Afghanistan, their voice would be listened to in any future conflicts. A year later, when the next conflict arose, their concerns were heard – but politely ignored.

From Moscow, Blair went on to Islamabad. Everywhere they went, security was extremely tight. Nobody knew what al-Qaeda might be planning next. They had seen what they could do with aircraft. Blair's VC10 circled high above the Pakistan capital, then dived down sharply. Blair talked to Anji Hunter about death, about his own mortality. When they landed they all breathed a collective sigh of relief. The streets were eerily empty for their motorcade. They had been cleared hours ago. The only people Blair could see out of his window were police and soldiers.

Just as Putin did, Musharraf gave Blair what he needed. Pakistan would not stand in the way of military action. It would round up any al-Qaeda operatives. Its intelligence service would hand over information to the Americans. And its army would try to seal the porous mountainous border. In return, Pakistan would get relief on its debt, access to world markets and would be allowed back in from the international cold. This was pure old-fashioned *realpolitik*, but as Blair might have said, traditional values in a modern setting. Given the situation four weeks ago, the achievement was remarkable.

Blair had rarely suffered doubts about his own powers of persuasion. During this period what few he still harboured were cast aside. He saw himself on a global mission. If the Americans weren't too accomplished at charming people, Blair told one of his aides, he would have to help them.

His approach to diplomacy was intensely personal. He would talk about looking in the whites of people's eyes. He believed in loyalty, friendship, but most of all in his own powers. One close aide put it like this: 'Tony is the great persuader. He thinks he can convert people even when it might seem as if he doesn't have a cat's chance in hell of succeeding. Call him naïve, call it what you will, but he never gives up. He would say things like "I can get Jacques [Chirac] to do this" or "Leave Putin to me". He has a strong sense that he can tap into people's good sides, find the best in them.'

On one occasion, after a particularly bellicose remark by Bush, a senior Cabinet colleague told Blair, 'You don't need to defend him.' Blair replied: 'Call me stubborn, but I will.'

It was during this period of intensive Blair diplomacy, when on one level he seemed to be succeeding so well, that Chirac began to have doubts about him. 'Blair has a problem of recognition,' remarked one senior French official at the time. 'We get the sense that he needs to be appreciated, to be seen to be at the heart of the action. There is not a single problem that Blair thinks he cannot solve with his own personal engagement – it could be Russia, it could be Africa. The trouble is, the world is a little more complicated than that.'

Blair too saw diplomacy in very personal terms. 'It's a strange paradox in today's world that in some respects governments are less powerful, but at certain critical moments governments are very, very powerful indeed, and the personal relations between people are of fundamental importance, far more so than people can ever guess from the outside. You need to be able to know that you can trust the other person.'

7

WALKING AWAY

TONY BLAIR LED BRITAIN INTO WAR IN AFGHANISTAN almost single-handedly. Between 11 September and the first missile strikes on 7 October he held only two meetings of his Cabinet. Both were devoid of debate.

In the back of his bulletproof Daimler en route to Downing Street, returning from his trip to Pakistan and Russia, Blair took a call from Bush. They agreed the timing of the first attacks. The Prime Minister told the President he wanted his forces to take part in the first night of raids, as a gesture of solidarity. He then informed the Queen and leaders of the opposition parties of the imminence of the war.

On the night of 7 October three US cruisers and a destroyer in the Arabian Sea let fire a salvo of fifty missiles. A wave of aircraft swept across Afghanistan: twenty-five F-18 strike aircraft from the USS *Missouri* and fifteen B-1 and B-52 bombers from Diego Garcia. Britain's nuclear-powered submarines, *Triumph* and *Trafalgar*, launched cruise missiles. Combat operations against thirty-one al-Qaeda and Taleban targets had begun. Blair told the nation the attacks would have been justified even if no British lives had been lost in the World Trade Center. 'This is a moment of utmost gravity for the world. None of the leaders involved in this action want war. None of our nations want it. We are peaceful people. But we know that sometimes to safeguard peace, we have to fight. Britain has learned that lesson many times in our history. We only do it if the cause is just.' Blair said he did not have information on any specific terrorist threats to UK targets, but he called for vigilance.

The statements were carefully co-ordinated. From the Oval Office the President also spoke of a noble cause, of good against evil. He said the air strikes on front-line positions around Kabul and Kandahar, the power base of the Taleban, had been 'carefully targeted'. Al-Qaeda's training camps near Jalalabad were also hit. Within hours, Bin Laden responded with a pre-recorded message broadcast on al-Jazeera around the world. Battle had been joined on two fronts – the military and the media. The clash of civilisations was being played out on twenty-four-hour television. His head swathed in a turban, his body clothed in fatigues, Bin Laden was filmed sitting outside a cave hewn into the mountainside. Beside him, a carefully placed AK-47 was on prominent display. America, he said, had been hit in one of its softest spots. 'America is full of fear from its north to its south, from its west to its east . . . These events have split the whole world into two camps – the camps of belief and the camps of disbelief.' That warning reinforced fears of further terrorist attacks.

The Americans were not making it easy for Blair. Even before a second night of air strikes had been launched, the British government had to account for Bush's statement that the war in Afghanistan was part of a 'broader battle' against states sheltering terrorists. Jack Straw, speaking after an EU meeting, tried to make light of it. 'There are always statements coming out of Washington. Washington is a very large place but this military coalition is about action in respect of military and terrorist targets in Afghanistan.' Blair took a different position in his statement to MPs. 'We are in this for the long haul. Even when al-Qaeda is dealt with, the job is not

over. The network of international terrorism is not confined to it.'
That was his most explicit warning yet that, like Bush, he too had
other countries in his sights. To Labour MPs, and to several in the
Cabinet, that was not part of the deal.

With each day, the air strikes increased in volume and ferocity,
inflaming passions across the region. But for all the hubris of
Donald Rumsfeld's claim that the US was 'running out of targets',
and his spokesman's assertion that they had 'eviscerated' the Taleban
forces, progress on the ground was slow. The 'principals' around
Bush were arguing among themselves while the military was blam-
ing the CIA. Bush was agitated.

Three days into the war, George Robertson offered Nato's help.
The alliance was keen to prove that it was not redundant in the new
post-9/11 world. On 10 October he went to the Pentagon to see
Wolfowitz. He offered troops, planes and ships. The Deputy Defense
Secretary replied: 'We can do everything we need to.' In other words,
thanks but no thanks. 'It left a sour taste,' recalls a senior official.
'People didn't expect an integrated military operation, but they did
think the offer might be taken up at least in part.'

Blair too was wondering out loud to his aides whether the US
had got the plan right. American commanders responded by promising that ground troops would be deployed 'within weeks'. They
came within days. By 19 October the first of around 300 US Special
Forces had slipped in to the country. British military chiefs agreed to
send up to 1,000 troops, including men from the SAS, for sensitive
operations. The situation in Pakistan was worsening. As US troops
and military aircraft stationed there were sent into action for the
first time, militants called a 'day of rage'. Protests against the
Americans and General Musharraf turned violent.

The Taleban was using its base in Islamabad to good effect.
From the serenity of his garden, its envoy to Pakistan, Mullah Abdul
Salam Zaeef, got the daily news cycle off on his terms. Progress was
slow, collateral damage was high, and Arab anger would manifest
itself at the very heart of Western capitals, he would proclaim each

morning, well in time for the *Today* programme and other outlets in
the UK and Europe.

Throughout this period, Blair played a double game. On no
occasion did he either explicitly or implicitly tell the Americans that
he would not support them if they widened the war on terror to
other countries. And yet in his conversations with Arab leaders, and
on his tours of the region, he sought to reassure them that it would
require extremely strong evidence of misdeeds elsewhere – such as a
link with the events of September 11 – for him to back military
action.

That was the message he gave to the Sultan of Oman as he was
visiting British troops there. He said the same to President Hosni
Mubarak of Egypt. That regional tour provided Blair with his first
diplomatic setback. A meeting in Saudi Arabia with Crown Prince
Abdullah was cancelled at the last moment. Shortly after leaving
Britain he was told it would be 'too sensitive' for him to be received.
That was after the heaviest wave of bombing. Wherever he went,
Blair's professions to be pushing the Americans into action on the
Middle East peace process were met with polite scepticism.

If Blair gained anything from that trip, it was the need to
improve the 'message' for the region itself. Campbell told him they
were losing the propaganda battle. As a small step, he set up the
Islamic Media Unit at the Foreign Office, a small group of Arabic-
speaking diplomats who could do interviews and place stories in
regional papers. That was the carrot. There was also the stick. Al-
Jazeera, the Doha-based pan-Arabian news channel, came into its
own in the Afghan war, broadcasting not just the words from Bin
Laden, but often being the first to the story. In Washington, its success was causing alarm. US officials asked the Emir of Qatar to stop
the station from transmitting any more from al-Qaeda. He told
them he had no power to do so. Just to bring home the point, US
fighter jets unleashed smart bombs on al-Jazeera's office in Kabul,
closing down its operation there.

Back home, three weeks into the war, public opinion began to move against Blair. Polls suggested many voters feared the war might increase their vulnerability to terrorism. Non-governmental organisations and aid agencies predicted a flood of refugees and a humanitarian catastrophe. Emergency aid that had been helping to relieve the effects of a long drought in Afghanistan would be disrupted, they said.

Some in the Cabinet were also being less than fulsome in their support. Gordon Brown would be glimpsed sometimes through a mountain of paperwork during meetings on the war. Blair had been through the same over Kosovo: optimism turning to frustration and then victory. He saw no reason to doubt that the current difficulties would pass. Privately, he and Campbell would curse the 'fickle' nature of press coverage, especially the armchair generals popping up on television. Campbell devised a strategy of playing down expectations while attacking the press. Straw was entrusted with the task of delivering the message. The war in Afghanistan and the broader war on terror, he said, may last 'indefinitely'. The press, he added, suffered from 'a reporting culture that is very, very short-term. It constantly wants to change the story forward. The other thing is that it lacks memory backwards.' He harked back to the war against Milošević. 'We had exactly the same headlines. This is why the press in a sense have almost no humility and no memory. Many commentators who are now saying that this is a mistake were saying Kosovo was a mistake.' Different words, same message: Geoff Hoon, the Defence Secretary, said: 'We are in for the long haul, with perhaps no end in sight.' Admiral Boyce gave his offering: 'It may take three or four years. The war against Communism took fifty years. I wonder whether we shouldn't be thinking like that.' This defeatist talk annoyed the Pentagon. 'Fine if they want to hang around,' one official said. 'We don't.'

There was a broader problem. Blair told Campbell and Manning he feared the memory of 9/11 was fading. He feared the pictures of Afghan victims of the war were giving rise to a moral equivalence he found abhorrent. On 30 October, as polls showed a twelve-point drop in support for the war and – for the first time – a majority in favour of a pause in the bombing, Blair used a speech to the Welsh Assembly in Cardiff to go on an emotional offensive to re-ignite public enthusiasm for the war. He claimed a 'flood' of new evidence had emerged over the past month confirming the guilt of Bin Laden for the 9/11 atrocities. 'It is important that we never forget why we are doing this; never forget how we felt watching the planes fly into the trade towers; never forget those answerphone messages. Never forget how we felt imagining how mothers told children they were about to die. Never forget the gloating menace of Osama bin Laden in his propaganda videos.' He concluded: 'The intelligence evidence, significant when I first drew attention to it on 3 October, is now a flood confirming guilt.' Blair had taken to sprin-kling references to 'intelligence' in his speeches. He believed it helped sell the message. It sounded convincing . . . professional.

Their worries did not fade. Campbell decided more drastic action was needed. He persuaded his opposite number in the White House, Karen Hughes, that the US and Britain should co-ordinate their message more effectively. The result was the establishment of the Coalition Information Centre (CIC). Operating out of Wash-ington, London and Islamabad, the idea was to get the message across at all times of the news cycle, to take on the Taleban's envoy.

Campbell sent two of his most senior media handlers to the Pakistani capital. He appointed Philip Bassett, a former *Times* jour-nalist who had become a senior figure in the government's Strategic Communications Unit, to head the CIC. Some twenty people were assigned. As there was not enough space in Downing Street they located themselves in the Foreign Office, for much of the time in a meeting room, K123, on the ground floor of the west wing. Lessons were being applied in reverse. Campbell had taught Nato a thing or two about presentation back in 1999, when it had been unable to cope with a stream of bad news during the Kosovo campaign. This time, he imported a piece of Nato, in the shape of one of its senior press officers, Mark Laity, a former BBC Defence Correspondent.

Campbell had a quiet word in the ear of George Robertson, the Nato chief. Officially this wasn't anything to do with the alliance, but they needed all the help they could get. As happened in Kosovo, part of the problem was shaking information out of the military system. Battle-damage assessments had always been slow, and generals did not operate on the same twenty-four-hour timetable as journalists. 'They still don't realise that collateral damage drives media reporting and we had to respond,' recalls one CIC official. The mantra was: get the information out, get the message out. For all their efforts, for all the new ways, there was a sense afterwards that again the military war had been won much more convincingly than the media war.

Blair sought volunteers on several fronts. On the eve of war, he turned to one of the most flamboyant and patrician figures of British diplomacy. He needed someone to slip in to Damascus to convey a message to its new young leader, Bashar al-Assad. Jonathan Powell suggested his elder brother Charles, who had been Margaret Thatcher's foreign policy guru. Blair raised his eyebrows, but agreed. He called Lord Powell, giving him one day's notice of his secret mission. He was not the first to go to Damascus. Peter Mandelson, out of office for a second time, had gone on a private trip and asked for an audience with Assad. Lord Levy, Blair's personal Middle East envoy, had had several contacts with the Syrians. He had even engineered a meeting between the Clinton administration and Hafez al-Assad, Bashar's father and the former president. A meeting was held. A *rapprochement* did not follow.

The US had long denounced Syria for harbouring terrorists. It provided a test for Blair's proposition that even the most implacable adversary could, with his time and personal engagement, be persuaded back into the fold. After all, Assad was young. He had spent much of his life in London. He had an English-born wife. Bush was sceptical. Donald Rumsfeld and Dick Cheney were hostile. Blair's policy of trying to bring so-called 'rogue states' back into the fold was one of the few areas where he could distinguish himself from the US. He had already restored diplomatic relations with Libya and Iran. Syria was the obvious next step. It was with some optimism that he arrived in Damascus for talks with Assad, the first such visit by a serving British leader.

The meeting started well. Privately the two men engaged politely and candidly. Within hours, however, it had all gone embarrassingly wrong. To the applause of Syrian reporters and to the horror of the man standing next to him, Assad used their joint press conference to condemn the bombing of Afghanistan and defend the Palestinians' use of terrorist methods against Israel. 'We cannot accept what we see every day on our television screens, the killing of innocent civilians. There are hundreds dying every day.' He condemned terrorists, he said, 'but we should differentiate between combating terrorism and war. We did not say we support an international coalition for war. We are always against war.'

Blair had set his sights high – very high for a Prime Minister of Britain, whose locus in the region was limited. He had two objectives: to wean Syria away from support for Hizbollah and to persuade it to re-enter talks with Israel about the Golan Heights. He secured neither. His humiliation that day played into the hands of those who regarded Blair as a diplomatic *ingénue*, always looking for the so-called big picture and missing the all-important detail. They could have told him that his host would have had no choice but to play to the domestic gallery. They could have told him to mention the Golan issue more prominently in the talks. They could have told him that any appearance before the press was asking for trouble. They could have reminded him that Bashar al-Assad had embarrassed the Pope with an anti-Israeli rant at a press conference in Damascus that May. 'What struck us was the naïvety of it,' recalls one senior Foreign Office official. 'The Prime Minister invests so much in his one-to-one relations, but it was clear to us all that Assad either didn't have the will or the power to enact reform.'

On the plane to his next destination, Saudi Arabia, Blair's spokesmen tried to play down the incident. Blair was deeply upset, as was Manning, who saw an opportunity lost. So was Levy. The reception was only marginally better in Riyadh – at least the Saudis had seen him this time – and in Amman. On the morning of his arrival in Jerusalem, the Israeli press, clearly briefed by their own government, described Blair as Bush's 'personal messenger'. It was a view, echoed by many, that was not designed to flatter. Ariel Sharon gave Blair little to go home with. He rebuffed his guest's passionate call at their press conference for an end to the 'cycle of violence', insisting that Israel would continue to assassinate Palestinians it regarded as potential killers. From Jerusalem, Blair went by heli-copter to the border with Gaza, where a convoy took him into the city. He was met with full military honours. This was his thirteenth meeting with Yasser Arafat since taking office, a record few other leaders could match. Bush had, even when in the same UN chamber, steadfastly refused to meet the Palestinian leader.

Blair's visit came on the historically charged anniversary of the 1917 Balfour Declaration, the British promise to establish a home-land for the Jews, normally an occasion for anti-British demonstrations in the territories. Shortly before Blair arrived, the Israelis had launched one of their raids. Usually, as a courtesy to guests, they waited until after they had left.

The visit was following a new and alarming pattern for Blair. In the space of a few weeks he had been rebuffed by the Saudis, humil-iated by the Syrians, and frustrated by the Israelis and Palestinians. On an earlier mission, Straw had run into trouble with Iran and Israel. But at least they had tried. In the three months following 9/11 Blair logged many more miles than Colin Powell, the US Secretary of State, in his efforts to promote an anti-terror coalition, meeting with leaders of more than seventy countries. 'He has often articulated the goals of the war against terrorism more eloquently than Mr Bush,' the New York Times wrote. 'He has not only been Washington's partner in facing the wider world, but on many occa-sions the world's ambassador to Washington. America should be grateful for both roles.' Many in the administration did not share that view. It seemed the hawks had gone out of their way to undermine Blair's efforts, stepping up the bombings in Afghanistan just at the most sensitive moments. To add insult to injury, Paul Wolfowitz proclaimed that 'allies, coalitions and diplomacy' were of little immediate concern.

The coalition on Afghanistan was under intense strain. It wasn't just on the diplomatic front that the contradictions were being exposed. Blair's actions during this period were based on a highly selective, or hypocritical, application of ethics. This was supposed to be a moral campaign to root out terrorism, and yet the governments he and Bush had chosen as their allies had a less than distinguished human rights record – the Pakistanis, the Russians, the Saudis and the leaders of the Central Asian states.

Some European countries looked on with a certain bemusement at the way Blair had taken to such high-level diplomacy in the service of Bush. The French, in particular, suspected an element of grandstanding. 'In Afghanistan, the Brits sent a few missiles but Blair gave the impression he was running the war,' said one senior official in Paris. 'That was his style. We weren't that bothered. We had grown used to it.'

Shortly before his latest trip to Washington, Blair convened a meeting in Downing Street that was unprecedented in international diplomacy. Britain had no formal leadership role to perform. It was not holding the presidency of the EU. Nor was it temporarily in charge of the UN Security Council. Yet such was Blair's belief in his own capabilities that he decided to summon European leaders for dinner on a Sunday night. The original plan was to confine the meeting to the 'big three' countries – Schröder, Chirac and Jospin, and the host himself. As soon as word got out, other countries cried foul. The meeting was then expanded to include prime ministers José María Aznar of Spain, Silvio Berlusconi of Italy, and Guy Verhofstadt of Belgium, as well as Javier Solana, the EU's foreign policy chief. Romano Prodi, the EU Commission President, for whom Blair had scarcely disguised disdain, sat fuming in Brussels.

The Dutch premier, Wim Kok, arrived an hour and a half late after forcing a last-minute invitation. He had been so angry that he phoned Blair to complain about being excluded, pointing out that Dutch military personnel were already working at the US military central command in Tampa, Florida. As for Verhofstadt, who was supposed to be running the European Council for that six-month period, his invitation had come so late – Sunday lunchtime – he had considered declining, and had accepted only after consulting others who had been left out.

This was a minor squall in the scheme of things, but it left a residual suspicion of British arrogance. This was, in effect, a council of war, with Blair going through the military progress so far, and the plans for a ground offensive. Chirac made clear his concern at the saturation bombing tactics, and the effect they were having on Middle East opinion. 'We know what is likely to happen,' he said. 'A mosque will be bombed by accident during Ramadan. What do we do then?'

To counter the general criticisms at home and abroad, meanwhile, George W. Bush stepped up the rhetoric, warning that al-Qaeda could unleash a nuclear Armageddon. 'They're seeking chemical, biological and nuclear weapons,' he said. 'Given the means, our enemies would be a threat to every nation; and, eventually, to civilisation itself.'

The language was becoming looser. The comparisons were becoming more colourful, the grasp on history more tenuous. While Bush would liken al-Qaeda to the 'Soviets' – a strange comparison between a terrorist network and a highly organised central state – Jack Straw popped up and called them 'Nazis'.

As the war entered its fourth week, Blair was facing frustration from all sides. British defence officials recognised that Washington was calling the shots. But there was growing impatience about American delays in deploying ground troops. Some SAS forces were in Afghanistan and awaiting orders from Central Command. One

senior minister close to Blair spoke disparagingly about General
Tommy Franks, the US commander of Operation Enduring
Freedom, noting that he spent his time at Centcom's headquarters in
Florida. Senior British embassy officials visited the White House
every day for meetings at the National Security Council, to hear
what the President was being told about the bombing campaign so
far and to get some indication of Bush's thinking on the next phase.
They reported back that the military campaign was going better
than portrayed in the media, but they expressed fears that the US
administration had done virtually no post-war planning.

With the Northern Alliance making very gradual progress, the
UN entrusted the task of finding a political solution for a post-
Taleban Afghanistan to one of its most experienced diplomats.
Lakhdar Brahimi, a former Algerian foreign minister, had already
served as special envoy from 1997 to 1999. He made it clear he could
not work from a set timetable and would not involve the current
regime. While promising to go 'as fast as is humanly possible', he also
said, 'The people of Afghanistan have responsibilities, we go just as
fast as they can themselves.' What Brahimi did not say, but what
many in the UN feared, was that the Northern Alliance could take
Kabul before a political blueprint had been agreed. Blair was growing impatient. Several times he asked his UN Ambassador, Sir
Jeremy Greenstock, to intercede, to urge Brahimi to speed things up.
'We desperately wanted to be in Kabul,' one senior diplomat recalls.
And yet Greenstock was wily. He pushed, but also recognised the
strategic constraints. He was quite prepared to use his own discretion. His motto was: 'Tailor the national instruction to the best
collective outcome.'

On 7 November Blair was back in Washington, this time via
Concorde for only six hours, and this time the atmospherics were
less cordial. After a brief meeting in the Oval Office, the President
and Prime Minister held a joint press conference to boost the cause.
After dinner with aides they went upstairs to confer alone. Blair
urged him to get to grips with the Middle East peace process and to

engage with Arafat. Bush refused, point blank. This was one of the low points. British morale deteriorated further when Donald Rumsfeld, in his inimitable style, addressed a black-tie audience of defence contractors, congressional staff and ranking military. He received a series of standing ovations when he said: 'The coalition must not determine the mission.' In other words, America decides, and if others want to join, so be it. Rumsfeld likened American successes to the Second World War. Then it had taken the US eleven months to launch its land campaign against Germany. This time the US had pulled together a coalition in weeks, and after just one month had flown more than 1,800 sorties in Afghanistan and dropped over a million rations. The speech, to British ears, went from bad to worse. 'We will not stop for Ramadan. We will not stop for winter. And after the Taleban and al-Qaeda, we'll get after the rest.'

Rumsfeld's optimism was justified. Two days later the strategic northern town of Mazar-i-Sharif fell. The Northern Alliance pressed on towards Kabul with impressive and then alarming speed. Jack Straw had just arrived at the UN, for the annual meeting of the General Assembly, which had been delayed after the events of 9/11. His Political Director and fixer Peter Ricketts was already there, and told him about the news from Mazar. They were all extremely cautious. Nobody realised how quickly events would then unravel, how quickly the Taleban would be overrun. The highlight of the meeting was Bush's first speech to the UN. He was in defiant mood, telling them that every country had a duty to fight terrorism. No country could be neutral at a time when terror groups were seeking weapons of mass destruction: 'Every nation has a stake in this cause. For every regime that sponsors terror there is a price to be paid. And it will be paid. Civilisation itself – the civilisation we share – is threatened. History will record our response and judge or justify every nation in this hall.'

Early in the war, Blair had appointed his own special representative, Robert Cooper. He had come to the Prime Minister's attention several years before with a series of papers highlighting the dangers posed by weapons of mass destruction and rogue states. Cooper was a rare Foreign Office mandarin, not shy in coming forward, and eager to appear in print. He was given licence to do that, and caused major waves in the diplomatic community with an essay entitled: 'Reordering the World: The Long-term Implications of September 11'. The world, he argued, comprised pre-modern states too weak to enforce the rule of law; modern states pursuing their national interests in the classic nineteenth-century sense; and post-modern states which reject power politics in favour of integration and systems of mutual interference. Britain, by implication, belonged to the latter group and therefore had a licence to impose its will on others. His writings did not endear him to many of his colleagues, but those around Blair approved. An Asia expert, Cooper was given the job of trying to hasten things along in Afghanistan. But even he had to restrain his boss.

Brahimi's efforts had not exactly forged ahead. 'Why isn't he getting on with it?' Blair complained of the UN envoy. Brahimi wanted the Tajik-dominated Northern Alliance and the Pashtuns in the south – from where the Taleban had drawn much of their support – to arrive in Kabul at the same time as the allied forces to prevent a bloodbath. Cooper had gone on a secret mission to Rome to see the exiled former king Mohammad Zahir Shah, to see if he would raise the standard of revolt. At the same time, Brahimi was making contact with Hamed Karzai, a Pashtun leader and member of the same clan as the king. These overtures needed time and no little subtlety. 'In the long-term interests of Afghanistan, we didn't want victory too quickly,' recalls one official closely involved in the process. 'That's not the kind of thing Tony seemed to understand. I suggested we liberate Herat first. David Manning said to me: "The Prime Minister wants to win this war, and taking the capital seems like a good thing to me."'

Blair's impatience was getting the better of him. He bombarded intelligence officials with questions about how long the war would last. He feared a campaign extending into the winter and spring. 'He was looking for good news all the time,' recalls one insider. 'He was looking for the point when the war would turn. It was difficult sometimes to bring it to him. We were cautious, that's in our nature.'

The intelligence chiefs said it would turn, but not as quickly as it did. Just after dawn on 13 November, after five years of perhaps the most extreme religious system anywhere on earth, Kabul was a free city. Overnight, Taleban lines had crumbled. It took next to no time for thousands of Northern Alliance fighters to cover the last few miles to the outskirts of the capital. Some fighters were halted there by their commanders, on the orders of the Americans who feared looting and revenge attacks by an army let loose on the city. Some police, or at least men dressed in police uniform, were sent in to clear the city. However, within hours looting had begun, at which point the troops were sent down the hill into the city. Some of the scenes were ugly. In the streets, in the ditches, lay the bodies of foreign volunteers for the Taleban, especially Arabs and Pakistanis. The foreigners were particularly loathed, so they were lynched before being shot. The new rulers on the streets announced that women could go back to work and girls back to school – activities that were banned by the Taleban. Men were allowed to shave off their beards.

Watching from Downing Street with amazement and awe, Blair was struck by the television footage of a few women tearing off their burkhas. He and his people cited this gesture of liberation as vindication of everything they had done. (Many women put their burkhas back on a few months later.) Military chiefs said the speed of the fall of Kabul had proved the effectiveness of a bombing campaign that only a week before was being criticised for its brutal impact on civilians.

Blair and his aides had a point to prove. Campbell believed that most of the British press, and the BBC in particular, was biased against war. Downing Street published a roll call of shame of journalists it claimed had been proved wrong by a hundred days of victory. In parliament, Straw ridiculed Labour MPs for suggesting

that the US and Britain might still be fighting in Afghanistan twelve
months down the line. On that score, he would be proven only half
right. For the Americans, the 'eureka' moment came as journalists
and alliance soldiers combed through al-Qaeda safe houses, documents and computer records revealing that Bin Laden's network
had been trying to acquire weapons of mass destruction. The
assumption, which they struggled to prove, was that they had been
looking to Iraq for supplies.

The final stages in Afghanistan saw three processes running
simultaneously – the search for a new political order, the desperate
need to provide humanitarian supplies, and the hunt for Bin Laden,
the Taleban's leader Mullah Omar and the remnants of al-Qaeda.

Blair would later admit to his advisers that he had read the
latter stages of the war incorrectly. He had put Greenstock in the difficult position of applying pressure on Brahimi, even though the
ambassador himself was wary of the approach. The Americans were
on Brahimi's side. Downing Street wanted the UN meeting on
Afghanistan's future to be held as soon as possible, in either Kabul or
in Saudi Arabia. Germany volunteered and offered Berlin, but
Brahimi wanted something more secure and serene. They settled on
a government guesthouse overlooking Bonn. On 5 December the
four Afghan factions involved signed a deal. Given the complexities
and the bitter divisions, it was a diplomatic *tour de force* by Brahimi.
The plan was for a power-sharing council, with Karzai at its head, to
take over on 22 December and to run the country for six months
until a *loya jirga*, a traditional meeting of the clans, was convened to
confirm a post-war settlement. The major powers were united in
welcoming the agreement. This was one of those telling moments of
Europe and America coming together. Nobody was starry-eyed. The
consent of several powerful warlords was still awaited, the future of
Afghanistan was still fragile, but it was as much as could have been
achieved in the circumstances.

It had been Brahimi's idea to sound out Karzai for the interim
leadership of Afghanistan. Well educated, fluent in English and just

Westernised enough, Karzai had the vital attribute of coming from the south. He had served as a deputy foreign minister in Afghanistan's first Mujaheddin government in 1992, but fell out with the Taleban. One of the major points in his favour was that he had not been involved in the bloodletting during the early 1990s. In October, Karzai had slipped across the border from Pakistan to gather support. As the Taleban retreated to Kandahar, their last remaining stronghold, Karzai led a team of fighters to flush them out. But it could all have gone terribly wrong. Just a few hours before the historic deal in Bonn, a stray American 'smart bomb' killed three US Special Forces soldiers, injured nineteen others and nearly killed Karzai. Robert Cooper, Blair's envoy, recalls how he was in Brahimi's UN office in New York as Brahimi was on the satellite phone. At the other end of the line was Karzai, standing on a hill outside Kandahar. Suddenly the line went dead and crackling was heard. The Special Forces team he had been with had phoned through the wrong co-ordinates.

The military job was far from complete. Bin Laden was on the run; the Taleban had fled to Jalalabad and Kandahar. For the Americans the top priority by far was to hunt down Bin Laden. Blair wanted to commit 6,000 more troops to support those American operations. Within days they were stood down. Downing Street shrugged off suggestions of a snub, but it was hard to portray it in any other light, so clear had Blair's views been. This would have made Britain the first country to put a sizeable ground force in Afghanistan. A few hundred US Special Forces and roughly 200 British soldiers were in the country at the time. The Northern Alliance complained to the Americans that they had not been properly consulted about the British plans. A contingent of 100 British Marines was confined to Bagram airbase amid confusion about their role. A Royal Navy spokesman said the Marines were there at the 'specific request of the Americans'. But a Pentagon spokesman said there was 'probably a misunderstanding as to what their mission was', a comment that angered the British.

To the Americans, the question of staying for the duration to rebuild Afghanistan was secondary. To Blair it was vital. During the Labour conference, he had declared: 'We will not walk away from Afghanistan, as the outside world has done so many times before.' On 19 December Geoff Hoon announced the despatch of up to 1,500 British soldiers, the bulk of them paratroopers, to Kabul, with an advance party of 200 Marine commandoes flying in immediately to head the International Security Assistance Force (ISAF). Some seventeen other countries also declared their willingness to participate, but Britain was very much in the lead. This was important to Blair, to demonstrate his willingness to show off the peacekeeping role of the military, even after 9/11. To guard against accusations of overstretch, he agreed that leadership of the force would be handed over to Turkey the following April.

On the reconstruction of Afghanistan, Blair met resistance in Washington at every turn. In an unholy pact with the Northern Alliance, the Pentagon tried to keep the numbers and remit of the ISAF down to a minimum. General Franks, the US commander, feared the new force would 'confuse the battlefield'. He simply did not want other countries interfering on his patch. In the end, the role of the multinational force was to be confined to training a new Afghan police force, guarding Bagram and other strategic sites – not to escort aid convoys or disarm the local population. All its activities were, in any case, subject to veto by an American administration that was insisting that its flailing, global war on terrorism took priority over rebuilding a single country.

Clare Short complained to Cabinet that the Americans were not taking the aid situation seriously enough. There was a more fundamental difference. Both the Foreign Office and the State Department wanted to extend ISAF's remit beyond Kabul. The Pentagon and the Ministry of Defence did not. Blair saw it as desirable rather than essential. One of his close aides says now: 'Anybody who knows anything about Afghanistan regrets that decision.' American minds were already elsewhere. The talk in Washington was of the start of 'phase two' in the war on terror – branching out to other countries. The only person who could have put pressure on Bush was Blair. He chose not to. As so often, he trod carefully with the President.

This was still a fearful American military participation. There was no commander in Afghanistan above the rank of Lieutenant-Colonel. Loath to risk an extended ground presence, the Americans were forced to look on helplessly as warlords cut private deals, carving up the country and allowing certain senior Taleban figures to walk free. At the same time, the CIA was given $1 billion of extra funding to identify local groups and provide them with the cash and weapons to do America's work. The more this happened, in the name of hunting down their prized catch, Osama bin Laden, the more the Americans undermined the interim administration and destroyed hopes of building a viable central administration for Afghanistan.

Beyond Jalalabad rise the White Mountains. In the vast bowl of crags one peak, Tora Bora, stands highest of all. Two days before the fall of Kabul, on 10 November, a convoy of trucks believed to contain Bin Laden was seen heading out. He disappeared into the network of caves excavated by the Mujaheddin in the war against the Soviets. US B-52s began to pound the hillsides. The American air force was confident it could blast al-Qaeda's positions apart. There was talk in the press of the latest bombing gadgetry, 'daisy-cutters' and 'bunker-busters'. On the ground, members of the Special Forces were tasked with guiding the bombs to their targets by 'painting' the mouths of caves with laser devices. Throughout December, American bombing in the east was as intense as at any time since the war began. It was in inverse proportion to remaining, legitimate targets. The Americans were in a hurry. They wanted the campaign over and done with. One predictable consequence of this unguided thrashing-about was an attack on 29 December on the village of Qalaye Niazi that wiped out a wedding party. At least 100 people were said to have died. The single biggest incident of 'collateral damage' did incalculable harm to public confidence in the Afghan project. It also further undermined Karzai, who was not being helped by the Americans to consolidate his political position. Several members of his shaky ruling coalition demanded a halt to US operations.

During the first few days of December, according to UK and US intelligence, Bin Laden slipped out of their grasp. 'We thought Bin Laden was in Tora Bora until the 9th or the 10th,' one intelligence operative says. 'We don't know what happened to him after that. We had some knowledge of him intermittently. He would come up on our signals, only to disappear again.' The Pentagon had left it to Pakistan's General Musharraf to seal the 100-mile stretch of rugged, lawless countryside that marked the border. British Special Forces, the SBS, thought they had tracked him. Suddenly, however, they received orders from the Americans not to proceed. They had been pulled off the job, so that the US Special Forces could do it themselves. In those intervening hours, Bin Laden got away. The British on the ground were furious. When word got back to Whitehall, Blair promised to take it up with the White House. He did, politely, but that, as far as he was concerned, was the end of the story.

In early January reports came through that Mullah Omar had escaped on a motorbike from the siege of his mountain redoubt. Despite all this aerial frenzy, none of al-Qaeda's senior leaders was killed or caught in the operation. Taleban 'holdouts' suddenly materialised for the Americans, only mysteriously to disappear once the B-52 bombers had taken to the air.

By this point, Bush was signalling that he might not achieve his original goal. To sugar the pill for an American public believing that this war had been about the search for the culprits of 9/11, he sought to rewrite history. 'Our objective is more than Bin Laden,' he said. 'I just don't spend that much time on him, to be honest. Focusing on one person indicates to me that people don't understand the scope of this mission. Terror is bigger than one man.' A Pentagon spokesman said the US had decided to stop 'chasing shadows'.

At just before midnight on 7 January 2002, Blair made his most perilous journey yet. Under cover of darkness he and Cherie flew into Bagram airbase in an RAF C-130 Hercules troop carrier, where he was met by Karzai. This was the first visit by a foreign leader and Blair's personal security had sanctioned it only a few hours earlier. His aim was to show solidarity with the interim leader, and to thank the British troops. The windows of his plane, which was bristling with anti-missile weaponry, had been blacked out during the flight from the Pakistani capital Islamabad, to protect him against an attack by rogue Taleban forces. The tight security served as an uncomfortable reminder of a war unfinished. Blair admitted as much. 'It is true that until our objectives are met, our mission is not complete. But substantial progress has been made,' he said. He repeated to Karzai the pledge he had made at the Labour conference. 'Afghanistan has been a failed state for too long and the whole world has paid the price – in the export of terror, the export of drugs and finally in the explosion of death and destruction on the streets of the USA. It is in all our interests that Afghanistan becomes a stable country, part of the international community once more.'

In Washington, talk of international community was interpreted flexibly. Shortly after Blair's visit to Bagram, the first of hundreds of al-Qaeda suspects shuffled chained and hooded on to a USAF cargo jet at Kandahar airport into a world of legal limbo. Camp X-ray at Guantanamo Bay, a US naval base in Cuba, became the most potent symbol of an American administration that saw its own security interests as overriding international law. So many were brought in so quickly in such degrading circumstances that flights had to be suspended while new cells were constructed. Politicians across the world questioned the judicial basis for their indeterminate detention, and expressed outrage at the conditions they faced. Chris Patten, the EU's external affairs commissioner, said the controversy showed the administration's dangerously 'absolutist and simplistic' strategy towards the rest of the world. Many Labour MPs expressed their horror, to which Rumsfeld responded, with one of his characteristic put-downs: 'It's amazing the insight parliamentarians can gain from 5,000 miles away.' With three British citizens among the captives, Blair was embarrassed and frustrated. He urged more humane conditions but expressed understanding for the Americans' position. These men would, in time, provide valuable intelligence, he said. The Americans refused to call them prisoners of war, arguing that the Geneva conventions did not apply. A new term was conjured: enemy combatants. 'Nobody should feel defensive or unhappy about the quality of treatment they've received,' Cheney said. 'It's probably better than they deserve.'

In March, Geoff Hoon announced the deployment of a further 1,700 combat troops to support the Americans' less than successful attempt to flush out what was left of al-Qaeda. This now constituted Britain's largest combat deployment since the Gulf War. Boyce was cautious. He had warned in December that a 'single-minded aim' of destroying the Taleban and al-Qaeda with a 'high-tech Wild West' operation would not be enough to win the hearts and minds across the Arab world. Much to their fury, the British forces were held back by the Americans. When they did finally go into combat they did not find a single Taleban fighter to engage with.

The war in Afghanistan had been won, but the peace most certainly had not. For more than a week in June 2002, some 1,500 representatives, elected or appointed from thirty-two provinces, gathered under a tent. The *loya jirga* confirmed Karzai as Afghanistan's leader. The hope was that the meeting would do more, would begin the process of healing the country's divisions, of taking it down the road to stability and away from warlordism. That required not just goodwill among the protagonists, but the active participation of the major international power. Karzai was already complaining that the Americans had abrogated their responsibilities. His writ extended not much further than Kabul's city walls.

Having survived several assassination attempts, Karzai became one of the most protected men in the world. Heavily armed US forces and CIA agents were deployed around the clock to keep him alive, and the hopes for a better life for Afghanistan invested in him. But with each month he became angrier at the West's broken promises. The 14,000 foreign troops in his country – 5,000 peacekeepers under ISAF; the rest, Americans still on combat missions – had failed to wrest control from the warlords. Infrastructure had not been rebuilt. Crime and disorder were rife. By mid-2003 fears were growing that the Taleban was regrouping. The only part of the economy that seemed to be working was opium. Poppy harvests were back to record highs.

This was not what Blair had intended. He saw the war in Afghanistan not just in the narrow immediate terms of routing al-Qaeda, but also in removing the Taleban. Both short-term goals were achieved. Al-Qaeda's global network was dispersed and severely damaged, but it did not take long to regroup elsewhere. As for the Afghan people, the Taleban's demise led, in much of the country, to the return of warlords and a combination of repression and anarchy. Democracy and civil society were as elusive as ever.

Afghanistan was now nothing more than an encumbrance to the US. This would become a familiar pattern, with Blair entreating Bush to engage in a process of nation-building that was alien to him. It mattered little to the American President. He had moved on. It mattered a great deal to the British Prime Minister. But he would have to settle for much less.

8

EVIL AXIS

ON 29 JANUARY 2002, GEORGE W. BUSH REWROTE THE RULES
that had guided the world for more than half a century. America, he
told Congress in his annual State of the Union address, would 'not
wait on events while dangers gather'. The war on terror had only just
begun. Listing Iraq, Iran and North Korea, he declared: 'States like
these, and their terrorist allies, constitute an axis of evil, arming to
threaten the peace of the world. By seeking weapons of mass
destruction, these regimes pose a grave and growing danger.' The
doctrine of US primacy and pre-emption was born.

Tony Blair was caught unaware. He hurried to catch up. Just
over two months later, on 6 April at the President's ranch at
Crawford, Texas, the British Prime Minister committed himself to
an invasion of Iraq. The only points left open were the timing and
the terms.

Blair told his inner circle he was one of only a few world leaders who
understood the 'new realities' of the global order, post-9/11. 'The
Prime Minister has an extremely acute sense of American power,'
says one of his entourage. 'Very few people understand just what that

means. He does. He understands that the Americans can bring to bear a capability of a different order to anything the world has seen. There is no historical precedent. America's reach is everywhere. They invented a new way of fighting a war. Afghanistan showed them that they have a capability that even they didn't know they had.'

The fall of Kabul had given Bush new confidence. The nervous President in those critical September days was gone. A more assured US administration became less prone to defer to anyone, including Blair. Bush wanted to tell his people, and the world, that he would not flinch from the next fight. He used the State of the Union occasion to do just that. The speech is the high point of the presidential calendar. The address is the product of months of work by a team of speechwriters. Everything is tested out first. Nothing is left to chance. Bush had emulated that other hero of the modern American right, Ronald Reagan, whose description of the Soviet Union in 1983 as an 'evil empire' had gone down in folklore as precipitating the downfall of Communism.

Across the world, reaction to Bush's words ranged from surprise to consternation to alarm. In Downing Street and at the Foreign Office, everyone was taken aback. They tried to make light of it. One official recalls: 'We all smiled at the jejune language. It was straight out of *Lord of the Rings*.' In Washington, Colin Powell knew what was going to be said, but he did not fight it. By this point he was looking increasingly sidelined. State Department officials puzzled over drafts and tried to convince themselves that the words did not represent a policy shift. They did report back that nobody abroad liked it. And yet it had an inexorable logic. This is what the hawks had been pushing for in Clinton's final years in the hope of influencing his successor.

Operation Desert Fox in 1998 had left Iraq in limbo. The UN inspectors were out. Saddam was free to do as he pleased. Sanctions were still in force, causing human suffering but achieving few political ends. In December 1999, after a year-long tussle, the UN Security Council passed Resolution 1284, with Russia, France and China

abstaining. Blair had been coming under increasing political pressure
to address the social consequences of the decade-old embargo. The
resolution was supposed to provide carrot and stick, to prod Saddam
Hussein to co-operate again. The first set of measures removed a cap
on Iraqi oil sales and established a 'green list' of humanitarian items
that could be imported into Iraq. At the same time it established a
new monitoring group, Unmovic, demanding that it be given 'immediate, unconditional and unrestricted access to any and all areas,
facilities, equipment, records and means of transport'. The second set
of measures held out the prospect of a suspension of sanctions and
possible foreign investment in the oil sector. This would occur if the
Iraqi government was found to have 'co-operated in all respects' for
a continuous period of 120 days with Unmovic. The meaning of
this requirement was kept deliberately vague by Britain. Iraq immediately rejected it, saying it would not implement any resolution that
did not immediately lift sanctions.

In September 2000, as the presidential election campaign
approached its climax, the Project for the New American Century
published a document entitled 'Rebuilding America's Defenses:
Strategy, Forces and Resources'. Behind it were the familiar faces of
neoconservatism – Donald Rumsfeld, Paul Wolfowitz, Dick Cheney
and Richard Perle. In their paper they called for a massive increase
in defence spending so that the US could 'fight and win multiple,
simultaneous, major-theatre wars'. They pondered that some 'catastrophic and catalysing event, like a new Pearl Harbor' was needed to
assure US global power. 'While the unresolved conflict with Iraq
provides immediate justification' for intervention, 'the need for a
substantial American presence in the Gulf transcends the issue of the
regime of Saddam Hussein,' it said. In other words, they were looking for a reason to expand US influence in the Middle East and
elsewhere.

For all the rhetoric, Iraq did not feature in George W. Bush's
election campaign. When Condoleezza Rice first signed up as his
foreign policy adviser in 2000, she did raise her concerns about the

issue. Bush said he wanted Saddam 'dealt with', but left open the 'how'.

Blair would later say that around the start of 2001 he became increasingly exercised by the issue of weapons of mass destruction, and urged Bush to act. Certainly in the preceding months, the Joint Intelligence Committee was collating information about Iraqi oil being sent illegally through Syria and Turkey. Flights were arriving in Baghdad in spite of a supposed embargo. In December 2000, Saddam staged a huge show of military strength in Baghdad, partly to quash rumours of ill health, and partly to serve a warning to the incoming US President. The containment policy had broken down. Resolution 1284 was not working. That was not in doubt. Bush ordered a 're-invigoration' of sanctions and set in motion a broader review of the policy on Iraq. He was keen on the idea of increasing funding to the INC and other groups, in the hope of fomenting an uprising.

One of Colin Powell's first decisions was to try to tighten the porous UN embargo while allowing more humanitarian support for innocent Iraqis – so-called 'smart sanctions'. Powell was clear in his mind that, while imperfect, the policy was better than any alternative. 'Though they may be pursuing weapons of mass destruction of all kinds it is not clear how successful they have been. We ought to declare this a success. We have kept him contained, kept him in his box,' he said. Blair eagerly agreed. At the time that is all he was thinking of. One senior US government official recalls:

They were horrified at all references to regime change. When we were negotiating [Resolution] 1284, the Brits were adamant this had nothing to do with regime change. I don't remember so much as a whiff or a whisper from the Brits about using more force. The idea that Blair was pushing this kind of war, or the idea of overthrowing Saddam Hussein, was fanciful. It's a rewriting of history. Rolling rationalisation is one of the less attractive features of British foreign policy.

Bush's Iraq review dragged on. By the summer the policy remained essentially the one inherited from Clinton – containment. Then 9/11 intervened.

Blair had no idea how vigorously some of the 'principals' in the Bush foreign policy team had been advocating military action against Iraq so soon after the attacks on the Twin Towers. It was in the first emergency meeting of the National Security Council on 11 September itself that Rumsfeld asked: 'Why shouldn't we go against Iraq, not just al-Qaeda?' From that moment on, he and Wolfowitz used every available opportunity to press the case. Wolfowitz described Iraq as a 'brittle, oppressive regime that might break easily'. Powell countered: 'The goal is terrorism in its broadest sense.' Cheney suggested: 'To the extent we define our task broadly, including those who support terrorism, then we get at states. And it's easier to find them than it is to find Bin Laden.' Rice was enigmatic. She instructed her officials on the NSC to 'think about how you capitalise on these opportunities'. She meant 9/11. Bush hedged his bets. 'Start with Bin Laden, which Americans expect. And then if we succeed, we've struck a huge blow and can move forward.' Undeterred, Rumsfeld and Wolfowitz held secret meetings about opening a second front – against Saddam. Powell was excluded. The strategy envisaged the use of air support and the occupation of southern Iraq with ground troops, to install a new government run by Ahmed Chalabi's Iraqi National Congress. Under the plan American troops would seize the oil fields around Basra, in the south, and sell the oil to finance the opposition.

Blair was alarmed. He asked John Scarlett, the head of the JIC, to provide an assessment. The response was categorical. 'We quickly established there was no link between Saddam and the Twin Towers,' says one official. When parliament convened in emergency session on 14 September, Blair stressed that the immediate focus was al-Qaeda, and securing the broadest possible international support for an attack. He repeated the same message in his conversations on the phone with Bush, and while in Washington. He believed he had convinced the President, and that there was no cause for worry. At the same time Blair believed he should not be seen to be disagreeing with Bush. So in a gesture of solidarity with the White House, he told MPs in that same debate: 'Our next issue is weapons of mass destruction.'

Blair's political aides and senior intelligence officials agree that Saddam posed no greater threat on 12 September 2001 than he had on the 10th. They accept that the intelligence on that is clear.

Yet that autumn Blair allowed himself to be persuaded of three things – that America had to be supported more than ever in its time of need; that it saw the world in a different light; and that the world would face a threat of an altogether different scale if Saddam made his chemical and biological weapons available to terrorist groups. The first was a value judgment. The second was fact. The third was a hypothesis based on an assumption.

Throughout this period, the issue of Iraq was not discussed at all in Cabinet. The focus was on the threat from al-Qaeda and the war in Afghanistan. 'None of us saw Iraq as a military adventure coming on to our radar screen,' recalls one Cabinet member at the time. 'It moved from being a gleam in the eye of hardliners in Washington to becoming a settled programme.'

In public, Blair spoke only of a broader threat. 'The first phase is the action in Afghanistan. The next phase is against international terrorism in all its forms,' he said in October. The next month, at a summit in London, Blair agreed with Jacques Chirac there was no need to extend the war on terror to Iraq. He was looking both ways, and had not yet decided which way to jump. By December, with Afghanistan fading from attention, he was putting down a stronger marker. 'We have always said there will be a second phase, but people shouldn't rush to conclusions about what the second phase will be. Nothing will happen without consultation with allies. It will be done in a very considered way.'

Of more immediate concern to Blair were warnings he was

receiving from Scarlett and Sir Stephen Lander, the head of MI5, of threats to the UK itself. Security services were picking up constant chatter. At this point Scarlett was having daily meetings with Blair. The security services and anti-terrorist police were put on a particularly high alert for the annual Armistice Day commemorations in Whitehall, when the royal family and the political elite would be out in force.

On Blair's orders, the security services had expanded their network abroad in the war on terror. In Iraq, however, the British 'hum-int' capability, human intelligence, had never recovered since three SIS agents were hanged outside the British Embassy in Baghdad in 1979. For all the claims to the contrary, the British were struggling to keep tabs. Within a few months, the intelligence services reported to Blair that, since 9/11, new agents had been successfully recruited in Iraq. They told him that given the difficulty of penetrating a society under such tight control, they were impressed with the quality of their intelligence. Blair saw no reason to doubt it. As he liked to say, 'These people were professionals.' In fact so impressed was Blair by the response of the intelligence agencies in those critical months that he wrote to Scarlett, Lander, Sir Richard Dearlove, the head of the SIS, and Sir Francis Richards from GCHQ, thanking them for their efforts in the war against terrorism. Blair told them they were the 'unsung heroes' of the campaign.

The fresh intelligence that winter confirmed the original assessment of September that links between Iraq and al-Qaeda and the events of 9/11 were, at best, tenuous. The intelligence, which was shared by the CIA, was by now departing from Bush's political agenda. Downing Street and the Foreign Office had been caught on the hop by the State of the Union address. Some officials believed it was simply Bush's way of diverting attention from the failure to find Bin Laden. Jack Straw was similarly unimpressed. He suggested during a trip to Washington that the President's speech should be 'best understood by the fact that there are mid-term Congressional elections coming up in November'. That did not go down well with his hosts and produced a tart response from Rice. 'This is not about American politics, and I assume that when the British government speaks about foreign policy, it's not about British politics.' Blair did not appreciate that kind of spat, and told Straw to refrain from offending the Americans in future. Manning then phoned Rice to apologise on the government's behalf.

Gradually the seriousness of Bush's message seeped through. Blair would rather have focused his efforts on routing out terrorist networks. But he and Manning concluded that the game had moved on to Iraq. Either Britain would stay out of it – something he would not dream of – or it would have to engage on the Americans' terms. This was no longer a case of US unilateralism, more multilateralism *à la carte*. Bush was putting into practice Rumsfeld's adage that the mission defines the coalition. Blair needed to be part of it – whatever it would be.

The reference to Iran in the State of the Union address was particularly difficult. Blair had personally backed mediation with Tehran as a key part of the strategy against al-Qaeda. He had proposed it as part of his memo on 12 September. Then, Bush had listened. This time he was more blunt. 'The Iranians should be told that if they wanted a proper relationship with the West, they had to give up their links to terrorism,' he said. Bush gave a sympathetic hearing to please Ariel Sharon, the Israeli Prime Minister, who urged the Americans to keep Iran in diplomatic isolation.

In the spring of 2002 the British government struggled to keep up with the Americans. Bush was listening to Blair, but listening to Cheney and Rumsfeld more. His anger, real or manufactured, was strong. *Time* magazine reported in March that on one occasion he poked his head into Rice's office at the White House and told three senators sitting there: 'Fuck Saddam. We're taking him out.' At the Pentagon, Rumsfeld asked for contingency plans to be drawn up for possible military action against Iraq later in the year. The dates they were working from were between the mid-term elections in November and the end of January 2003. Bush secretly signed an intelligence order directing the CIA to mount a comprehensive covert programme to topple Saddam, including authority to use lethal force to capture him. General Tommy Franks went to the White House every three or four weeks to give Bush a private briefing on planning for Iraq.

The neocons set about giving an intellectual imprimatur to the new policy. The two P's lay at the heart – pre-emption and primacy. But the motive was not simply national self-interest. Emboldened by their experience in Afghanistan, they saw the opportunity to root out hostile regimes in the Middle East and to implant a very American interpretation of democracy and free markets, from Iraq to Iran to Saudi Arabia. Wolfowitz epitomised this view. He saw a liberated Iraq as both paradigm and lynchpin for future interventions. At the State Department, however, they saw all this as utopian fantasy. Older hands argued that Iraq would fragment into ethnic enclaves, that US garrisons would be targets for an eruption of Arab fury, that oil supplies will be endangered – and that Americans lacked the patience to midwife a pro-Western Iraq.

Opinion polls in Britain were pointing to a marked decline in sympathy towards the US, or more specifically a growing hostility to the Bush administration. Blair's advisers picked up a dangerous shift in sentiment. Whereas opposition to military action in Afghanistan was, in parliament, confined roughly to the same 'usual suspects' who had opposed the war in Kosovo, scepticism about American intentions was becoming mainstream and increasingly vocal. For those on the left who had supported the notion of 'liberal intervention' – military action in defence of human rights and democracy – Blair's alliance with Bush was becoming increasingly hard to defend.

On 11 March 2002, six months to the hour after 9/11, Blair played host to Dick Cheney in Downing Street. The British always found him the hardest nut to crack. Unlike the loquacious Rumsfeld, the Vice-President was inscrutable. But Blair and Manning were under no illusions that he wielded considerable influence with Bush, and his were the most hawkish instincts of all. Their talks focused on the 'second phase' of the war on terror that had imperceptibly moved from rhetoric to planning. 'There is a threat from Saddam Hussein and the weapons of mass destruction that he has acquired. It is not in doubt at all,' Blair said. The coalition partners now needed to 'reflect and deliberate' on how that problem should be addressed. Cheney spoke of a 'potential marriage' of groups like al-Qaeda and those who would help them or were handing on knowledge about lethal weapons. This was the most concerted effort so far to justify action against Iraq as an integral part of the war against terrorism. This was all co-ordinated. In Washington, Bush said of Saddam: 'Men with no respect for life must never be allowed to control the ultimate instruments of death.'

The Anglo-American position rested on a list of assumptions – that Saddam had weapons of mass destruction, that they were battle-ready, that he intended to use them and/or he was looking to sell them to terrorist groups such as al-Qaeda. These were stated as facts.

Within the Labour Party, concerns were mounting. Chris Smith, the former Culture Secretary, had been a friend of Blair's for years. He had been part of his leadership team in 1994. Even after being reshuffled out of the Cabinet in June 2001, he spent a day with the Blairs at their holiday villa in south-west France that August. They had had a long walk through the garden, talking politics. Blair told him that day he had three priorities for his second term of office: to improve public services in the UK; to take Britain into the Euro; and to show that he could work with the Republicans. He was irked by the neocons' links with the Tory party. He was determined to do everything possible to prevent them driving a wedge between New Labour and the Republicans.

Smith kept his thoughts mainly to himself, and was reluctant to criticise Blair. But on 24 March 2002 he went on television to warn that many party colleagues 'would be worried if there were something being contemplated which was all-out invasion of Iraq simply going on the coat-tails of an American unilateral decision'.

The next day Smith received a call from Blair's diary secretary, inviting him in for a chat. Smith told Blair he was seriously worried about the build-up to war – the military feasibility, the humanitarian consequences, the impact on the Middle East and the damage to the coalition against terror. Blair told him these were all entirely valid points, and that if he were not satisfied he had an answer to them, he would not go ahead. Blair assured him no decisions had been taken. And yet Smith thought, from the body language and his tone of voice, that the Prime Minister had already taken the decision. He hadn't – but he was about to.

By April Bush had begun to use the term 'regime change'. With each speech, he and the 'principals' in the administration gave the term more prominence. Bush stepped up CIA funding for operations inside Iraq. The CIA Director, George Tenet, the only hangover from the Clinton administration, estimated there was only a 10 to 20 per cent chance of ousting Saddam without accompanying military action. Tenet had forged a good working relationship with Bush. Clinton had asked only for a written intelligence submission each day. Bush, whose father had been director of the CIA, wanted it in person. The trouble for Tenet was that the CIA was one of only several sources. The Defence Intelligence Agency (DIA) inside the Pentagon had a similar remit. All the agencies were still trying to live down their failure to understand the al-Qaeda threat until it was too late.

Rumsfeld and Wolfowitz believed that while the established security services had a role, they were too bureaucratic and too traditional in their thinking. They hoovered up too much general information, but did not process it 'cleanly'. Their assessments were couched in the conditional. Their bets were too often hedged. Within days of 9/11 they wanted a group of experts around them who could cut to the chase, who would produce definitive information on the nexus of terror. That nexus would have to include Iraq.

They set up what came to be known as the 'cabal', a cell of eight or nine analysts in a new Office of Special Plans (OSP) based in the US Defense Department. Rumsfeld denied this was an attempt to bypass the CIA, but that is how the rest of the intelligence community saw it. The CIA has long maintained a moderate stance on Iraq. It argued in 1991 against overthrowing Saddam at the end of the Gulf War, saying it would undermine Middle East stability. During the 1990s, it argued against supporting a domestic insurgency.

The job of the OSP was to find evidence of what Wolfowitz and Rumsfeld already believed to be true. Its director was Abram Shulsky, one of the original neocons, who had worked on intelligence for three decades, specialising in the Soviet threat. Crucial to their 'intelligence' gathering was information provided by the INC. The CIA had for years been instructed to funnel millions of dollars to the INC. Those payments ended in the mid-1990s when doubts were cast about Chalabi's reliability. As the administration geared up for conflict with Saddam, Chalabi was welcomed in the inner sanctum of the Pentagon. Within a few months of being set up, the OSP rivalled the CIA and DIA as Bush's main source of intelligence on Saddam's weapons and links with al-Qaeda. Shulsky, Rumsfeld and Wolfowitz did not see fit to challenge any of Chalabi's information, even though Shulsky himself admitted in a 1991 textbook on intelligence that the reliability of information from Soviet defectors had 'bedevilled US intelligence for a quarter of a century'. Such volunteer sources, Shulsky wrote, 'may be greedy, they may also be somewhat unbalanced people who wish to bring some excitement into their lives, they may desire to avenge what they see as ill treatment by their government'. That assessment would be particularly prescient when it came to accepting intelligence from Iraqi opponents of Saddam.

Those around Blair did not receive any intelligence that spring suggesting that the threat from Saddam had suddenly increased. The Americans received the same message from Middle Eastern intelligence services they trusted. Whatever the CIA might have been saying, the White House wilfully ignored it, relying on steers from

the OSP. Some of the disinformation belonged to fertile imagina-
tions, such as the supposed testimony of an ex-lover of Saddam,
known as 'The Blonde', who claimed that Bin Laden had paid
Saddam a visit in the 1980s. Even the Pentagon did not try to push
that one too hard.

Then there was talk of a meeting between Mohammed Atta,
the suspected leader of the 9/11 hijackers, and an Iraqi contact in
Prague in April 2001. That turned out to be bogus, but not until the
Americans had offered it as 'fact'. Even after the CIA and FBI had
investigated it, concluding that the rendezvous had never happened,
the story was still offered up as 'evidence'. At the JIC there was exasperation. 'From the very beginning we didn't believe the Atta story,'
says one senior official. 'It was clear to us that Atta had been
misidentified by the Czechs. But the Americans wanted to believe it.
The way it was chased about the place was surprising. We were surprised that rational, objective people would want to believe a flaky
story. Our training is to see facts as they are, not as we want to see
them.'

Then came rumours of a Baghdad school for hijackers, complete with its own luggage-screening X-ray machine. Two further
attempts were made at drawing a link, involving Ansar-ul-Islam, a
militant group with a base within Iraq but outside the area controlled by Saddam. Ansar's links with Bin Laden were clear, but with
the regime in Baghdad? That was based on lurid accounts from
defectors held in Kurdish jails, which turned out to be false. The
other person fingered was Abu Musab al-Zarqawi, an obscure
Jordanian militant. He was in Baghdad with Saddam's support, they
said. Hawks even linked him later with the plots to use ricin in the
UK. No links were ever found.

Blair knew all this was going on. He accepted the JIC's assessment of the raw facts. At the same he let it be known that the
'realities' had changed, that US attitudes towards Iraq had changed,
so, 'like it or not, we have to deal with their new priorities'.

The first concerted attempt to present the evidence to Labour

MPs was made on 5 March 2002. Michael Williams was a rare breed of special adviser. With long experience at the UN, he had none of the brashness of some New Labour colleagues. If anyone could be trusted, it was him. At the request of Downing Street and party headquarters he put together a document entitled simply 'Iraq Briefing', which he presented to a meeting of the Parliamentary Labour Party (PLP). Its arguments were concise, the language carefully chosen. It described Saddam's regime as 'a demonstrable threat to the stability of the region' – nothing less, but notably, nothing more. It catalogued human rights abuses and violations of UN resolutions. 'If Iraq's weapons programmes remain unchecked, Iraq could redevelop offensive chemical and biological capabilities within a very short period of time and develop a crude nuclear device in about five years,' the document said. The international community could not afford to ignore the threat. It concluded by saying that steps should be taken to ensure that UN weapons inspectors were sent back. The controls imposed by previous teams had 'contained the regime's military ambitions'. There was little there for anyone to dispute. Nor was there a rationale for war. That was the problem.

Blair was becoming increasingly agitated by all the questions, from party activists, members of the public and MPs. Why Iraq? Why now? He told Manning he needed an intelligence-based dossier. He wanted as much intelligence as possible to be put out in the public domain. He asked Scarlett to persuade his security colleagues to declassify some of the assessment material. The idea then was to put it in a form that the public understood. 'You know what we want. See what you can do,' Scarlett was told. He was given helpful advice: 'maps, graphics, that sort of thing'. Downing Street was growing fond of 'dossier politics' – assessments stamped with the authority of the security and intelligence agencies. Pleased with his Afghan dossier, Campbell planned a bigger, glossier Iraqi version, to help Blair make the case for action. The trouble was, there were many external experts and there was much more freely available information on Iraq than there had been on Afghanistan.

By March, a number of versions were being worked on. Apart from Michael Williams' presentation, which did not contain intelligence material, the JIC put together one position paper on WMD that went much further than Iraq, ranging to North Korea, Iran, Syria and Libya. It included political judgements about specific regimes and their leaders. Blair was told the paper was 'ready to go' from Easter. He and Campbell thought of putting it out, perhaps in a more concise form, but concluded that the material was too complex and not persuasive enough. 'We had a lot of discussions about those papers. Then they were shelved. We decided we needed a completely different exercise,' recalls one official. Another official who saw it commented: 'It didn't look great.' One senior defence official told his counterpart in Downing Street: 'If you've got better stuff than this, you had better put it out.' His colleague at Number 10 said he understood the problem and accepted that people might not be persuaded. But he was confident that Blair would 'pull people in behind him. That's what leadership is about.'

Scarlett was asked to persuade the intelligence services to declassify more material. A round of meetings was hurriedly convened. He reminded the intelligence chiefs that he was the first JIC chairman from SIS and not from the Foreign Office. He came from their 'community'. They could trust him. 'The JIC gave as much as they dared, and much more than had ever been previously attempted,' one senior official says. Scarlett, according to one involved in the discussions, 'tried to make it as daring as possible'. A second version, amounting to six pages, limited to Iraq, was put together. Campbell had wanted to present it on the eve of Blair's summit with Bush in Texas. A date was then set, 25 March. Why was it postponed?

Blair was worried on two counts. Although he wanted to make the case, he was persuaded that the publication of a dossier at this point would inflame the party. 'We feared people would think it was six weeks until we bomb Baghdad,' one Downing Street official recalled. There was another reason. The dossier provided, in the words of one official who worked on it, 'meagre pickings'. Straw showed a draft to a group of senior loyal MPs. They said it was distinctly unimpressive. They told him the document did not compare well with Williams' briefing paper to the PLP that had relied entirely on open-source material. It alleged that Saddam had made fresh attempts to upgrade his arsenal, notably biological weapons and long-range missiles. But it provided no new evidence of an increased threat – no new grounds to go to war.

By the time Blair arrived at Crawford, Bush had already decided to go to war. In a rare British TV interview broadcast on 5 April, the eve of Blair's arrival, the President said: 'I made up my mind that Saddam needs to go. That's about all I'm willing to share with you.' It came as no surprise to Downing Street. In one meeting to prepare for the summit, Blair told his aides: 'We're not going to be with the other Europeans. Our policy on Iraq has always been different to them. We've always been with the Americans on this one.'

Given what was at stake, Bush's casual demeanour set a vivid contrast with his gaunt, sleep-deprived, black-suited guest. Blair was ever mindful of protocol, and Britain was still in mourning for the death of the Queen Mother. Staying at Bush's Prairie Chapel ranch with Cherie and Kathryn Blair had put him in a small foreigners' club whose other members include only Putin and Vicente Fox of Mexico. He spent what Downing Street officials – most of them housed in nearby Waco – called 'the vast majority of his time' one-on-one with the President. Sometimes he was accompanied by David Manning. Blair was flattered to share the President's CIA briefing, but had been told in advance that their information was less complete than his own.

At their joint press conference, Bush heaped praise on his guest. 'History has called us into action. The thing I admire about this Prime Minister is that he doesn't need a poll or a focus group to convince him of the difference between right and wrong.' Back home, among senior diplomats at the Foreign Office, there was growing concern about Blair's sudden enthusiasm for a strike on Iraq. 'He's caught some of Bush's moral fervour,' said one official. Blair himself went further than he had done before in backing the military option. Pressed on television whether this was 'down the road potentially', he said: 'It depends on what happens. As President Bush has said, there's no doubt there is a problem. We have to deal with it.'

Crawford was the turning point for Blair. That weekend he and Manning concluded nothing would stand in the way of Bush and his mission. The question was not *if* there would be war, but on what terms it would be fought. They told the President that he had the power to do it on his own, that Britain would support him come what may, but in order to maximise his case he should try to build a larger coalition, preferably through the UN. Bush told them: 'We don't want to do it alone.'

They took that as an aspiration. What they needed was a cast-iron commitment. For all the talk over the next several months that nothing had been decided, Blair and his aides knew that military action was – barring a miracle such as a popular uprising or a last-minute change of heart by Saddam – all but inevitable. Publicly, Blair said nothing of the sort, to his Cabinet, his party or his diplomats.

Blair set about his immediate task of preparing the public for military action, while maintaining the front that it was 'not inevitable'. His first opportunity came straight away, in a speech to an audience of the Texan great and good at the George Bush Senior Presidential Library. His aim was to try to marry American impulses with the imperative of collective action. 'Like it or not, whether you are a utilitarian or a utopian, the world is interdependent,' he said. He sought to argue that – from Kabul and Kosovo to free trade and the *intifada* – enlightened self-interest and *realpolitik* both pointed to engagement against the global ills of poverty and terrorism. He talked of Iraq's weapons of mass destruction as a suitable case for treatment, but insisted: 'I know some fear precipitate action. They needn't. We will proceed, as we did after September 11, in a calm, measured, sensible but firm way.'

So clear was he in his mind on his return from Crawford that he asked Gordon Brown to redraw his financial calculations for the budget he was due to give later in April. Secretly, officials from the Treasury and Downing Street got down to work immediately on 'the numbers' – the amount of extra money that would be required to pay for the war preparations. They pencilled in an initial down-payment of £1 billion, to be announced as and when required, but they estimated the total cost to be several times that. 'We were all told to make a hard assumption that there would be war,' says one senior official. 'It was very delicate. We had to do it on the quiet, because we were saying politically and diplomatically that nothing had been decided, whereas in actual fact the decision had just about been taken.'

For eleven months after that, Blair would insist that he was not set on war, that he had not fixed himself on to George W. Bush's radar screen. Those around him knew, however, that he had, that war with Iraq was a price well worth paying for demonstrating his credentials to the White House. He assumed that the US adminis-tration would at least try to make that war palatable for British and European voters. That was an issue of presentation. On the princi-ple, his conscience was clear.

Bush and Blair had also talked about another pressing interna-tional crisis. India and Pakistan had been moving closer to war, a potential nuclear war, as their long-standing dispute over Kashmir reached another peak. In December 2001, gunmen burst into the Indian parliament, killing twelve people. India blamed it on Pakistani-based militants. The two countries deployed troops to their common border. The following months saw a number of serious gun battles and attacks from both sides. Blair and Bush agreed the need to intervene. Straw and Powell were sent to Delhi and Islamabad in two co-ordinated trips. This marked a return to old-fashioned diplomacy. The difficult missions appeared to succeed. Both governments drew back from the brink.

The issue had brought out the best in the Blair approach – and also the worst. The early part of Straw's visit was dominated by controversy over arms sales. Just as he was trying to defuse tension, he had to answer charges that, in spite of Robin Cook's best intentions back in 1997, the British government had reverted to type and was flogging as many arms as it could. In this case it was 148 weapons licences for India and 18 to its enemy. Straw made a valiant attempt at defending the indefensible. 'I am quite clear that the licences that were issued earlier this year have made no difference whatsoever to the level of tension across the line of control,' he said. These ones in particular had been approved in February, he said, before tensions had reached a peak. Those tensions, however, were still very high.

Blair had already demonstrated his personal enthusiasm for selling British hardware to the region. He had devoted much of his visit to India in January – spun as his 'peace mission', trying to persuade India's Prime Minister, Atal Behari Vajpayee, and its defence minister, George Fernandes, to sign up to a £1 billion deal to sell India sixty Hawk fighter-bombers made by BAE Systems. The export credits guarantee division of the Trade Department was spending around half its budget underwriting arms contracts. One Downing Street aide said of BAE's Dick Evans: 'Whenever he heard of a problem he'd be straight on the phone to Number 10 and it would get sorted.' Powell was particularly keen to be supportive. Government departments, British embassies abroad and BAE had regular secondments both ways. The word passed down to ministers and officials was to assume that all sales were right and proper, and that they had to make a very good case to the contrary.

Competition for the Hawks contract was intense. The Americans had a counter-bid in alliance with the Czechs. The Italians were vying for it too. Blair sent several of his ministers to lobby. Three weeks after his trip, the British High Commission gave a party for a group of defence exporters who had arrived for a big defence fair, Defexpo. This was part of a long-term strategy. Britain had one diplomat in Delhi in charge of 'defence supply'. A list of twenty-two 'highly valuable priority markets' targeted for British arms sales put India and Pakistan near the top. Several members of Blair's Cabinet were uneasy about the Hawks affair. Patricia Hewitt, the Trade and Industry Secretary and the minister responsible for checking licences against the government's own criteria, was known to be unhappy. She was overruled. The flaws in the argument were summed up by the Liberal Democrats' defence spokesman, Menzies Campbell: 'What on earth is the British government doing granting arms licences as recently as last month when a million soldiers were facing each other across the Line of Control with the overhanging spectre of a nuclear exchange?'

This was a government that proclaimed countries that had WMD posed a serious danger to the world. This was a government happy to arm two nuclear neighbours on the brink of war.

Blair's approach to human rights and ethics had always been inconsistent. After 9/11 it was entirely selective. Countries seen as 'on-side' in the war on terror saw export controls loosened irrespective of their records. The Central Asian autocracies that had allowed the US to set up military bases, such as Tajikistan, Turkmenistan and Uzbekistan, were considered beyond reproach. China had *carte blanche* over Tibet; Russia over Chechnya. The influence of the human rights lobby began to wane. The imperative of countering Soviet and Chinese imperial advances trumped concern about the regimes' abuses. The new element in determining American foreign policy was what assets – bases, intelligence and diplomatic leverage – a particular country could bring to bear, first against al-Qaeda, then against Iraq.

By the early summer of 2002 the neoconservatives were setting the agenda for Iraq. At the State Department, officials continued to brief the media that war had not been agreed. They were correct only in the sense that a formal decision had not been taken, and that the planning was still at an early stage. What mattered was that Bush had accepted the principle of war. As one senior administration official told the *Weekly Standard* in July: 'It was over by the State of the Union.'

Blair had grown used to dealing with an administration that, even by the standards of Washington, was split by departmental in-fighting. Downing Street was aware of Colin Powell's weakness. Rumsfeld, Wolfowitz and Cheney were calling the shots. Their efforts were making a war extremely hard for Blair to sell to his party.

Time and again when Blair tried to demonstrate how the spe-cial relationship was paying dividends for the UK, the Bush administration would take a unilateral decision that flew in the face of that assertion. He signed into law subsidies for US farmers that violated all the tenets of free trade that Blair so passionately advo-cated. He imposed tariffs on foreign steel producers that set off a bitter trade row with Europe. Most damaging, however, for Blair's efforts to portray the administration in a positive light was its refusal to ratify the establishment of the International Criminal Court unless US forces were given a blanket immunity from prosecution. The Americans ended up in the same camp as the Chinese, Russians and Israelis. Rumsfeld said the exemption was needed to avoid 'political harassment that can take place unfairly, particularly when you are fighting the global war on terror and the terrorist training books are encouraging people to make those kinds of charges and allegations'. To press the point, the Americans threatened to with-draw peacekeepers from the Balkans unless their terms were met. They got their way – thanks to Blair's support.

At a graduation ceremony on 1 June at the US Military Academy in West Point, New York, Bush spoke under a cloudless sky to throngs of cadets. 'For much of the last century, America's defence relied on the Cold War doctrines of deterrence and containment. In some cases those strategies still apply. But new threats also require new thinking. Deterrence – the promise of massive retaliation against nations – means nothing against shadowy terrorist networks with no nations or citizens to defend,' Bush declared. 'If we wait for threats to fully materialise we will have waited too long. We must take the battle to the enemy, disrupt his plans and confront the worst threats before they emerge.' He had laid out what came to be known as the Bush Doctrine.

Blair accepted this new reality. He did so because he saw it as Britain's duty to be at the right hand of the US. He did so because Bush's view coincided with his. Blair was not dragged into war against Iraq. He was at ease with himself and his own beliefs.

9

MAPPING THE ROAD

MICHAEL LEVY'S FIRST CLAIM TO FAME WAS THAT HE discovered Alvin Stardust. His second was that he helped bankroll New Labour just when it needed the cash most – when Blair was trying to transform it into a putative party of government in the mid-1990s. Levy persuaded the super-rich, often over a game of tennis at his mansion in Totteridge, north London, that if they wanted to get on the right side of Blair they should open their chequebook. They did sign the cheques, and they did get on the right side of him. Levy's third major achievement was that he made Blair interested in Israel and the Middle East peace process.

The Israeli Embassy in London is assiduous in courting up-and-coming politicians. In 1993 one of those it identified was the shadow Home Secretary, Tony Blair. He was invited over to Jerusalem, shown the sights, introduced to the movers and shakers and taken on a helicopter tour of the country. An aerial view provides visitors with two strong impressions: first, Israel's vulnerability, when you see that at its narrowest point it is only a few miles from the West Bank of the river Jordan to the sea; second, its military power over the Palestinians. The man who organised the trip was

Gideon Meir. Two weeks after Blair returned to London, Meir organised a dinner party for him. There he met Levy, and from that moment one of modern politics' most intriguing friendships developed.

Born in Hackney to a humble home, Levy made his fortune as a pop impresario. A leading figure in the Jewish community, and a patron of Jewish charities, he served as a bridge between the Jewish community and New Labour. When Blair became leader of the opposition, Levy organised his controversial 'blind trust'. When Blair became Prime Minister, it was the soon-to-be-ennobled Levy who secured the even more controversial £1 million donation to Labour from Formula One chief Bernie Ecclestone. It was only in February 2000 that Blair was forced to reveal an extra role that his friend was playing. Levy, it transpired, had become his special envoy to the Middle East, visiting the region nine times in 1999 – more than Robin Cook, the Foreign Secretary. The difference was that Blair trusted Levy.

When he took office, Blair, as he admitted himself, knew very little about Israel's history or the complexities of the peace process. The first Gulf War had prompted George Bush senior to push ahead with what he hoped would be a defining settlement. Two years later came the Oslo accords. For the Israeli left, this was a moment of unbridled optimism. The same applied to the British left, whose views on Israel had fluctuated from idealistic support of this nascent Kibbutzim socialist state to despondency over its treatment of the Palestinians. In the Labour Party of the 1980s and early '90s, the cause of the Palestinians was synonymous with internationalism and unilateral nuclear disarmament – the very symbols that Blair and the reformers around him began to disdain.

As he began to remodel the party in his own image, Blair saw a pro-Israeli position as a defining symbol of New Labour. From his first party conference as leader in 1994, Blair made a point of spending time networking at the Labour Friends of Israel receptions. Year after year this was the red-letter event of Blair's week at the seaside.

While he might pop his head in at other events, this one he would attend from start to finish. His message as he worked the room was: 'I'll never let Israel down. I'll never do anything to harm it.' At the same time Levy was busily tapping in to the Jewish community for cash. They were keen to be raising money, and to be seen to be raising money, for Blair, and Blair was keen to be seen with them. It was a symbiotic relationship.

Levy was also prominent on the Israeli left. Although he spent most of the year in London, he and his wife Gilda went to their holiday home in Herzlia, north of Tel Aviv, as often as they could. It was at this house that several of the most secret negotiations over the Oslo deal took place. The Israeli justice minister, Iosi Beilin, and the Palestinians' chief negotiator, Mahmoud Abbas, also known as Abu Mazen, were frequent visitors. When they reached an impasse in their talks, Levy would invite them to go downstairs and play table tennis to clear their heads.

The assassination of Yitzhak Rabin, as he addressed an election rally in Tel Aviv on 4 November 1995, shattered the dreams of the Israeli left. The man who had signed Oslo with Yasser Arafat, earning both the Nobel Peace Prize, was gunned down by an Orthodox right-wing extremist in protest at the land-for-peace formula on which Israeli–Palestinian agreement was based. Shimon Peres, the foreign minister, took over. He was the last of the leaders drawn from the old school, many of whom had lived through the Holocaust and who had witnessed and fought for the creation of the Jewish state. Most held views that were left of centre. The Olso formula soon unravelled. Six months later Peres was ousted from power by a new face, Benjamin 'Bibi' Netanyahu, a charismatic, fluent English-speaker with impeccable links to the American right. His policy was to unshackle Israel from the old tenets of negotiation, to allow new settlements to be built in the occupied West Bank and Gaza Strip, and to use military might far more readily to root out Palestinian guerrillas.

David Manning was packing his bags, preparing for his new

assignment as Ambassador to Israel, on the day Rabin was killed. The job is difficult at the best of times. Britain's colonial role and the Balfour Declaration that created the conflict are rarely far from the lips of Israeli interlocutors. Netanyahu took a serious dislike to Manning. The feeling was mutual. Relations between London and Jerusalem had for some time been decidedly tetchy. They were not made any easier by the itinerary for Cook's first visit as Foreign Secretary in March 1998. Cook had instructed Manning that he wanted to visit Jebel Abu Ghneim, where the year before Israel had started to build a housing project called Har Homa. The construction, in a part of Jerusalem that Palestinians consider to be their future capital, had plunged the peace process into another crisis. Cook had made his intentions known well in advance. Just before he left, however, the Israelis kicked up rough. As a compromise, he allowed himself to be shown around by two Israeli government officials rather than the Palestinians' representative in Jerusalem. This satisfied neither side. Israeli protesters hounded Cook as he toured the plot of land. Television pictures of him trying to hold up his EU umbrella in the driving rain, as he was jostled by settlers, left Blair furious. To compound it, Netanyahu cut short their meeting later in the day and cancelled a formal dinner. Cook and Manning felt they had been double-crossed by Netanyahu. 'They were determined for the trip to go badly. They did everything possible to undermine it. They wanted to teach Cook a lesson,' recalls one official.

The experience bruised Cook and left an indelible mark on Manning. A month later it was Blair's turn. Campbell spun that visit as sorting out the mess Cook had left behind. Blair would always receive better treatment from the Israelis than his underlings. That was part of the game. He was, in any case, internationally unassailable at that point – only a week earlier he had acted as midwife to the Good Friday Agreement in Northern Ireland. From there he went to Spain to offer advice to its government on dealing with the Basques. If he could crack the problems of Ulster, why not the Middle East? He knew that, for decades, Europe had had precious

little pulling power on Israel. But that, to his mind, was defeatist. He
invited Arafat and Netanyahu to London for talks. They did not get
off the ground.

A year later Blair had real cause for optimism. Barak had con-
founded all expectations and won a landslide victory over
Netanyahu in elections in May 1999. Bill Clinton seized the initiative
and tried one last push for peace, to revive the Oslo process. A year
later, in July 2000, amid high hopes, he invited Arafat and the new
Israeli Prime Minister to Camp David. For fifteen days the three
were locked in discussions over every detail of their long dispute.
The talks ended in failure on the specific question of the status of
Jerusalem. But within weeks the process had unravelled. Clinton
would try again in January in the Egyptian Red Sea resort of Taba in
the dying days of his presidency, but the second failure only confirmed in the minds of his successor the flaws in his approach.

Blair understood that Europe could play only a minor role.
Israel looked to the US to lead the way. The Palestinians knew the
reality. They might get reconstruction money from the EU, but for
them too relations with the White House were all-important. Blair,
eager to embrace Barak's government, felt frustrated throughout
1999 and 2000. He saw Clinton as a control freak wanting to run the
whole process. 'I would leave it to Bill if only he'd do something
about it,' Blair confided once in Peter Mandelson. Asked why he was
supportive of Israel, Blair would speak of its courage, of a people
who bear fortitude and who strive for excellence. Implicit in Blair's
actions was the belief that he, as a friend, understood Israel's interests better than many Israelis – that meant a secure but not enlarged
country. Ireland provided his framework – the will of the majority
and equality for all, translating in a Middle East context to security
for Israel and a state of their own for Palestinians. The detail would
match the principle, not the other way round.

Clinton was not interested in deferring to his friend on the
Middle East. 'On some issues Tony was listened to, but not Israel,'
one senior Clinton aide recalls. 'Blair has never influenced us on

Israel. The more multilateral the world tries to be, with its quartets and its other institutions, the more the Americans stand firm. Blair knows he has no influence on US–Israeli policy. He can help elsewhere in the world, but not there. It comes down simply to the relationship between the US President and the Israeli people.'

Paradoxically, Blair held out hope that a Republican President might be more flexible. The prospects when Bush took office were mixed. Bush was exposed to three separate messages – the disengaged 'anything but Clinton' message; the traditional Republican analysis that assumed the majority Jewish vote went to the Democrats; and a new strain of thought that linked southern Christianity to Israel's right to its biblical lands.

Many evangelicals began to identify the return of the Jews to Israel as a sign of the imminence of the Second Coming – and see the attacks on Israel as portending the Antichrist. Bush, for all his religiosity, was not obsessed with Israel, did not thank the Jewish lobby for delivering him an election victory. There were no Jews in his Cabinet, and few on his staff. And yet he vowed not to repeat his father's mistake of alienating the conservative heartlands. The last time an American administration had fallen out with Israel was in the final year of Bush senior's presidency, when his Secretary of State, James Baker, famously told Yitzhak Shamir, 'When you're interested in peace, here's my phone number.' He threatened to withhold funding unless Israel stopped building settlements in occupied territories.

On his single trip to the Middle East, while governor of Texas in 1998, Bush got on well with Sharon, then foreign minister, who took the time to take the presidential scion on a helicopter tour of the occupied territories. The running commentary as they flew over the West Bank and Gaza was heavy on security. He would later say of that trip: 'For a Texan, a first visit to Israel is an eye-opener. At the narrowest point, it's only eight miles from the Mediterranean to the old armistice line. That's less than from the top to the bottom of Dallas-Fort Worth airport.'

Bush's inauguration coincided with the elections that brought Ariel Sharon to power. This was three months after the start of the second *intifada*. The new US President was convinced that Yasser Arafat had conned Clinton into believing he was serious about peace. He made it clear, right at the start of his presidency, that he had no intention of dealing with him.

Each suicide attack reinforced that antipathy. The summer of 2001 saw two particularly horrific incidents. In Tel Aviv, 21 people were killed and 120 were injured when a suicide bomber blew himself up outside a disco along the seafront promenade. That was on 1 June. Two months later, in central Jerusalem, a bomber blew himself up at the Sbarro pizza restaurant, killing fifteen Israelis, among them six children. Successive attempts to secure a ceasefire, by George Tenet and by George Mitchell – the senator who helped craft the peace process in Northern Ireland – came to nothing.

Bush was convinced that Arafat was either looking the other way or encouraging the bombers. His gut instincts were confirmed by 9/11. In the new global order, the world would be divided into terrorists and those who gave them succour, and those who sought to resist them. Arafat fell into the former camp and Sharon, for all his faults, into the latter.

Sharon did not play the initial stages well. Instead of rallying to America in its time of need, showing a willingness to reverse roles, he tried to use the crisis to clamp down further on the Palestinians. After comparing Arafat to Bin Laden, something Bush did not do even in his angriest moments, the Israeli premier rebuffed calls for ceasefire talks and ordered advances across the occupied territories, including the third invasion of Ramallah in less than a week. He pulled back only after heavy pressure from a US government in the early stages of efforts to create an international coalition against terrorism. Key to that, in British eyes, was improving relations with states long considered pariahs, like Iran.

Jack Straw's talks in Tehran, as part of a Middle East tour that included Israel, were crucial. On the eve of his visit, he wrote an article for an Iranian newspaper in which he said: 'I understand that one of the factors which helps breed terrorism is the anger which many people in this region feel at events over the years in Palestine.' The offending paragraph barely made any impact in the Iranian press, but in Israel the reference to 'Palestine' and the link he made between frustration and terrorism was seized upon by Sharon as evidence that Straw would fall into the traditional category of an 'Arabist' British Foreign Secretary. The article was drafted by diplomats at the Foreign Office and was widely circulated before being sent to Tehran. Straw personally approved it. So did Blair. Nevertheless, Blair had to intervene in a phone call to urge Sharon to meet Straw. That went ahead, but Shimon Peres, the foreign minister, wanted to cancel the planned dinner. Michael Levy intervened, and they compromised on a working supper of sandwiches. It could have been worse.

Blair hoped that in spite of the Palestinian terrorist attacks and the Israeli reprisals, Bush might be galvanised by the carnage of the Twin Towers to take a more active role in the Middle East. He was proved right. On 2 October 2001, Bush did what no US President had done before and announced he was prepared to back the creation of a Palestinian state. This, he assumed, would remove many of the reservations other countries in the region might have to supporting the US in the wider war on terror. It was certainly a bold initiative, signalling a new departure for the administration. The timing, however, could not have been less fortunate. On the same day, Palestinian gunmen burst into a settlement in Gaza, randomly shooting civilian residents and killing a young couple. The pressure on Bush to draw back from his pledge was intense, both at home and in Israel. Some eighty-nine senators signed a letter asking the President not to try to restrain Israel from using 'all strength and might' to respond to suicide attacks.

By this point, Colin Powell was telling his officials that Sharon's behaviour 'borders on the irrational'. Sharon was convinced that Bush was planning to sacrifice Israel's security as a *quid pro quo* with Arab countries for supporting a war on Afghanistan. 'Do not try to appease the Arabs at our expense. It is unacceptable. Israel will not be another Czechoslovakia,' he said. The implicit comparison with Chamberlain infuriated Bush. Sharon quickly retracted. The damage could have been more severe, but over the next few months two events pulled the US President firmly in one direction. In October four members of Arafat's personal entourage entered an East Jerusalem hotel and shot dead the tourism minister, Rehavam Ze'evi, one of Israel's most hardline politicians – an advocate of deporting Palestinians to Arab countries. On 3 January 2002, the Israeli navy intercepted a ship in the Red Sea, the *Karine A*, containing a vast weapons arsenal, including anti-tank missiles and Katyusha rockets. The Israelis said it was part of a smuggling operation co-ordinated by the Palestinian Authority, the Lebanese militant group Hizbollah and Iran. The Israelis went to great lengths to convince Washington that this proved Arafat's links with international terrorism. Bush accepted their version. For him, this was a point of no return. The seizure had a profound effect on him ahead of his State of the Union speech.

In one of his more unguarded moments, Bush confided in Blair that he did not like Sharon personally. But the Israeli Prime Minister played Bush like a dream. After one visit, on 16 October, Sharon emerged beaming: 'As far as I can remember – I can look back for many years now – I think we have never had such relations with any President of the US as we have with you.' During 2002 alone, Bush met Sharon seven times. They talked on many more occasions by phone. He did not once meet Arafat. That was left to Blair. One of his aides explains the dilemma: 'We saw Arafat as the elected leader of the Palestinians. It was a matter of using him for what we wanted to achieve, but recognising that other Palestinians had to be developed in time.'

Blair left most of the talking with Arafat to Michael Levy. For all his Israeli contacts, Levy spent more time in the region as a go-between with the Palestinians. He did Blair's blunt talking for him.

One conversation, in mid-December 2001 during one of the worst periods of suicide bombings, was particularly difficult. Levy said to Arafat, repeating it slowly six times like a metronome: 'No more suicide attacks.' A few days later Palestinian militia announced a ceasefire. British intelligence lines were buzzing to see if he could deliver. Arafat's security services were operational enough to get the message to Hamas, if not to direct them. The ceasefire held for four weeks.

With Sharon it was no easier. On one occasion, Levy met him at his farm. This was in January 2002. Sharon had just defeated Barak but had yet to take office. They talked for three hours. Most of the time they sat on their own in Sharon's kitchen over tea and cake. Every twenty minutes his nervous security guards would walk in to check that Levy hadn't killed him. He reported back to Blair that Sharon should not be demonised, that provided the circumstances were right, he could make painful concessions. Blair took the advice. He rarely doubted his own powers of persuasion, but with Sharon he had few illusions. 'We always knew we had almost no locus with the Israelis, although Tony has a fraction more than most British Prime Ministers,' says one of his people. 'In their conversations with us the Israelis always knew they had American support before we walked in the room.'

Most of the time, in private, Sharon was gentlemanly and softly spoken. He had an almost exaggerated air of politeness. Other meetings were different. At a meeting that autumn, he expressed his anger that Blair was continuing to meet Arafat and was dealing with Syria on the UN Security Council. He saw that as double standards after 9/11. Anyone who saw Arafat had blood on his hands, Sharon said. Levy asked him to clarify whether that meant any leader who allowed one of his officials to see Arafat would have blood on his hands. At that point Sharon lost his temper, accusing Levy of twisting his words, before adding in Hebrew: 'The British Mandate is now finished.' After he had stormed off, his people came in to apologise.

Sharon was contemptuous of those who did not share his worldview. One who fell into that category was Colin Powell, the US Secretary of State. Throughout 2002 Powell was systematically undermined by Donald Rumsfeld, Paul Wolfowitz and Dick Cheney – on foreign policy in general but policy towards Israel in particular. Blair and Straw watched on in horror.

It began with what should have been an innocuous trip to Central Asia. No sooner was Powell out of Washington than his detractors started scheming behind his back. The Israelis were tightening the screws in all parts of the West Bank and Gaza, confining Arafat to his headquarters in Ramallah. Air raids and tank invasions were daily occurrences. Yet Ari Fleischer, the White House spokesman, used Powell's absence to describe Sharon as 'a man of peace'. Wolfowitz appeared at a pro-Israel rally in Washington, which was called to oppose US pressure on the Sharon government. Cheney and Rumsfeld urged Bush to take one final step and cut all links with Arafat. On his return, Powell scrambled to turn policy round, but Blair and Straw had an early glimpse of just how marginalised Powell had become. 'It took Tony a long while to adjust to the reality of the neocon hegemony, but these incidents finally brought it home to him,' one of Blair's aides recalls.

Shortly before Sharon arrived in Washington to a warm welcome, Bush declared Arafat 'irrelevant'. At the same time, Sharon expressed regret for not having killed Arafat when, as Israel's defence minister, he besieged his compound in Beirut in 1982. The language between Washington and Jerusalem became uncannily similar. Powell's diplomatic efforts were being rebuffed at every turn – by his own Cabinet colleagues, by Sharon, and by an upsurge in Palestinian suicide bombings. A peace plan presented by Saudi Arabia's Crown Prince Abdullah was received coolly by the White House, which didn't bother responding formally for a week. On the ground, Bush's special envoy, General Anthony Zinni, was proving out of his depth. The British had thought from the beginning that his appointment was a mistake.

On 27 March, what remaining hopes Powell or Blair might have had were extinguished. A Palestinian suicide bomber walked into the lobby of a hotel in Netanya crowded with Israelis gathered for their Passover meal, blowing up himself and twenty-nine people with him. More than 140 were wounded. Sharon launched Operation Defence Shield, first attacking Arafat's compound, the Mukata, in Ramallah. As the Palestinian leader was struggling to stay alive, Bush warned him that he must do more to root out terrorism. At the same time, the Israelis moved into the refugee camps in Nablus and Jenin, and lay siege to the Church of the Holy Nativity in Bethlehem, where Palestinian militants had taken shelter. The surrounding of one of Christianity's most symbolic sites led to howls of outrage from Europe. Bush, however, laid the blame at Arafat's door. Behind the scenes, the British Ambassador to Israel, Sherard Cowper-Coles, played a major role in brokering a solution, in which the six Palestinians holed up inside were eventually sent into international custody abroad. There was devastation in Palestinian towns the length of the West Bank. The number of casualties in Jenin was a matter of bitter argument. Eventually, on 1 May, Arafat was freed, but throughout their operation the Israelis had a nod and a wink from the White House.

Bush was sending out dangerously contradictory signals. At the start of April, in a speech in the Rose Garden, he demanded that Israel withdraw from the towns it had besieged. His language was emotive. 'The future is dying,' he said. 'Enough is enough.' Speaking as a 'committed friend of Israel', he declared: 'To lay the foundations of future peace, I ask Israel to halt incursion into Palestinian-controlled areas and begin the withdrawal from those cities it has recently occupied. The United States is on record supporting the legitimate aspirations of the Palestinian people for a Palestinian state.' He reinforced the message with a twenty-minute call to Sharon. Such was the domestic lobbying on Bush that following his call on Israel to withdraw its tanks, the White House received 100,000 angry e-mails from the Christian right. Bush was influenced less by the Jewish vote than the opinion of the self-styled 'Christian Conservatives' – who according to his pollster Karl Rove constituted at least 15 per cent of the electorate.

Bush had spoken to Blair hours before making his speech. It was two days before the Prime Minister was due at the presidential ranch in Crawford. Blair discussed it with him 'again and again over the phone'. Downing Street issued a statement welcoming the speech, endorsing the call for an end to suicide bombings, and repeating the call for an Israeli withdrawal from Palestinian towns and a resumption of negotiations. Bush, Rice, Blair and Manning spent hours at the ranch discussing the Middle East. They decided to send Powell back to the region. Powell was reluctant. He was now increasingly nervous of leaving Washington for fear of what his colleagues might get up to in his absence. Powell left just as the summit ended.

The Secretary of State's first stop was Madrid, for a meeting of a new grouping that had been formed to try to apply broader international pressure on both sides. The original idea of the Quartet – the US, Russia, the UN and the EU – was to share the burden, not leaving it all to the Americans. It didn't work like that and no matter how hard the diplomats tried, they couldn't escape the impression that – just as with the Contact Group for Bosnia and Kosovo – the bigger the problem, the grander the organisation set up to tackle it. In its statement, the Quartet repeated the tried and tested formula, the two-state solution in which Israel and Palestine would live in peace side by side, in a settlement based on the principle of land for peace. They also called on Sharon to withdraw from besieged Palestinian towns. If that was not particularly effective, the rest of the trip provided a masterclass in failed diplomacy. Powell spent much of his time in the region talking to Washington on secure embassy phones. He felt as if he was being hung out to dry – which he was.

The British were hopping mad. In each of his meetings with Israeli ministers, Powell had the impression that they knew his negotiating position ahead of time. He suspected Sharon and his team had been on the phone to either Cheney or Rice first. Rice's job was to pass messages to and from Bush. Cheney was influenced on Israeli by his veteran chief of staff 'Scooter' Libby, one of the most pro-Likud members of a pro-Likud US administration. Jack Straw, who was called by a despairing Powell several times during that trip, would say of Libby: 'It's a toss-up whether he is working for the Israelis or the Americans on any given day.'

As Powell left Israel, Sharon launched new incursions into Palestinian villages, including several close to Jerusalem. To compound the defiance, the best he gave his visitor to take home was a promise that Israel would 'prepare' to withdraw 'within the next few days or a week'. Publicly, Powell directed his frustration towards Arafat. His anger was actually directed more at his own people. He confided as much in Straw, phoning him as soon as he returned to Washington. From that moment he decided to ask the British to lobby Bush on his behalf on Middle East policy. Blair was becoming despondent, complaining privately that Sharon had been 'running rings' around Bush. That led him to rewrite the job description for a British Prime Minister. Blair decided that he and Powell should act as a lobbying organisation working within the Washington administration, seeking to influence Bush. Rumsfeld, Cheney and the neocons were pitted against them on the other side.

For all the mutterings of dismay at the Americans and Israelis – and that is usually all they were – Blair and Straw were loath to go too far in antagonising either government. The Israeli air force, which often took the lead in actions against the Palestinians, had put in a request for more F-16 warplanes from the US. Under the existing contract, the 'head-up display units' – the military version of a dashboard – were supplied BAE Systems. Blair did not give a second thought to the approach. His aides told him that Britain's cherished position as one of the world's leading and most reliable weapons suppliers would be jeopardised if it pulled out, even though Downing Street was forced to admit that these amounted to 'only 1 per cent of that particular aircraft'.

Straw dutifully announced that he would allow the components to be exported to the US, from where the completed planes
would be sent to Israel. His junior foreign minister in charge of
Middle East relations, Ben Bradshaw, was dismayed that Straw,
having expressed to him his misgivings in private, gave the green
light. Patricia Hewitt was another Cabinet member unhappy with
the decision, but she once again fell into line. 'The Israelis had given
us assurances that the planes wouldn't be used in the occupied territories,' said a senior government member at the time. 'We knew
those assurances to be worthless. We knew similar planes had been
used to bomb refugee camps.' Bradshaw was shunted out of the
Foreign Office soon after taking his stand.

Blair and his chief of staff, Jonathan Powell, were annoyed by
the row. They made sure the export criteria drawn up at Cook's
insistence in 1997 were watered down. As part of the F-16s
announcement, Straw also published what was called 'supplemen-
tary guidance', making sure that components incorporated in
systems sold by a second country to a third country could not be
impeded. Downing Street said the guidelines reflected the 'new realities' of the multinational defence industry. A few weeks later,
Colin Powell was forced to announce a review of Israel's use of
American weapons in operations in the occupied territories after a
bomb dropped by a US-made F-16 killed fifteen people, including
nine children, in Gaza.

In many cases, however, Britain was careful. It did not admit as
much, but it had tightened up its licensing since the start of the
second *intifada*. The DTI was embarrassed when a letter from its
director of export controls to the British Embassy in Tel Aviv was
leaked to an Israeli newspaper. It said that Israel's military tactics in
the territories in the past two years had led to a discreet review. As a
result of that, 'We have not approved licences for equipment we
have licensed before.'

In the middle of June, Rice told Manning to expect a big
announcement. Bush was going to set out his grand vision for the

Middle East. The mood was so lugubrious in Downing Street that whatever Bush said could be construed as progress. The speech was delayed by several days after two suicide attacks. It later transpired that Bush was planning to call for a regional conference in September when a Palestinian theological student blew himself up on a bus, killing nineteen people. The speech he gave in the Rose Garden on 24 June, with Rumsfeld on one side of the lectern, Powell on the other, was rewritten at the last minute. This was now draft number twenty-six. Bush laid out conditions for the eventual establishment of a Palestinian state – the foundations for what would later be known as the 'road map'. But he prefaced that with a new demand: 'Peace requires a new and different Palestinian leadership, so that a Palestinian state can be born. I call on the Palestinian people to elect new leaders, leaders not compromised by terror.' The explicit call that Arafat must go was added to it only hours before delivery.

This could, remarked one of Blair's people, 'have been written by Likud', for whom the removal of Arafat was a major goal. Everyone tried to put a brave face on it. Egypt's President Mubarak denied it amounted to the political death of Arafat. Blair described it as 'helpful and constructive'. After all, it showed the US was engaging with the Middle East. That was as much as he could muster. On the Israeli right, there was jubilation. They had achieved a clear shift in policy.

Two days later Blair was due to meet Bush in Kananaskis, a Canadian mountain resort. This was the first annual meeting of the G8 since the events of September 11, and it was chosen for its remoteness and security. Before leaving for Canada, Blair wrote Bush one of his very personal handwritten letters, focusing on the Middle East peace process. He told him he could not and would not publicly back the call to remove Arafat. Blair and Bush had an unscheduled 7 A.M. meeting in a gym that had been converted into a meeting room. Bush shifted in his seat. Both looked uncomfortable, as Blair did what he was reluctant ever to do with the President.

He confronted him head-on: 'It is for the Palestinians to elect the people that they choose to elect. It's not a question of saying we are going to tell people who they will elect or not.' He pointed out that the Palestinians had actually chosen Arafat in elections specifically demanded of them by the US. Bush told Blair he'd 'think about it'. That was his standard parting line. Blair emerged from these meetings hoping he'd got through, but never being entirely sure.

By now these summits had fallen into a pattern. Christopher Meyer, the British ambassador, knew the Bush body language better than anyone. He, even more than Blair, would conclude that you could never quite be sure what had been achieved. Each time, he would do the rounds of the 'principals' – Powell, Rumsfeld, Cheney and Rice – a day or two later to see whether the balance of forces had changed, to see whether any of the discussions with Blair had 'percolated out'. His conclusions, as he would tell his bosses back in Downing Street, were: 'I'm afraid you made less progress than you had hoped, maybe none at all.'

10

THE UN ROUTE

AT THE END OF JULY 2002 TONY BLAIR SENT HIS FOREIGN policy adviser, David Manning, on a secret mission. He had done this several times before. Manning could slip in and out of foreign capitals without anyone, least of all journalists, being alerted. He went on specific missions, and would report back immediately. The Prime Minister would not have to contend with the bureaucracy of the Foreign Office.

This assignment was his most important and most sensitive yet. Blair wanted him to go straight to Bush with a message. After agreeing at Crawford in April to go along with the Americans in principle, he was starting to get cold feet about the war on Iraq. Public opinion was not rallying as he had expected. The neoconservatives were making his case virtually untenable. Until this point, Blair had been confident that he could reconcile the humanitarian interventionist instincts of the Labour Party with the new Bush Doctrine of primacy and pre-emption – all in the name of tackling one of the world's most evil dictators and his weapons of mass destruction. Just as he had seen himself as a bridge between Europe and America, so he saw himself as a bridge between these two

competing, although in his view not incompatible, approaches. He
was now beginning to have doubts.

Blair now had two conflicting priorities. He was worried about
embarking on military action that could be deemed illegal under
international law. He was even more worried that the Americans
might go it alone, without the United Nations, even without him.
Sally Morgan, Blair's adviser on domestic affairs, warned him that
any agreement to go to war without being sanctioned by the UN
would break the party and government. Several ministers would
resign. Morgan, a former teacher and Labour official who had taken
over from Anji Hunter, had a clear idea of what the party could
take, and what it could not. She reminded him that every Labour
manifesto since 1945 had referred to the UN Security Council as the
highest international authority. At the Foreign Office there was considerable disquiet about the diplomatic consequences of any
decision to go it alone.

Manning took with him to America a personal letter from the
Prime Minister. Blair had taken to dropping notes of a page or two
to other world leaders. This one, written in the formal but personal
style that he found worked best with Bush, hinted, ever so gently,
that without a UN resolution, Britain might not be able to join a
military campaign in Iraq. Manning was left to fill in the gaps.

His first meeting was with his opposite number, Condoleezza
Rice. They were similar characters – their reserve masking brilliant
minds. Given that they spoke once or twice a day on the phone, she
usually knew what Manning was about to say before he said it. She
always gave the British a sympathetic hearing. On a bookshelf opposite her desk stood a photograph of three people with their arms
around one another. One was Blair. The other was Bush, in his
leather bomber jacket. In the middle was Rice. For a foreign adviser
to be given face-time with the US President was virtually unheard of.
But Rice had told Bush he needed to see Manning. She accompanied
him into the Oval Office. Manning set out Blair's position. In his
soft-spoken tones, he explained there were some things that Blair

could do, and some things he could not. Everyone, he said, had a bottom line. Prompted by the President, he got to the point. A war against Iraq without international backing would put Britain in an 'extremely difficult position'. He added: 'We would be unable to do it.' For a while Bush said nothing. As he stood up to end the meeting, he said only that he understood. Manning did not know what conclusion he had come to.

On his return to London, Manning went straight to Chequers to brief Blair. He told him he was reasonably confident that Bush had accepted the argument, but he could not be certain. They knew Bush was also listening to Cheney. The two were having weekly lunches, and Cheney was intensely suspicious of Blair. He saw Blair as Colin Powell's spokesman, and Powell as Britain's ambassador. Cheney told Bush that if he were to 'go down the UN route' – to seek a resolution at the UN for action against Iraq – it must be framed purely as a test of the UN's resolve.

Powell did not enjoy anything like the personal access to Bush that Cheney did, but he prevailed upon Rice to allow him a thorough presentation of his concerns. Their dinner on 5 August *à trois* – Bush, Powell and Rice – was crucial in persuading the President. It was a pattern of the Bush presidency, however, a pattern experienced by Blair as much as by Powell, that you could never be entirely sure you had won the argument with him. Sensing that, the principals themselves tended to re-open discussions about decisions already made by Bush, forcing him to decide all over again. 'The sale still isn't closed,' remarked a British diplomat at the time. 'Sales never seem to close with this administration.'

In this period of indecision, senior Congressmen were complaining about a lack of consultation. Several with access to classified intelligence briefings said they had not seen or heard any new evidence suggesting that Saddam posed an imminent threat to US security. They urged Bush to set out the case more clearly. Veterans of George Bush senior's administration, people like Brent Scowcroft, his former National Security Advisor who still carried some clout around Washington, took issue with the whole focus of the war on terror. 'Co-operation is waning,' Scowcroft said. 'The Europeans conceive that, in essence, we've stiffed them in Afghanistan, did not accept or utilise the force they offered until much of the conflict had been completed. And on other issues, whether it's the conflict in the Middle East, the second *intifada*, whether it is Iraq, these are interfering with the concentration on the war on al-Qaeda.'

In the middle of August, Bush held a video conference from Crawford with his foreign policy insiders. They agreed on the broad outlines of a strategy to go through the UN, but not to allow the UN to delay a war or to dictate terms. The bottom line would be to send in weapons inspectors for one last, brief time to flush out Saddam's weapons and to test the international community's resolve. The following day Cheney went out of his way to undermine the strategy.

'A return of inspectors would provide no assurance whatever of Saddam's compliance with UN resolutions,' Cheney told the Veterans of Foreign Wars national convention in Nashville, Tennessee. 'On the contrary, there is a great danger that it would provide false comfort that Saddam was somehow back in his box.' In other words, what was the point of the inspectors? They wouldn't show any steel and they wouldn't get anywhere. They had been dismissed as weak and irrelevant even before they had been reactivated. Cheney concluded by predicting that after liberation, the streets of Baghdad and Basra would 'erupt in joy in the same way as the throngs in Kabul greeted the Americans'. He had not bothered to tell Powell about his speech. But he did clear it with Bush – a painful reminder to Powell and Blair that the President was still distrustful of the whole process.

With Blair only just finishing his holiday, Jack Straw was on Iraq watch. He was sitting in a BBC caravan in a car park in Edinburgh doing a radio interview on how we should learn to like Europe when he was told about Cheney's speech. He nearly fell off his chair. The following day, Rumsfeld told US Marines at Camp

Pendleton, California, that doing the right thing 'at the onset may seem lonesome'. The US would readily go it alone if it had to.

Blair tried to switch off briefly from Iraq that August. But it was not easy. He confided to a house guest in Italy: 'This could lose me my job. I may have to pay the price for doing what I think is right.'

He returned to London at the end of August to a renewed sense of crisis. He was furious that the neocons had 'loosened off stories into the media vacuum' of August. He summoned his inner circle. Manning, Powell, Campbell and Morgan had little over a week to plan for their most important summit yet with Bush. It was arranged for Camp David on 7 September, just five days before Bush was due to address the UN General Assembly.

It was symptomatic of Blair's style that he had come to rely on this small group in Downing Street for each and every decision. He took them on his trips and into his discussions with foreign leaders – while the professional Foreign Office team was kept outside. His entourage meant everything to him. Blair's top ambassadors, such as Sir Christopher Meyer, would talk directly to him or Manning rather than the Permanent Secretary or Political Director at the Foreign Office. Meyer would later confess that he rarely bothered with the Foreign Office at all during his time in Washington. The FCO was regarded as an annexe, to do specific tasks as and when required. The concentration of power in the hands of unelected officials, some with considerable experience of international affairs, others with very little, infuriated many British diplomats.

Blair needed to see for himself where Bush stood. He was keen to nail down Bush's commitment to the UN. Rice told Manning on the phone that they had it. But still they could not be entirely sure that at the last minute someone – by that they meant Cheney or Rumsfeld – might not prevail upon the President to change his mind.

Blair also felt that he had allowed the message back home to drift. The public and the party had been given the impression that he was seeking to restrain Bush. While that was not unhelpful in one sense, Blair knew it misrepresented his position. He was keen to push the President down a more multilateral path, but he knew he had to strike a delicate balance. He called his monthly press conference for as early as possible, on 3 September in his Sedgefield constituency. He worked out what he was going to say in his statement on the plane back to the UK from South Africa, where he had been attending the Earth Summit. Blair, Manning and Campbell agreed that he should give out a particularly hawkish message: he was determined to 'disarm' Saddam Hussein, and if that meant military force, so be it. 'The history of Saddam and weapons of mass destruction is not American or British propaganda. The history and the present threat are real. The only decision that's been taken at this stage is that inaction is not an option,' Blair told the journalists. Then he used the following line for the first time, carefully agreed with Manning. 'The UN has to be the way of dealing with this issue – and not the way of avoiding dealing with it,' Blair said. This was code. To make it easier for Bush to go down the UN route, Blair wanted to make it clear that if he did so, the British government would go to war as his staunchest ally.

Four days later Blair was back in the US. On his plane over – as was his habit on these journeys – he leafed through copious amounts of reading material. This included a briefing prepared by his private office detailing how since the 1991 Gulf War Iraq had hidden its weapons, ignored UN resolutions on weapons inspectors and circumvented sanctions. He also read an advance copy of a report due to be published two days later by the International Institute for Strategic Studies. The report reinforced Blair's hopes that he could make the case, that Iraq's weapons of mass destruction did pose a danger. It pointed to the gaps in information on WMD left behind since the departure of the weapons inspectors in 1998. It asserted that it would be 'incredible' if there had not been more weapons built since then. Blair walked to the back of the plane to talk to the press, one of those rituals that were part of prime ministerial travel.

This time he was in bullish mood. He spoke to the press three times in less than a day. He wanted to get across the 'very real' dangers. 'If these weapons are developed and used, there is no way that any conflict Saddam initiated using those weapons would not have direct implications for the interests of Britain,' Blair declared. His apocalyptic predictions had the desired effect. The Sunday papers were full of 'Blair's nuclear warning'. That was the easy part.

Persuading Bush to give the UN a chance would, he feared, be harder. Blair confided to his team that this was going to be the most delicate diplomatic meeting of his premiership. He was not wrong. As Blair was en route, Bush held a meeting of the principals. Cheney told Bush he wanted to attend Camp David, to keep an eye on Blair. What neither Blair nor his aides had reckoned on was the sight of Cheney as they arrived at the retreat. He was not on the original list, but to the Britons' surprise was included, along with Rice, in Bush's inner team. The only person Blair took with him for the longest and most detailed parts of the discussion was Manning. They then asked other members of the delegations to join them.

They came to a deal. Bush promised that if the UN did deliver genuine disarmament, he would pursue the diplomatic route. Blair promised that if that failed, he would go to war. He set out his position. He would, he assured Bush, remain unfailingly loyal. Britain had no interest in being anywhere other than at America's side.

Blair made it clear to Bush that they both wanted Saddam out, but while an American audience would probably go along with regime change as the reason for war, he would not be able to get that past the Labour Party and the British public. He outlined that autumn's political timetable, including a difficult party conference a few weeks later. For domestic reasons, Blair explained, they had to go through the UN and to be seen to be going through the UN. If, however, at the end Saddam had not 'engaged seriously', then war should ensue, in which Britain would play its full part. Blair went to Camp David to urge the President to give diplomacy a chance, to win over the UN before waging war. In return, he promised him he could deliver the Europeans; he would convince them to embrace the primacy of America in the new world order and the validity of its cause.

Bush accepted. A war that the Pentagon believed could be fought in December or January would now take a little longer to prepare. They then moved on to the detail. They agreed that a UN resolution should be based on 'coercive compliance', that the Iraqis would have actively to demonstrate their *bona fides* to the inspectors, not the other way round. The UN team should have considerable powers vested in it, to verify sites and also to question scientists. Finally they agreed that Blair would publish the dossier his intelligence services had been drawing up since March. Bush said that would be 'very helpful' and promised to give it his imprimatur.

On their way home, to Balmoral for a truncated annual stay with the royal family, Blair expressed relief. He told his entourage he was pleased he had neutralised the talk of him losing influence on the Americans. He had constructed a formula with Bush that gave him enough to persuade the party. This was the period of the 'big sell'. That began straight away. Just as he did on the journey there a few hours earlier, on the home leg, Blair went down the plane to tell journalists that Saddam's arsenal of chemical and biological weapons, and his pursuit of a nuclear option, spelt danger. 'I am not saying it will happen next month, or even next year, but at some point the danger will explode. This is not an American preoccupation. It is our preoccupation. It must be the preoccupation of the entire world.'

He reinforced the message two days later at the TUC conference in Blackpool. Blair needed to tailor his message carefully. Sally Morgan, his political adviser, had been exercised for some time that everything about Bush and his demeanour was making the sell that much harder. The problem, she felt, had got so bad that she and Campbell decided at Camp David to bite the bullet and tell the Americans about it. They told Andrew Card, Bush's chief of staff, and Karen Hughes, his director of communications, that some of the language Bush used was 'a bit alien. You have to understand that it doesn't work in Britain, even less in Europe,' they told them. They also suggested that Bush should take longer to prepare his joint press conferences with Blair. The Downing Street media team were shocked that Bush would leave just a couple of minutes at the end of meetings to prepare for the press.

Blair accepted that Bush had a 'media problem' abroad. But he was adamant that it did not provide the real picture of an 'intuitive and instinctive' politician of 'great ability'. Blair's inner circle would repeatedly discuss 'the problem'. Blair would bemoan the fact that the British people did not appreciate the President's 'sharp brain, acute powers of concentration and readiness to listen'.

Still, in his speech to the TUC, Blair did not mention Bush by name once. Publicly he criticised the left for its 'anti-Americanism', but Blair accepted privately that he would have had far fewer problems if Bill Clinton or Al Gore – or a moderate Republican, for that matter – had been in charge. Although he did not admit the deal he had just struck with Bush two days earlier, Blair set out its terms: 'If the will of the UN is ignored, action will follow.' He again tried to put the case that Britain faced an imminent danger: 'I for one do not want it on my conscience that we knew of the threat, saw it coming and did nothing.'

Blair saw his relations with Bush on a simple template – private candour and unflinching public loyalty were the only ways he believed he could exercise any influence. But throughout this period, and the desperate months that lay ahead, Blair would fatally underestimate the contempt of many of Bush's advisers for the very concept of multilateralism. Officials in Washington were openly scornful of the view espoused by Blair that a new international order could be built on the ruins of the World Trade Center. The administration would pursue its legitimate security concerns. If Britain wanted to go along with that – all the better. Blair was both master and prisoner of his influence. His leverage came with constraints.

Still, in the short term he got what he wanted. But it was a close shave. By the time Bush stood up before the General Assembly on 12 September, Blair was confident that Bush would mention the UN resolution as promised. The lobbying had gone on until the final hours. This was the twenty-eighth draft of the speech. 'We were all watching intently on our TV screens. We weren't sure what Bush would say even when he got to the podium,' recalls one member of Blair's team. 'If Colin Powell wasn't sure, how could we be sure?' They all stood in front of a television in Downing Street. Momentarily, their worst fears were confirmed. The crucial sentence was missing. But then Bush declared: 'We will work with the UN Security Council for the necessary resolutions.' The sentence had slipped from the autocue. Bush remembered what it was, and ad-libbed it in. The trouble was, he said 'resolutions' in the plural. What seemed a small mistake helped fuel confusion later.

That night, Straw went to Powell's hotel. The Secretary of State gave him a real-time read-out of what had gone on in the drafting process. Shortly after, Straw saw Bush at a reception. The President told him: 'Jack, you know how much time we spent on getting there, and then the crucial line went missing. I knew the words in my head. I put them back in, but not in the right place.'

For the first time, Blair felt he needed the active support and endorsement, not just the compliance, of his Cabinet. For the first time, candid discussion was encouraged. The long summer break had produced a vacuum, and Blair wanted to hear what his colleagues were thinking.

Robin Cook had let it be known in August that he was unhappy with developments. Clare Short also spoke of her anxiety, but usually confined it to her humanitarian responsibilities. The two of them did not think of co-ordinating their message. Personal animosity and distrust got in the way of political leverage. Apart from these two members of the awkward squad, Blair was not seriously challenged on his strategy. It was not done for Cabinet members to air their reservations before their colleagues. The only exasperation they showed was towards Short herself, who had a habit of butting in whenever the Prime Minister was speaking. Blair knew that she needed to be kept on board. She had form. She had first quit the Labour front bench in 1988, over Northern Ireland. She was brought back only to resign again in protest at Neil Kinnock's support for the first Gulf War. Blair indulged Short, but ignored her interventions.

As for Gordon Brown, a long period of silence had given rise to suggestions, from inside Number 10 as well as outside, that he was hedging his bets. There had been similar periods during Kosovo and Afghanistan, but as the accusations of disloyalty were getting out of hand, Brown used several media appearances to pledge his 'unwavering support'. That message was reinforced around the Cabinet, but with one urgent proviso. Progress in the Israeli–Palestinian conflict had to go hand in hand.

It was with some fanfare that Blair presented to the House of Commons on 24 September his second dossier in exactly one year. The prosecution document the year before against Osama bin Laden and al Qaeda for destroying the Twin Towers had not drawn on much intelligence. It did not need to make the case in much more than rhetoric, because few doubted the veracity of the accusation. But with opinion polls showing a dogged resistance to war and to Bush's rationale for war, with Labour MPs increasingly agitated, Blair knew he had to make the case on Iraq. Journalists were primed that the fifty-page document, 'Iraq's Weapons of Mass Destruction: The Assessment of the British Government', provided 'conclusive proof'.

Opening the debate, Blair described what he said was Saddam's arsenal of weapons, based on the report of UN weapons inspectors after they left Iraq in December 1998 – 360 tonnes of bulk chemical warfare agents, including 1.5 tonnes of VX nerve agent; up to 3,000 tonnes of precursor chemicals; growth media sufficient to produce 26,000 litres of anthrax spores, and over 30,000 special munitions for delivery of chemical and biological agents. All of this was missing or unaccounted for. Operation Desert Fox, the three days of air strikes, had set the programme back, but not ended it, Blair said. The following was the most important and contentious passage. Saddam's chemical, biological and nuclear programme 'is not an historical leftover from 1998. The inspectors aren't needed to clean up the old remains. His WMD programme is active, detailed and growing. The policy of containment is not working. The WMD programme is not shut down. It is up and running.'

Active, detailed and growing. No ifs, no buts, no caveats, no discussion of the nature of the intelligence he was using to reinforce his argument. Blair did throw in the rhetorical suggestion that some might wonder why he was relying on the 'good faith' of the intelligence services. He assured MPs and the public that 'the intelligence picture they paint is one accumulated over the past four years. It is extensive, detailed and authoritative.' That was a subjective assessment. Blair had no reason to dispute the good faith of his security services. From his first day in Downing Street he had spoken of his admiration for their professionalism. He needed and wanted to give them the benefit of the doubt.

The report itself was carefully structured. It began with a Foreword by the Prime Minister and an executive summary. Part 1 set out the role of intelligence and the history of Iraq's WMD programmes from 1971. The most important section was Chapter 3, detailing the position from 1998 to the present day. The two parts that followed were designed as providing ballast for the broader argument, about Saddam's violation of UN inspectors and his human rights and war record.

Blair's Foreword covered similar ground to his statement to MPs. It included a series of bald and bold assertions, for example: 'Despite his denials, Saddam is continuing to develop WMD.' The picture presented to Downing Street by the Joint Intelligence Committee 'has become more not less worrying'. He expanded on that: 'I am in no doubt that the threat is serious and current, that he has made progress on WMD and that he has to be stopped.' Blair acknowledged that the publication of material such as this was controversial. By definition, intelligence agencies had to be circum-spect for fear of revealing sources or compromising themselves in other ways. Few would have disputed that. That, he said, was 'why we cannot publish everything we know'.

In fact, according to one senior figure intimately involved in the process, the agencies used 'just about everything we had'. Sometimes facts were generalised in order to maintain the confi-dentiality of a source, but no facts of any importance were left out. That was what the British spooks knew – or thought they knew. It was a little, but not much more, than they knew in March when they decided to shelve their first report.

As Blair, his ministers and security chiefs would admit, intelli-gence information from Iraq – one of the most secretive, centralised and repressive regimes in the world – was extremely hard to come by, especially since the murder of the three SIS agents in 1979. Britain shared its intelligence not just with the US, but also with the Australians, the Germans and, crucially, the French. The various agencies worked extremely closely, pooling what few resources they had. For all the confident assertions, that was the backdrop that informed this report.

As anyone who has seen intelligence reports would testify, they are a compilation of raw material, closely but confidentially sourced, that is then turned into assessments of prevailing threats. This is a world of best guesses, cautious conclusions and often circumstantial evidence. The information from the SIS, MI5, GCHQ and defence intelligence is usually derivative, weighing one fact up against another. This is then pulled together by the Joint Intelligence Committee. With its eighty-strong staff on the second floor of the Cabinet Office, it bears no resemblance to the James Bond image. It is more like a series of university professors' rooms. The JIC tends to shun extravagant claims, couching its reports in caveats, making clear the strength of a particular piece of information. 'The security people were always clear and candid to us in private about the limits of their knowledge,' says one Cabinet minister.

For all the arguments that would ensue between their governments, the SIS, the CIA and France's DGSE, the Direction Générale
de la Sécurité Extérieure, worked well together. They would continue
to do so right up to, during and after the war. There was, according
to one senior official, 'no difference in the intelligence received, in
quality or quantity'. He added: 'There was not that much to share.
Most of it had come from the inspections up to 1998. After that we
didn't have that much. People forget how much Unscom actually
destroyed.'

That was certainly not the impression in the report presented
to MPs. John Scarlett, the Chairman of the JIC, was providing Blair
and a select group of ministers and officials twice-weekly assessments of the threat. Blair devoured the assessments as soon as they
were presented to him. On his return from holiday, Blair had asked
that the material be presented in a way that would be digestible and
convincing.

During a four-week period Scarlett, Campbell and other
Downing Street officials had six meetings, mostly in Campbell's
office along the corridor in 12 Downing Street. They discussed in
detail how to present the document. Sometimes Manning and
Powell joined in. Blair took part in the final stages. Between those
meetings, drafts of the document were, according to one involved,
'moved around the building' by e-mail, on the secure intranet
system, with suggestions sought on how best to present the information available. Scarlett had already cleared with his intelligence
chiefs what could be used and what could not. He was comfortable
with the principle. He had no quibble with the request from
Campbell and Blair for a document to help the government make its
case. He knew that senior figures in SIS in particular were unhappy
with the use of intelligence material for political ends, and with the
consequences for their future work of making the intelligence
public. But he believed that, if sensitively handled, these concerns
could be overcome.

Scarlett had the specific task of compiling the report. He signed off what was published. Downing Street considered having a firm conclusion, setting out the reasons for military conflict, but then dropped the idea. Scarlett was comfortable with the message that containment was not working, but he insisted to his colleagues that it was 'not intended to be a document that justifies war'.

The salient section, Part 1, Chapter 3, was largely written by Scarlett. All the facts later contested were contained in that section. In the first half of 2000, the report said, the JIC received intelligence on Iraqi attempts to procure dual-use chemicals and to reconstruct production at sites formerly associated with the chemical warfare programme. There was also intelligence, it added, that Iraq was starting to produce biological warfare agents in mobile production facilities. It went on:

> In mid-2001 the JIC assessed that Iraq retained some chemical warfare agents, precursors, production equipment and weapons from before the Gulf War. These stocks would enable Iraq to produce significant quantities of mustard gas within weeks, and of nerve agent within months. The JIC concluded that intelligence on Iraqi former chemical and biological warfare facilities, their limited reconstruction and civil production pointed to a continuing research and development programme. These chemical and biological capabilities represented the most immediate threat from Iraqi weapons of mass destruction.

Those observations were hard to prove or disprove. The language was carefully crafted, combining hypothesis and assumption with alarm. The following pages produced the bigger problems. The document said: 'Iraq has made repeated attempts to acquire a very large quantity (60,000 or more) of specialised aluminium tubes. The specialised aluminium in question is subject to international export controls because of its potential application in the construction of gas centrifuges used to enrich uranium.' However, it qualified this by adding: 'There is no definitive intelligence that it is destined for a nuclear programme.' Earlier, the document had pointed to further 'evidence' of a nuclear programme. 'There is intelligence that Iraq has sought the supply of significant quantities of uranium from Africa.' That was based on intelligence from the Italian security services, citing documents from Niger that would later turn out to be blatant forgeries.

Under a sub-heading 'Recent Intelligence', Scarlett wrote that 'subsequently intelligence has become available from reliable sources which complements and adds to previous intelligence and confirms the JIC assessment that Iraq has chemical and biological weapons'. The evidence to support this was the assertion that 'Saddam attaches great importance to the possession of chemical and biological weapons which he regards as being the basis for Iraqi regional power'. Without it, his political weight would be diminished. That might be so, but there was nothing to back up the claim. A second piece of evidence was the assertion that Saddam knew how to play the inspectors. 'Sensitive equipment and papers can easily be concealed and in some cases this is already happening. The possession of mobile biological agent production facilities will also aid concealment efforts.' He was concealing it. Therefore he must have it. Therefore it must pose a real threat to the world. That was the crux of it, an extrapolation of his past record in lieu of fact-based evidence. They all wanted to believe it.

The third and most eye-catching example of 'Recent Intelligence' said: 'Intelligence indicates that the Iraqi military are able to deploy chemical or biological weapons within 45 minutes of an order to do so.'

The 'subsequent' intelligence referred to in the report did arrive late in the day. It caused great excitement in the JIC and Downing Street. One official recalls: 'Over the summer our sources were reporting good stuff. We had very good information. Suddenly things got illuminated.'

So just how strong was the evidence? When Blair received JIC assessments, he would turn to his spy chiefs and ask: 'We are sure about the intelligence, aren't we?' They would tell him they were as sure as they ever could be, which was not quite the answer he wanted.

For all his public assertions that the intelligence was rock solid, Blair had his doubts throughout. He confided only in a small number of people in his entourage. They too had their doubts. If any of this hesitation about the intelligence had been known at the time, war would have been much harder to sell. This was a policy based on hope more than anything else. 'We hoped we were right,' recalls one official. 'We *felt* we were right.'

Given all the doubt, was there anyone who tried to reflect this caution publicly? All the major Western intelligence agencies saw the raw material. Even the CIA was somewhat dubious about its strength. Its top officials did not think of highlighting it in their presentations to the administration. In testimony to the Senate Intelligence Committee a few weeks later, George Tenet, the Director of the CIA, suggested that while Saddam did possess chemical and biological weapons he did not pose an imminent threat and was unlikely to attack the US unless provoked. That was seen in the US, and in Whitehall, as further evidence of CIA misgivings about the rush to war. It was quickly cast aside.

In Moscow, Vladimir Putin was dismissive of the dossier. 'Fears are one thing, hard facts are another,' he told Blair. Jacques Chirac, who was still getting on relatively well with the Prime Minister, told him on the phone that the document had offered 'no proof, only indications'.

The Europeans were distinctly dubious about this supposed intelligence illumination. 'We received nothing that summer that changed the situation,' recalls one senior official. The French were so wary they asked London to send someone to Paris to discuss it. Peter Ricketts, the Political Director at the Foreign Office and Scarlett's predecessor as head of the JIC, went over to the Quai d'Orsay. They were still unmoved. 'Ricketts would say he had more,' recalls the official. 'He would send more people to Paris. It was not very impressive.'

The bottom line was not the raw data. The main intelligence agencies received the same. This is the version of one senior European official:

> We know that in terms of the nuclear programme there was nothing of importance. Any assertion to the contrary was a pure lie. We knew they had ballistics. They had some remaining capacity. On biological and chemical weapons we know the Iraqis attempted to get it. But we had no indication, no presumption that they had any capacity. It's one thing to have the elements, the ingredients and the precursors. There was no indication about the weaponisation of those elements. There was even less evidence about any ability to deliver weapons we didn't think they had.

The difference lay in the assessment of the threat. 'The Brits admitted to us that there was no immediate threat, but they would say that there was a potential threat from the combination of a dictator willing to possess WMD and from terrorist groups willing to acquire it. Their argument then was that we had to act pre-emptively. Our position was that there was no immediate threat, and the potential threat was too weak because the weaponry had been significantly reduced.' The issue was not the intelligence, but the interpretation of the intelligence. As the official put it: 'Out of the same grapes in a vineyard you can make a very different wine.'

The mismatch between the claims made in the document and the facts as they subsequently transpired caused considerable soul-searching in the JIC and the intelligence agencies. Senior intelligence figures would later show contrition about the Niger allegation. They accepted that the paperwork in question was fake, but said they had been assured by 'another party otherwise' – another intelligence agency. They had not seen the raw data themselves, nor had they been able to cross-check it. Still, they say the claim itself was not wrong. 'Other reporting from other sources pointed to this really going on.'

And what of the forty-five-minute claim? As ministers would later concede, it came from a single uncorroborated source. It sounded alarming. In fact the source had actually said '20–45 minutes', but the JIC took the more cautious timeframe. Set against other assertions in the report itself and in explanations to ministers, the claim was meaningless. It was, as Blair and all those around him knew, a red herring designed to scare. The Iraqi military, the report said, was able to deploy biological and chemical weapons within forty-five minutes *of an order to do so*. It was a claim of hypothetical command and control, which revealed nothing about the level of threat. At the same time the document itself noted that Saddam was concealing his weaponry to avoid it being found, so the chemical and biological agents and the delivery mechanisms, assuming they still existed, were unlikely to have been in the same place.

But it was even more nebulous than that. One serving member of the Cabinet recalls a discussion during one of Scarlett's presentations to groups of ministers early in 2003. 'I pressed them strongly on the use of chemical weapons. I asked about troops on the battlefield. I was told it would be hard for the Iraqis to get the delivery mechanisms to the front line because of dispersals. I was told the previous year that, in July 2002, they had started moving it out, and dispersing it.' In other words, this minister, a loyalist, suggests he was told dispersal had started before the September document was published. Government officials insisted that this kind of dispersal began only *after* the UN inspectors arrived. 'It was only then that we received indications that Saddam had ordered the stuff to be dismantled, destroyed or hidden. At the same time we were getting indications that various units were being issued with chemical kits,' the minister says. Even if the government were given the benefit of the doubt, that it was giving the information as it knew it at the time, it made no attempt at any point, right up until the start of the war, to clarify the impression that the chemical weapons were ready to be used within forty-five minutes. Even if Downing Street and the intelligence community were confident at the time of the document that Saddam's WMD threat was 'real and growing', the closer they came to war, the more the evidence seemed to show that the threat was diminishing.

So why, to use the most charitable explanation, did Blair's entourage alight on the worst-case scenario? Why did they all turn inconclusive raw intelligence into something more? This was not about one individual – Alastair Campbell or anyone else. The whole of Downing Street was in this together. The mood was a febrile mixture of hubris – they felt they could do what they want – and fear – of letting Saddam out of their sights. The politicians and the security services were still exercised by the experience of 9/11. The SIS and the CIA had been compiling all kinds of data against al-Qaeda, but that had not been translated starkly enough to ministers. They had been swamped by the detail. They did not want a repeat of that. Then there was Saddam's own history. Throughout the 1980s he had run rings around the International Atomic Energy Agency, hiding an advanced nuclear weapons development programme that was discovered only in the first Gulf War. Blair was convinced that Saddam was not only evil and dangerous, but that he was a pathological liar. His record in the 1980s and with Unscom in the 1990s had already proven his guilt. On WMD, he would not even contemplate erring on the side of caution – and everyone in Whitehall and in the intelligence community took their cue from him. 'My worry was not that the stuff was made up, but that we were seeing only a part of the picture and failing again,' says one aide close to the Prime Minister.

At the same time, the intimate relationship with Washington had brought about an unprecedented level of not only intelligence-sharing, but, as one official put it, 'conclusion-sharing'. George W. Bush provided a telling insight into his thought process, and the level of proof required. 'We all know that Iraq and the al-Qaeda

terrorist network share a common enemy – the USA,' he told a meeting in Cincinatti on 7 October 2002.

> We know that Iraq and al-Qaeda have had high-level contacts
> that go back a decade. Some citizens wonder: after eleven years
> of living with this problem, why do we need to confront it now?
> There is a reason: we have experienced the horrors of
> September 11. We have seen that those who hate America are
> willing to crash airplanes into buildings full of innocent people.
> Our enemies would be no less willing – in fact they would be
> eager – to use a biological or chemical weapon or, when they get
> one, a nuclear weapon. Facing clear evidence of peril, we cannot
> wait for the final proof – the smoking gun – that could come in
> the form of a mushroom cloud.

The JIC had always been disdainful of the intelligence assessments
being sent to Bush from Rumsfeld's Office of Special Plans suggesting a Saddam link to al-Qaeda and 9/11. But the British still
drew from many of the same sources as the OSP – including the
exile groups whose political purpose was clear. 'We relied on a
number of people for information who were relying on us to help
them get rid of Saddam. Some agents were obviously enticed by
money. But with others it was a symbiotic relationship. They knew
what we wanted to hear from them,' says one official who has seen
many of the papers.

Although senior ministers were on the distribution list of JIC
reports, the formal structures were bypassed. The Ministerial
Committee on Intelligence, comprising the Deputy Prime Minister,
Foreign Secretary, Defence Secretary, Home Secretary and chaired
by the Prime Minister, was supposed to meet regularly. It did not
meet once. Blair wanted his ministers to help him make the case, but
at the same time he sought to control the information flow to them.
Clare Short had long had good relations with the SIS, usually to
discuss Africa and tensions in the developing world. She would have

lunch at its heaquarters across the Thames in Vauxhall with Sir Richard Dearlove, still quaintly referred to in Whitehall by the acronym 'C'. Other senior officials came to see her at her offices at the Department for International Development. In October she asked for specific WMD briefings, beyond the JIC reports. Downing Street initially blocked them until she complained to Blair. Short now says that Dearlove told her the date for war had already been set for mid-February, and that she was given the same message by Sir Andrew Turnbull, the Cabinet Secretary, and Gordon Brown.

That was not the message Blair gave to his increasingly fretful party. He devoted most of his speech to the Labour conference on 1 October to a call for greater boldness. He told them that he was set on war with Iraq. But this would be the consequence of non-compliance by Saddam. Then he added the following passage:

> Some say the issue is Iraq. Some say it is the Middle East peace process. It's both. Some say it's poverty. Some say it's terrorism. It's both. And yes, what is happening in the Middle East now is ugly and wrong. The Palestinians living in increasingly abject conditions, humiliated and hopeless; Israeli civilians brutally murdered. I agree UN resolutions should apply here as much as to Iraq. But they don't just apply to Israel. They apply to all parties. And there is only one answer. By this year's end, we must have revived final-status negotiations and they must have explicitly as their aims: an Israeli state free from terror, recognised by the Arab world, and a viable Palestinian state based on the boundaries of 1967.

That pledge earned Blair the longest applause of the speech. It was just what the party wanted to hear. They might be able to coun-tenance a war on Iraq as long they were convinced that this was not double standards, that Israel was going to be made to abide by its UN obligations. The problem was that nobody in any position of responsibility in the UK government, nor anywhere else, had any idea that Blair was going to say this.

'Nobody' meant not Jack Straw; not Mike O'Brien, the Foreign Office minister responsible for the Middle East; not Lord Levy, Blair's special representative in the region. Not even David Manning knew. As a civil servant, he was not at the party conference. The first he heard about it was when he watched the speech on television. The first Sherard Cowper-Coles, the British Ambassador to Israel, heard about it was when he was questioned by the Israeli media. The line was inserted at the last minute by Blair and Jonathan Powell while going over the speech in the 'green room' behind the stage in Blackpool. There was no time to put it in the autocue. They did it to head off dissent within the party – or in the words of one who was involved in the speech, 'to sweeten the pill of Iraq'. Blair had sought to overturn carefully crafted Middle East policy on a whim to gain support from his party.

In the Foreign Office and elsewhere the phones were buzzing. A line was quickly worked out, that Blair was putting himself in the lead of peace efforts. The Americans, the real brokers, knew nothing of it. The other partners in the quartet – the Russians, the EU and the UN – were similarly in the dark. Nor did the Israelis, who were furious, nor the Palestinians, who were perplexed. 'We had to explain it away when they all called us,' recalls one senior Foreign Office figure. 'Nobody in this building knew. It might have turned out for the best, but it's not the best way of conducting foreign policy.'

Blair was already planning to call Bush from Blackpool to reassure him that the invitation to Bill Clinton to address them was not intended as a snub. He and Manning also had to explain to Bush and Rice exactly what this new Middle East initiative-on-the-hoof was all about. Others in government might not have been, but Blair and Powell (and Manning, once he found out) were pleased with what had been done. They believed that – even as they assumed the deadline could not be kept – they had applied some pressure on Bush, who had signalled he wasn't going to move on Israel until after the mid-term elections. It was the job of Straw and his officials to make something out of it. 'After the PM's line we had to scramble an initiative,' says one senior FCO official. 'We needed to activate a plan. Everything we did after that was to give the speech a rationale, to make the timescale look realistic.'

Blair had been making no headway on the Middle East with Bush. The President had told him he was not willing to risk his political currency on the issue. Blair thought he had built up enough credits, but it seemed he had not.

The Israeli–Palestinian crisis was discussed openly in Cabinet. Blair accepted the view of his ministers that the conflict was inextricably linked to Iraq and the broader Middle East picture. Mike O'Brien, the junior Foreign Office minister responsible for the region, reported to Cabinet that he had been shocked when he went to see Arafat in July. His Mukata headquarters in Ramallah resembled a bombsite. O'Brien would keep a set of photos in the drawer of his FCO office to show people the extent of the damage. By September the violence had again got out of hand. The British feared the Israelis were about to make a martyr of Arafat, with American acquiescence. Israel accused him of sheltering fifty suspected militants inside his Mukata compound. On 21 September, the Israelis had cut water and power supplies. Arafat remained defiant; Blair was desperately worried. Manning, who had been talking about it almost daily with Rice, called her again that Saturday night. Straw called Powell.

'We received word that there were those in the Israeli Cabinet who wanted him taken out, period, or taken out of the country by force – preferably the former,' recalls a senior British official. Sharon vacillated. There were some around Bush who were telling him: 'We'd be better off without him [Arafat].' 'We were saying to the Americans – you've got to stop this.'

Straw needed to get a 'bankable promise'. Powell phoned the Israelis and reported back to him that he had. Straw had no reason to doubt Powell's intentions, far from it, but could he deliver? After all, he had been overruled and humiliated so many times before by the neocons. Just to make sure, Straw asked Cowper-Coles to talk to Sharon's office. The White House had already conveyed a message that it did not want Arafat killed, but according to a senior British official, 'it was a close call'.

A few days later the US reluctantly criticised Israel over its attack on the compound. Israel withdrew its bulldozers. For a rare moment, Blair's views had prevailed. Britain's role in that crisis was kept quiet, for fear of antagonising the Americans and the Israelis.

The problem went deeper than simply doing a favour for his staunch ally. Much of the Bush administration had become an outpost of the Likud party. In fact, many of them were to the right of Ariel Sharon. In their determination to prevent any compromise, to dash all hopes of reviving a settlement based on land-for-peace, the hawks were being consistent with their past record. In the Foreign Office and other parts of Whitehall the fear dawned that the emotional thrust of the neoconservatives' campaign against Iraq was predicated more on the security needs of Israel, which Saddam really threatened, than that of the US, which – even with the most wilful exaggeration – his weapons of mass destruction had no chance of reaching.

Relations with Washington were going through one of their intermittent difficult patches. The British were unhappy with the way the Americans were negotiating the early draft of the resolution on Iraq. They were particularly unhappy that one of the drafts had been leaked to the *New York Times* – in the middle of the Labour conference. Blair spent much of his time in Blackpool talking to Sir Jeremy Greenstock, the British Ambassador to the UN. For all the talk of this being a joint declaration, the hands of the hawks were all over the leak. 'Sure, the British proposals informed the draft, but by the time we got to write it there wasn't a whole lot of Blair in it,' one US official said. Several points in the published document were of particular concern – the stipulation that the inspection team could be joined by experts from 'any permanent member of the Security Council' (for that, read the Americans), and most crucially that any breach of compliance 'authorises member states to use all necessary means to restore international peace and security in the area'.

The French and the Russians, whom Blair had desperately sought to sign up to a resolution, had made clear their opposition to what in UN-speak was called 'automaticity' – a single resolution linking the inspections to war. Blair had an 'open mind' on that point. He was not, he told his aides, 'theological' about the details. What he wanted was a tough resolution, but one with the widest possible endorsement.

The Americans were in no mood to compromise. Bush had just been given the go-ahead by Congress to use the military 'as he determines to be necessary and appropriate' against Iraq. Blair remarked to one of his advisers if only Britain's parliamentarians would be so eager to do the right thing.

Bush's authority, it seemed, was unassailable. Now the administration was working from a fully fledged policy template. The US National Security Strategy unveiled on 20 September gave an official imprimatur to the doctrines of pre-emption and primacy. It set out the right of the US to use its unsurpassed, indeed unsurpassable, military power to overthrow governments by force if, in its view, they attempted to acquire weapons of mass destruction or harboured terrorists. Dick Cheney suggested this included no fewer than sixty states. The strategy cast aside all the traditional tenets of international law as well as the UN and Nato charters. It abandoned the concept of deterrence, considered the bedrock of stability throughout the Cold War and cited by successive British governments as justification for their nuclear arsenal. Talking of 'freedom's triumph', Bush wrote in his preamble: 'As a matter of common sense and self-defense, America will act against such emerging threats before they are fully formed. We cannot defend America and our friends by hoping for the best.'

Blair's talk was to marry the new US doctrine with the multilateral process to which he had committed Bush. The negotiations in New York dragged on for seven weeks. Much of that time, however, was taken up by the rival factions in the US government arguing among themselves. The other Security Council countries had to wait until they were told what the official US position was on any given day. The British were content to be perched between the Americans and French. The discussions were long and detailed, but they were conducted cordially. Colin Powell worked well with his French opposite number, the erudite poet *manqué*, Dominique de Villepin. Straw was talking to Powell on the phone several times a day. He notched up a record seven conversations on one particular day. On one occasion he had to go through an arcane question of wording while conducting a constituency surgery. The French were certainly in confident spirits. Chirac had just returned from a triumphant tour of the Middle East. In Beirut, a summit of fifty-five Francophone states had endorsed his cautious line on Iraq.

There was another point of contention. The British suspected throughout October that the Rumsfeld–Cheney axis was seeking to undermine the credibility of the man in charge of the inspection team – Hans Blix.

The avuncular former academic was brought out of retirement by a phone call from Kofi Annan, who asked him to head the UN Monitoring, Verification and Inspection Commission (Unmovic). He thought long and hard. He had had an unhappy experience of Iraq as head of the IAEA from 1981 to 1997. He admitted: 'The IAEA was fooled by the Iraqis.' Blix was a compromise choice. The US and Britain had wanted Rolf Ekeus, who had run Unscom from 1991 to 1997, to come back.

So worried was the Pentagon by the choice of Blix that it asked the CIA to investigate him. When the agency failed to discover any evidence of wrongdoing, senior officials were said to have been furious. They tried another tack. They encouraged friendly

commentators in the US and UK to write pieces suggesting that
Blix did not have what it took to confront the canny Saddam, that he
would roll over the first time an obstacle was put in his way. 'The
people doing the briefing are the same people who didn't want Bush
to go to the UN in the first place,' one of Blair's aides commented at
the time. 'For us, the test in all this is to give Blix what he needs to do
the job. He's a good guy. We have to give him a resolution that is very
tough and serious but that is workable as well, not one that is just an
excuse for conflict.'

The French were prepared to accept a resolution that linked
Iraq's non-compliance with the threat of the use of force. What they
wanted to ensure, however, was that there was no immediate trigger
and that the Security Council would have to reconvene to discuss
consequent military action. Powell was determined not to allow that
to happen. Straw instructed Greenstock to come up with a compromise. The negotiations were enmeshed in linguistic nitpicking. The
French wanted wording that said Iraq 'might' face serious consequences. The US insisted on the word 'will'. Six weeks into the
process, the breakthrough was achieved. Igor Ivanov, the Russian
foreign minister, called Straw to tell him he had agreed not to veto a
deal. The next day De Villepin called Powell and the two came to an
agreement. Later, the Americans would allege that France's top
diplomat had gone back on his word and that he had promised his
country would back war if a second resolution were sought. The
French denied it, and the Americans struggled to produce evidence
to support the claim.

With the threat of vetoes lifted, the Americans and the British
wanted to extract the maximum possible authority for the resolution by ensuring that all ten non-permanent members of the
Security Council – elected for two-year periods – would also go
along with it. The hardest nut to crack was Syria. Bashar al-Assad's
mauling of Blair two months earlier did not augur well. The Syrians
were insisting on changes to wording already agreed with the
French. Chirac offered his services, spending half an hour with

Assad, trying to persuade him to accept what they hoped would be the final draft.

The British and Americans were determined to close the deal. On Wednesday, 6 November, Greenstock was asked by the Syrians to make one more concession. He rang Peter Ricketts, the Foreign Office's Political Director, on his mobile. He was asked by an usher to switch off his phone. He apologised for the break in protocol but told him it was important. Ricketts turned to Straw and asked if there were any more concessions to make. Straw replied: 'No – we're done.' The next day Straw and Colin Powell spoke to their Syrian counterpart. They knew at that point it was 14 to 1 in the Security Council. He urged them to delay a vote until after a meeting of the Arab League that weekend. Powell declined. Straw did the same. They called his bluff. Two hours before the vote, Greenstock called from New York to say the Syrians had come on board.

The UN Security Council passed Resolution 1441 unanimously on Friday 8 November. It was not exactly a British creation, but they did play a pivotal role in reconciling the differences. Or at least they *thought* they had reconciled the differences. Blair was proud of his diplomats' creative ambiguity.

Jack Straw was so pleased with the resolution he learned parts of it by heart. He could recite chunks from the first article denouncing Iraq's past practices, to the 'enhanced inspection regime' of article two, to article three that required the country to submit 'a currently accurate, full and complete declaration of all aspects of its programmes to develop chemical, biological and nuclear weapons' within thirty days. Article four set out the definition of non-compliance: 'False statements or omissions in the declarations submitted by Iraq pursuant to this resolution and failure by Iraq at any time to comply with, and co-operate fully in the implementation of, this resolution shall constitute a further material breach of Iraq's obligations.' Article five called for the inspectors to have 'immediate, unimpeded, unrestricted and private access to all officials'. They 'may at their discretion conduct interviews inside or outside of Iraq' and 'such interviews may occur without the presence of observers from the Iraqi government'.

Articles twelve and thirteen were crucial. The Security Council would, in the event of a material breach, 'convene immediately' upon receipt of the report 'in order to consider the situation'. The document concluded: 'The Council has repeatedly warned Iraq that it will face serious consequences as a result of its continued violations of its obligations.' These two articles gave all the negotiators what they wanted. The Americans did not have the automatic link between non-compliance and military action, but at the same time the French did not have the explicit requirement of a second UN resolution to authorise war. The Americans had an implicit threat of force that they could say was explicit, but 'serious consequences' fell far short of the standard formula – the 'all necessary means' of Resolution 678 in 1990, the precursor to the first Gulf War. The circumstances twelve years later had changed. Resolution 1441 contained an inherent contradiction. Either military action was automatic, or it required a second resolution. It had to be one or the other.

Blair knew this. At the same time, he could say that he had delivered Bush to the UN and the UN to Bush. He wanted to believe it would work. He also believed that in the harsh climate post-9/11 the only way for the UN to preserve its role in dealing with crises such as this was to approve American decisions. He assumed that it would.

This was the high point of Blair's diplomacy. It also laid the foundations for the crisis that was to unfold. Blair was committed to supporting Bush in his road to war. At the same time, he had foisted on him a process he was neither committed to nor understood. Blair found himself caught in the middle, the eternal triangulator seeking to reconcile two irreconcilable forces: American hyper-power and international diplomacy.

PART III

HOUNDED WARRIOR

11

COULD WE NOT DISAGREE
A BIT MORE?

THE SECRET DEAL STRUCK AT CAMP DAVID STILL STOOD.
George W. Bush had delivered on his pledge to pursue the diplomatic route. Tony Blair had promised that if the UN failed to force
Saddam Hussein to disarm, Britain would join America at war with
Iraq. But how and when was failure to be determined? This was
how Blair's adherence to the Americans' timetable would bring him
into conflict with his party, many in his country and much of the
world.

Five days after Resolution 1441 was passed, Saddam bowed to
the collective will of the international community and agreed to
allow the unconditional return of UN inspectors for the first time in
four years. At the same time he vehemently denied that Iraq had
developed weapons of mass destruction, 'whether nuclear, chemical,
or biological, as claimed by evil people'.

On 25 November 2002, the first experts from Unmovic and the
International Atomic Energy Agency arrived in Baghdad. Two days
later they set off from their headquarters early in the morning on
their first missions, splitting into teams and heading in opposite
directions. They were supposed to arrive at the sites unnoticed. They

gave no advance warning, but the surprise factor was somewhat ruined by car chases between journalists trying to keep up with the UN convoy. At one point, the cavalcade created an hour-long jam.

One team spent three hours at a military–industrial compound east of Baghdad, while another drove to a small complex west of the capital. The first day also took in a missile testing site and a graphite factory, all relatively close by. Unmovic and the IAEA declared themselves satisfied and said the Iraqis had given full co-operation. They accepted that the start had been relatively low-key, but once reinforcements arrived – giving them up to 100 inspectors at any one time – they would be able to fan out across the country. Still, the scenes on television of this very public investigation alarmed the people around Blair. They knew that this would play into the hands of critics in the US who had always regarded Blix as 'soft'. They were committed now. Blix had to be allowed to get on with it.

Under the terms of the resolution, Iraq had to provide within thirty days a 'currently accurate, full and complete declaration' of its arsenal. That was imminent. Blair knew that the Americans would seize on any obfuscation or lack of information as a trigger for war. London and Washington were already raising the stakes. They said the launch of ground-to-air missiles against US and British jets enforcing the no-fly zone constituted a 'breach' of Resolution 1441. The French, along with the Russians and Blix, said it amounted to no such thing. Blix was furious that the White House and Downing Street seemed to be dismissing the whole inspection exercise so soon.

The second week of inspections proceeded to the reasonable satisfaction of Unmovic. The experts made unannounced visits to two presidential palaces. The gates were opened and they were allowed in, something the Iraqis had refused to do when Unscom was around in the mid-1990s. The head of Iraq's National Monitoring Directorate and the liaison point with the inspectors, General Hassam Mohamed Amin, said Iraq would produce its declaration a day early. He said it would contain 'new elements', but added, ominously: 'We are a country devoid of weapons of mass destruction. This fact is known to all countries including the United States of America and Britain and all those concerned.'

Blair, meanwhile, exhorted his ministers to 'make the case' that, whatever Saddam might say, he posed a threat to the world. He turned to a method he had grown fond of – the dossier. This time, he wanted to paint a broader picture of the evil nature of the regime. On 4 December the Foreign Office presented a twenty-three-page document, 'Crimes and Human Rights Abuses', setting out two decades of atrocities, including torture, beheadings of women and the use of chemical weapons. A video showed footage of the Halabja massacre of 1988 and what appeared to be Iraqi soldiers ill-treating prisoners. Solemn music was played as a soundtrack. 'We're publishing this because, yes, it is important that people understand the comprehensive evil which is Saddam Husscin,' Jack Straw said. 'He's got these weapons of mass destruction, chemical, biological and, probably, nuclear weapons which he has used in the past against his own people as well as his neighbours and could almost certainly use again in the future,' he said. A few hours later he was forced to backtrack on the nuclear claim.

International human rights groups complained they had been trying to draw attention to abuses for years while British governments had been supporting Saddam. Amnesty International accused Blair and Straw of being selective, of ignoring other countries and suddenly picking Iraq's appalling human rights record to drive forward wider foreign and military goals. Even an Iraqi exile wheeled out by the government to reinforce the claims criticised Britain's 'silence' over the previous two decades. The assessment in Whitehall was not complimentary either. One senior official called it a 'shoddy piece of work, reliant on old material'.

The law of diminishing returns was beginning to apply to Blair's dossiers. Opinion polls were not budging. One survey, for Channel 4 News, suggested that one-third of Britons now believed that Bush posed a greater risk to world peace than Saddam. Blair had tried time and again to talk up the dangers. In a speech at the Lord Mayor's banquet, he spoke of the 'linked dangers' of terrorism and weapons of mass destruction. 'States which are failed, which repress their people brutally, in which notions of democracy and the rule of law are alien, share the same absence of rational boundaries to their actions as the terrorist.'

The public did see danger all around, but they were not attributing it to Iraq. Indeed, there was a sense among many that both Blair and Bush, in their desperation to soften up opinion for military action against Saddam, had taken their eye off the big war, against terrorism more broadly. Al-Qaeda was re-emerging as a serious threat. Its camps in Afghanistan might have been shut down. Osama bin Laden might have been driven out, injured or even killed. But, with an estimated 10,000 people trained by the network, eradicating the threat was a different proposition. Several worrying incidents had taken place in 2002. In March, five people, including two Americans, were killed in the bombing of a church in Islamabad. In April, a blast outside a synagogue in Djerba, Tunisia, killed twelve German tourists. In May, a car bomb in Karachi tore apart a busload of naval advisers, killing twelve Frenchmen and four Pakistanis.

The real wake-up call came on a Saturday night, 16 October, on the Indonesian island of Bali. The Sari Club, a popular drinking hole in the beach resort of Kuta, was heaving with young holiday-makers, mainly Australians. Approaching midnight, several car bombs were detonated outside the Sari and an Irish pub next door, sparking an inferno that would claim 200 lives. All indications pointed to the work of Jemaah Islamiyah, a militant Islamic group that had been operating in parts of the Indonesian archipelago with impunity.

A week later, a different terrorist attack took place, closer to home. Armed Chechen rebels, wired with explosives, seized a crowded Moscow theatre during the second act of a hit musical, *Nord-Ost*. For more than two days they held the audience and performers hostage. As fears mounted and conditions deteriorated,

Russian Special Forces used a previously untried gas to storm the building. All the rebels and 120 spectators died – almost all as a result of inhaling the toxic substance. The death toll was increased by the Russian government's refusal to tell anyone – even the doctors treating the victims – which gas they had used. Western leaders were in a predicament. They all knew they had to give public backing to Putin to stamp out terrorism. But there was alarm at the tactics used. Blair was one of the most effusive in his praise, phoning Putin within hours to congratulate him on ending the siege.

A month later came a third attack. On 28 November a troupe of Kenyan dancers was entertaining holidaymakers waiting to check into the Israeli-owned Paradise hotel in Mombasa when a four-wheel-drive car smashed through the entry barrier and pulled up outside. One man ran into the lobby and blew himself up. Two others detonated the car, which was packed with explosives. Some sixteen people – ten Kenyans, three Israelis and the three bombers – were killed. Minutes later, two ground-to-air missiles narrowly missed an Israeli charter Boeing 757 airliner leaving for Tel Aviv with 200 people on board. Another horror along the lines of September 11 had been narrowly averted. Nevertheless, terrorists had shown that they could strike anytime, anywhere. Al-Qaeda was all too pleased to claim responsibility.

It was not just 'non-state actors' who were causing alarm. North Korea, the last Stalinist redoubt of the Cold War, had been defying the international community for years in its desperate attempt to acquire nuclear weapons. In 1994, while Bill Clinton was president, the US had nearly gone to war with the secretive and impoverished state. William Perry, the US Defense Secretary at the time, would later admit 'we came much closer to a war then than most people in this room probably appreciate. We were willing to risk war because we believed that a nuclear weapons production programme in North Korea posed an unacceptable security risk.'

By December 2002 that risk had grown significantly when the government in Pyongyang announced it was restarting its one functional reactor, and re-opening other nuclear facilities frozen under the deal that had ended the previous stand-off. The Americans believed that in the intervening years North Korea had begun reprocessing spent fuel rods, providing enough plutonium to make several nuclear weapons. Some intelligence reports indicated they already had a small number of weapons. The Bush administration, obsessed as it was with Iraq, was only now beginning to engage with a problem that should have been one of its biggest international concerns. It had neither a strategy for military action – something that, with the number of US troops in South Korea, would almost certainly lead to a conflagration – nor for diplomacy. The Americans' caution towards North Korea highlighted how selectively the policy of preventing nuclear and other weapons proliferation was being applied. They avoided confronting countries they feared posed a danger too great.

On 7 December the neoconservatives had what they needed. With a flourish, General Amin drove to the UN compound in Baghdad to hand over crates of documents. He had earlier produced all the material at his headquarters for a photo call for the world's media. Piled on a long table were 43 spiral-bound volumes of documents, written in English, containing 12,159 pages, 6 folders and 12 CD-Roms. It was divided into three parts. The first covered the period from the end of the Gulf War. Most of the detail – 6,287 pages – focused on Iraq's 'missile activity'. Under UN resolutions imposed after the first Gulf War, Iraq was banned from holding missiles with a range greater than 150 kilometres. The section also explained Iraq's nuclear, chemical and biological activities. On the CDs, the second section comprised a series of six-monthly reports over the previous decade. The last section, 352 pages, covered the continuing monitoring process, including cameras, sensors and tags placed by UN weapons inspectors on suspect equipment. Amin said the declaration would answer 'all the questions which have been addressed during the last months and years'.

To add to the drama, Saddam issued a statement read out on state television apologising for the invasion of Kuwait in 1990: 'We apologise to God about any act that has angered him in the past and that was held against us, and we apologise to you [the Kuwaitis] on the same basis,' he said. He invited Kuwaitis to join his fight against the 'armies of occupation'.

The bulk of the documents were flown immediately to Unmovic's offices at the UN in New York. Those relating to a nuclear programme were sent to the IAEA in Vienna. Blix and Mohamed El Baradei, Director-General of the IAEA, had insisted their experts would need weeks to analyse the documents, and then months to cross-check the information inside Iraq. Blix said the material would be shared among the fifteen members of the Security Council.

That was too much for Bush. John Negroponte, the US Ambassador to the UN, who had gone along with Blix's original stipulations, was ordered by Bush and Powell to reverse them. The Americans claimed that the documents would contain information that could help rogue states construct the chemical, biological and nuclear weapons they were seeking to eradicate from Iraq. They demanded that they take charge of the papers. Kofi Annan complained, but the UN complied. The US then duplicated and distributed the documents to the other four permanent members of the Security Council and officially sanctioned nuclear states – Russia, China, Britain and France. The ten non-permanent members, who rotate every two years, were to be given edited highlights. Another reason for the reluctance was that the documents were believed to contain details of the extent to which the permanent members had helped arm Saddam in the past. One of those who did not appreciate such flashbacks was Rumsfeld, who as Ronald Reagan's Middle East envoy went to Baghdad in December 1983 – at a time when the Iraqis were using chemical weapons in their war against Iran – to discuss restoring diplomatic ties between Iraq and the US.

As the Americans went through the Iraqi declaration, they gave the British sneak previews. The news that came to Blair was gloomy. They told him most of the report was a recycling of information that was known either from public sources or from intelligence. One of Blair's key officials told him it was an 'exercise in obfuscation'. Another of his entourage recalls the moment when the Prime Minister believed that war had moved from being probable to being certain. 'Tony came into the room, looked at us and said, "He hasn't done it, has he?"' Blair told them this was 'the defining moment. That was his [Saddam's] big opportunity. He's blown it.' That was the consensus. 'We were surprised. This was a kind of declaration of war. We thought they would give us something – if not everything,' says one official.

Blair believed Saddam's last chance had gone. He concluded that a war he had committed himself to in principle in April 2002 was now unavoidable. He also knew the British public was not prepared for it.

Predictions among Blair's inner circle had varied. Some said Saddam just might do what was required of him. So important was his WMD programme that if he was forced to give it up, the nature of his regime would change. 'We didn't think it was a good chance. But we thought there was a chance he would conform,' recalls one aide. This was the scenario some members of the entourage were hoping for: 'We thought we could avoid war if the Security Council was united. We got that with 1441. We hoped then that Saddam might take fright and come clean. We knew we wouldn't get anything more than a one- or two-year delay from war, but that was good enough. I told the Prime Minister that even if others [the Americans] might not like it, we must accept this could happen.' The JIC assessments forecast that Saddam would not obey the UN resolution and that whoever had led the inspections, Blix or anyone else, the result would have been the same.

Blair told his team he would keep to his side of the Camp David deal. He knew it would not be easy to explain. They had bought into a UN resolution that was clear in the demands placed

on the Iraqis, but unclear about the mechanisms that would authorise military conflict. They had bought into a process that was based
on Saddam's WMD, nothing more. They feared they had bought
into an inspection process whose remit had been misunderstood.

The British were adamant that Blix had not been under any
instructions to find chemical or biological weapons. His job was to
verify those produced for him by the Iraqis and get credible explanations from them of what had happened to weapons they claimed
they had destroyed but which were still unaccounted for. British
diplomats involved in the drafting of Resolution 1441 would later
admit that Blix's role had been drawn up on a false premise. 'We
knew we had to get robust powers for the inspectors into the resolution to make it credible. Yet the idea wasn't for them to go fishing.
We knew he wasn't going to be able to show up at sites and find what
he was looking for. We should have made that clear to our publics,'
says one official. 'With hindsight we should have plonked Blix in a
hotel in Baghdad and told him to tell the Iraqis to come to him if
they had anything they wanted him to see.'

The neoconservatives had consistently argued that the onus
was on the Iraqis to go to Blix, not the other way round. It was not
simply out of disdain that Wolfowitz played down the role of the
inspectors. 'It is not and it cannot be their responsibility to scour
every inch of Iraq to search out and find every illegal weapon or programme,' he said. That is not how Blix chose to interpret it, nor
most of the world's governments or public opinion.

Saddam's 12,000-page declaration had played straight into the
hands of the hawks. In the Pentagon and in the Vice-President's
office there was relief that Saddam had not complied. They knew
that co-operation would have set back the prospects of a war they
were eager to prosecute. On the other hand, they felt angry and
frustrated with Blair and Colin Powell for persuading Bush to go to
the UN in the first place.

On 19 December Bush declared Iraq to be in 'material breach'.
A beleaguered Powell referred to 'omissions' and 'obvious false-

hoods', but stopped one step short of talking of war. 'Iraq's non-compliance and defiance of the international community has brought it closer to the day when it has to face the consequences,' he said. 'This declaration fails totally to move us in the direction of a peaceful solution.' Jack Straw offered a variant on the same theme: 'There has already been one trigger pulled. They [the Iraqis] now, in a sense, have their finger on the other trigger.'

Blix too was disappointed. Privately, he told his aides that Saddam was behaving 'like an old emperor of Mesopotamia'. He added: 'He might not like having foreigners crawling around his country, but if he wants to get out of this mess then he has to engage with us.' Blix agreed with the US and British assessment that most of the information had been rehashed and that on a strict reading of 1441 Saddam had not complied with the demands to account for his weapons. If he had got rid of chemical and biological materials and their delivery systems, he would surely have paperwork and other evidence to prove it. But, using the same logic, Blix was adamant that Saddam's documents did not provide evidence that he still actually had WMD. He suggested that if the Americans or British knew better, they should produce evidence of their own. 'The most important thing that governments like the UK or the US could give us would be to tell us sites where they are convinced that they keep some WMD. This is what we want to have. They have all the methods to listen to telephone conversations, they have spies, they have satellites, so they have a lot of sources which we do not have.'

From this point, the paths diverged sharply. Armed with a list of more than 1,000 scientists and technicians, Blix's team started conducting interviews with individual experts. The Iraqi authorities initially insisted that they be chaperoned. To the British and Americans, this was laughable. The scientists would be in fear of their lives and would not say anything under those conditions. They reminded Blix of the terms of 1441, which also provided for the scientists to be taken outside Iraq. Britain had offered military bases in Cyprus. Blix said there was no question of 'abducting' any of them, while those who might want to leave voluntarily would have to consider the consequences for any family members left behind.

Blair was becoming alarmed. He feared the UN process was unravelling. His confidence in Blix was beginning to wane. He was convinced that the Iraqis were giving Unmovic 'the runaround'. But he also accepted it was vital for the inspectors to come up with something. He was prepared to give Blix more time – and to convince Bush to give him more time. He was prepared to provide British intelligence material to help him.

Britain's military chiefs were becoming agitated. The Americans had permanent stocks of matériel for desert conditions. The British, to save costs, tended to buy them in. They had some desert uniforms and boots from a major exercise conducted in Oman in the autumn of 2001. But they needed much more. They needed to sandproof tanks and artillery. They needed to charter ships. There was the question of mobilising reservists. They and their employers needed time. The regular soldiers and their families needed time. At the Pentagon detailed planning had already taken place for a potential war. Rumsfeld had, as a contingency, set an informal target date of 15 February 2003 for full deployment of US forces. Nothing like that was being done in the UK because the politicians were prevaricating. 'This was desperate for us,' recalls one senior defence official. 'With the US, the sooner you decide in a general way that you're happy to participate, the more influence you get. From September we had wanted to start planning, to buy kit, to explain the situation to our forces, warn their units and their families, but we were prevented from doing so.'

In the middle of December the military told Geoff Hoon they needed deployment decisions within weeks. Hoon told Blair. They were asked if they could leave the announcements as late as they practically could. At this time, senior Foreign Office officials were talking up the political difficulty of sending troops. They cited not just overstretch, with army units involved in the fire service strike in the UK, but also the political atmosphere. They talked openly of the US needing Britain far more politically than militarily. Blair was undecided about when to make the announcement of deployments. He knew he could not delay indefinitely. In his Christmas message to the armed forces Blair admitted the strategy was unclear. 'I am sorry about the uncertainty,' he told them. 'I am afraid it is inevitable though, because at the moment we simply don't know whether Iraq will be found in breach.'

Over the holiday period Blair spent time talking to his family and reflecting. The goodwill and the benefit of the doubt that he had enjoyed a year earlier after the war against Afghanistan, and with the country still traumatised by 9/11, had turned to confusion and, within his own ranks, anger. He confided to friends that he feared he was losing his moral authority over the Labour Party, if not his control. Although in public he used the refrain 'war is not inevitable', he knew that only a miracle could stop it. In any case, why should he want to anyway?

He was reconciled to war. In his New Year's message he painted an irredeemably bleak picture. 'I cannot recall a time when Britain was confronted, simultaneously, by such a range of difficult and, in some cases, dangerous problems.' He listed his worries as: 'Iraq, and the prospect of committing UK troops to act if Saddam Hussein continues to flout international law; the mass of intelligence flowing across my desk that points to a continuing threat of attack by al-Qaeda; the lack of progress in the Middle East peace process and more recently the disturbing developments over North Korea's nuclear programme.' He concluded by warning that the future of Britain was at stake: 'Whether we survive and prosper or decline in the face of this insecurity depends crucially on the political decisions Britain now takes.'

Within days that sense of insecurity was brought home, when police found traces of the chemical ricin in a raid on a flat in Wood Green, north London, during which North African men were detained. Each discovery, each terrorist alert, played both ways for Blair. They emphasised the seriousness of the global situation. At the same time they cast further doubt on his order of priorities. Why Iraq?

Like some of his predecessors – Margaret Thatcher in particular – Blair had become frustrated at the ways of the Foreign Office. He had handpicked a new team of diplomats at the top, but as an institution he still felt the FCO was unreliable, bureaucratic and soft, invariably citing reasons not to act. Jonathan Powell had suggested bringing back the entire complement of British ambassadors, from the prestigious postings like Washington, Paris and Moscow to those envoys in far-flung places from whom little was heard in Downing Street. The two-day get-together was organised by the FCO, but this was Blair's opportunity to set out his view of the world. He started off with a joke about how he arrived in one country, having been told there would be no welcoming party, only to see out of his window a red carpet, the host president and a military guard. His suits had all been packed in the hold. He was in T-shirt and jeans. Without being asked, a diplomat travelling with him, of a fortunately similar build, offered up his suit.

Blair listed the principles that guided his foreign policy. The order he placed them in spoke volumes. 'First, we should remain the closest ally of the US, and as allies influence them to continue broadening their agenda. We are the allies of the US not because they are powerful, but because we share their values. I am not surprised by anti-Americanism; but it is a foolish indulgence. For all their faults, and all nations have them, the US are a force for good; they have liberal and democratic traditions of which any nation can be proud.' He suggested other countries were jealous of those relations.

The problem people have with the US – not the rabid anti-Americans, but the average middle ground – is not that, for example, they oppose them on WMD or international terrorism. People listen to the US on these issues and may well agree with them; but they want the US to listen back. The price of

British influence is not – as some would have it – that we have obediently to do what the US asks. I would never commit British troops to a war I thought was wrong or unnecessary.

Important, but seemingly subordinate to that priority, were: being at the heart of Europe and engaging with China, Russia and India.

Blair described his fourth priority as drawing on Britain's influence as a former colonial power. 'Our history is our strength,' he declared in a mild rebuke to Jack Straw, who had said two months earlier: 'A lot of the problems we are having to deal with now, I have to deal with now, are a consequence of our colonial past.' Blair made clear: 'Our empire left much affection as well as deep problems to be overcome.' Fifthly, Blair focused on global inequality. 'There can be no new consensus, no new order, no stability, without tackling the appalling poverty that afflicts nearly half of the world's population.' His sixth point was related. He wanted to make the IMF and World Bank more responsive to the needs of the developing world, to provide more incentives for poor countries to reform their economies. Finally, he called on British diplomats to reach out to the Muslim world.

> It is about even-handedness. The reason there is opposition over our stance on Iraq has less to do with any love of Saddam, but over a sense of double standards. The Middle East peace process remains essential to any understanding with the Muslim and Arab world . . . Unless there is real energy put into crafting a process that can lead to lasting peace, neither the carnage of innocent Israelis nor the appalling suffering of the Palestinians will cease. At the moment the future of the innocent is held hostage by the terrorists.

The public part of the meeting over, Blair then presided over a question-and-answer session with his ambassadors. He asked for contributions about how Britain was perceived. The responses were

respectful but candid. The word 'poodle' was offered up, in embarrassment, several times. 'We could be less subservient in public.
While staying loyal to the Americans, we can still be ready to be
more outspoken when we disagree,' said one senior envoy. Blair said
he agreed. He then asked John Holmes, the Ambassador to Paris and
his former right-hand man in Downing Street, for a résumé of
French perceptions of Britain's position. Holmes said the gulf was
widening, adding whether 'it mightn't be a bad idea if we could disagree with the Americans a bit more publicly'.

12

OLD AND NEW

BACK IN 1997 IT HAD STARTED SO WELL. WITHIN WEEKS OF welcoming Bill Clinton to Downing Street on a glorious May morning, Blair was cycling to victory at his first EU summit in Amsterdam. There was nothing incongruous about those two meetings. This was exactly the role he wanted to play – the bridge between the old continent and the new. There had been problems – over Operation Desert Fox and, in a different way, over Kosovo – but they were overcome with minimum acrimony. Blair did not have to make the choice he always said he never wanted to make.

His cause was helped by a rare period of discord between France and Germany. The European motor that had been so powerful in the 1980s and early 1990s under Helmut Kohl and François Mitterrand, had spluttered when Jacques Chirac and Gerhard Schröder came together. By the end of the 1990s Blair had successfully positioned Britain as an influential counter-weight between Paris and Berlin.

Prompted by Peter Mandelson, who kept a close watch on German politics, Blair hailed Schröder's election in 1998 as an important opportunity. New Labour had been wooing the 'modernising' wing of the Social Democrats for some time. It was far closer to the Blair project than anything Lionel Jospin in France could offer – not that he ever wanted to. On 8 June 1999, Blair and Schröder marched on to the podium at Millbank Tower, Labour's headquarters, to launch their joint document 'The Third Way – Die Neue Mitte'. Blair declared that they had found the key; they had managed to reconcile continental social democracy with the leaner and meaner Anglo-Saxon version. They had found a new ideology that would guarantee power for Europe's centre-left for years to come. Blair praised what he said was 'a new generation of centre-left leaders' across Europe. Of the fifteen EU countries, eleven were either governed fully or in coalition by parties of the centre-left.

This was the high water-mark of the Third Way, characterised by a succession of summits, gatherings and 'think-ins' presided over by Blair, Clinton, Schröder and leaders and politicians from other countries, hopeful that some of their reformist zeal might rub off on them. But much of it turned out to be a chimera. Schröder was punished at the European elections, in regional elections and at party conferences for flirting with policies that were anathema to a more collectivist body politic. He quickly disengaged from New Labour thinking. Blair gradually became disillusioned with him. In Lisbon in March 2000 the British tried hard to push a set of economic reforms through the EU. But for all the millennial optimism of the 'dot-com' summit, little came of it. Blair, the man in a hurry, the man who liked to get his way, ran up against the frustrations of a group that was more quizzical about change *per se*.

These were unnerving times for the French elite. The cohabitation between Chirac, a right-wing President, and Jospin, a left-wing Prime Minister, stymied decision-making. France's clout internationally was also suffering. Neither men got on particularly well with Schröder, who had served notice that he would be less willing to compromise Germany's national interest for the sake of Europe as a whole. He was quite happy to do his line in Teutonic Thatcherite handbagging to get his way. The sight of Blair bestriding the European stage further undermined France's position. French newspapers started to goad Chirac for losing the leadership in European construction. They urged him to do something about the 'British takeover' of Brussels.

Blair always found Jospin 'cold' and 'stiff'. With Chirac, he trod carefully. On one level they enjoyed good banter, partly in English, partly in French, partly in Franglais. Blair indulged Chirac's need to be seen as the father figure, schooling his bright son. 'With Jacques you have to play him for what he likes,' Blair confided in his aides. 'Chirac doesn't like anyone to be his equal.' Chirac's relations with Bush got off to a reasonable start. The two men treated each other with caution, but respect. As French diplomats admit, Chirac blew an important opportunity when shortly after 9/11 during his visit to Washington he appeared to qualify his expressions of sympathy and solidarity by talking about the need for the US to engage in the issues that gave rise to terrorism. That was a miscalculation – wrong time, wrong place. This allowed Blair to consolidate his position as first among friends, seeking to influence Bush from the cosy inside, rather than from the prickly outside as Chirac was seeking to do.

As France's presidential elections approached in May 2002, with the polls pointing to a comfortable victory for Chirac in a run-off with Jospin, Blair was working on the assumption of a second term for Chirac. He was careful not to be seen to be endorsing the Socialists. The catastrophic result for the left in the first round would change the nature of Franco-British relations far more than anyone realised at the time. Chirac consolidated his thumping victory over Jean-Marie Le Pen of the far right National Front in parliamentary elections the following month, in which the left once again was humiliated. Cohabitation was over, and for the first time since entering the Elysée Palace seven years before, Chirac was the master of all he surveyed.

By that point the German elections were in full swing, but Schröder was in a very different position. Even though the right's candidate, Edmund Stoiber, presented an unappealing alternative,

Schröder began the campaign as the underdog. He seized on two developments for all they were worth. Floods had engulfed much of the country and the Chancellor's response, cancelling his scheduled events and rushing down to the banks of the Elbe to help stricken towns and villages – and to be seen by television cameras to be helping – reaped huge dividends. For once, he was showing leadership.

Iraq was the other issue. Schröder had been staunch in his support for Bush in the aftermath of 9/11 and in the war in Afghanistan. The Americans appreciated the solidarity, but expected as much from a country that had been on the front line of the Cold War and where tens of thousands of US troops had been based for decades. Whereas in sixteen years Kohl did not have to commit German troops to war, early on Schröder sent his forces to Kosovo. He did the same in Macedonia and Afghanistan. For the Chancellor, and particularly his foreign minister, Joschka Fischer, this was a considerable political risk, challenging the deep pacifist and non-militarist convictions of post-1945 Germany. Fischer argued passionately the case for liberal intervention against the resistance of most in his Green party. In November 2001, soon after the fall of Kabul, Blair was given a standing ovation at the SPD's annual conference after giving a ringing endorsement to Germany's more interventionist role.

For most Germans, however, the war on Iraq was beyond the pale. Public opinion moved steadily after Bush's 'axis of evil' speech in January 2002. Schröder knew he could not endorse the US position, but he was hoping to tread a careful line. During a visit to Berlin that May, the Americans say Schröder gave Bush a private assurance in a one-to-one conversation that he would choose his words carefully in the election campaign, that he would not seek to exploit the issue. Gradually, as the polls moved against him, so Schröder sharpened his rhetoric against the war. 'He was agnostic about the war. With the economy in trouble and with other things going wrong, the only area where his ratings were consistently high was opposition to US military plans,' says an aide of the German Chancellor. 'He got sucked into it.' He started talking of American 'adventures' and making it clear he would not support them. Matters came to a head when he was forced to sack his justice minister, Herta Däubler-Gmelin, after she drew parallels between Bush and Hitler. In a frenetic end to the campaign Schröder was making several campaign speeches a day. Increasingly they revolved around Iraq. In one, he took a swipe at Blair. 'With all respect for Tony Blair, he on his own does not speak for Europe on this issue or on others. We have absolutely no reason to change our well-founded position. Under my leadership, Germany will not take part in an intervention in Iraq.' So popular was this rhetoric that even the hesitant Stoiber was forced to announce that he would not allow American jets to fly over Germany on their way to Iraq.

Schröder scraped home, thanks in large measure to his position on Iraq. This now presented him with a desperate problem – how to repair relations with Washington. Bush was furious. The French had, since De Gaulle's time, kept one step removed, but not the Germans, who had the Americans to thank for decades of Cold War defence. Germany had been doing a lot that the US should have approved of. They had pushed hard against French resistance to get Turkey into the EU. They were taking the lead in peacekeeping in Afghanistan and in the Balkans. 'We wanted to be good without actually saying sorry,' says one senior German official.

Blair volunteered his services as a transatlantic marriage counsellor. In the last days of the German election campaign, as a favour to Schröder he gave several interviews to German TV expressing support and refusing to criticise him over Iraq, saying obliquely that Schröder had 'asked the questions that needed to be asked'. At Camp David he tried to reassure Bush. He told him Schröder had his back against the wall and with public opinion where it was, he had to say the things he did. Blair said he was sure Schröder would want to rebuild bridges. Crucially, Blair told Bush that after the election, if Schröder did win, he could 'turn him', bring him round to supporting the Americans, or at the very least to refrain from opposing them.

Two days after securing his tight election victory, Schröder went to London for dinner in Downing Street. That in itself was remarkable. The traditional first port of call for a German leader was Paris. But Schröder felt he did not have much to thank Chirac for. The French President had hardly endeared himself to Schröder by openly courting Stoiber and then, in the middle of the campaign, awarding the Bavarian opposition leader the *Légion d'honneur*.

Throughout this period, for all their differences, Blair and Schröder enjoyed, as one official put it, 'a very high comfort level'. Their dinner was a discreet affair, only the two of them plus an interpreter. Schröder asked for advice on how to repair relations with the US. Blair told him that while he understood his election predicament, Germany now had nothing to gain from a rupture with Washington. He suggested that the German leader make some kind of pledge of Atlanticism and make clear that his statements on Iraq during the campaign had been a 'one-off'. Schröder had been taken to Number 10 by Thomas Matussek, the German Ambassador to London and a young and modernising influence. Matussek told him in the car that he had met Henry Kissinger in London at a conference the day before. He told him what Kissinger had said: 'You guys are really in trouble. Don't come knocking at our doors, but show by your deeds where you stand.'

Overtures were made, but the reconciliation did not happen. Schröder did tone down his language, but he showed no signs of moving towards Blair's approach. The Prime Minister began to despair of him. Using the New Labour lexicon that comes naturally to Blair's aides, one put it like this: 'Tony likes Gerd on a personal level, but he knows he doesn't deliver.'

That autumn Chirac and Schröder, encouraged by their advisers, formed the beginnings of an awkward alliance. To the consternation of Downing Street, Paris and Berlin started producing joint papers for the first time in several years on internal European reform. Chirac, emboldened by his much stronger second mandate, needed an ally to reverse what he saw as the creeping Anglicisation

of the European Commission in Brussels. He also did not appreciate
British spin on Europe. He was reminded of how, back in December
1997, Blair summoned ambassadors to Waterloo Station for a piece
of showmanship marking the UK's six-month presidency of the EU.
It was all style – a Eurostar train gliding in to the platform. The
train had come not from across the Channel but from just a mile up
the line. When it came to the substance, Blair's hesitations on the
Euro convinced the French elite that Britain was not committed to
the European agenda and that it wished to remain in its traditional
position of straddling the two continents.

On the evening of 24 October, Blair had flown to Brussels for
one of those interminable EU meetings. This one was more important than most. It was due to discuss the financial consequences of
the accession of new members from Central and Eastern Europe.
Blair arrived later than most of the other leaders. He had had a lot
on his mind, including a reshuffle after the sudden resignation of
one of his Cabinet ministers, Estelle Morris. On the eve of the
summit, as an opening gambit, Chirac suggested that the rebate
Margaret Thatcher had negotiated for Britain back in 1984 should
be thrown into the negotiations. Blair rejected this out of hand and
saw it as nothing more than a gesture by the French to show who
was boss. But Blair and his Europe advisers made one of their most
serious miscalculations that day. They knew Chirac and Schröder
were due to meet, but they failed to see that the two were about to
stitch up an agreement on farming subsidies – the biggest burden on
the EU budget – and then present that to the others as a *fait accom-
pli*. Straw was meeting Britain's Ambassador to the EU, Nigel
Sheinwald, at a hotel up the road. They were told journalists were
reporting that the French and Germans had struck a deal on the
Common Agricultural Policy.

As Straw quickly swotted up on the documents, Blair was
meeting Chirac for a scheduled 'bilateral'. The Prime Minister
emerged from their short meeting in a state of shock. Chirac had, he
told his advisers, been at his most patronising. Instead of a discus-

sion, the President had delivered a lecture on the CAP, on the EU in general, and Iraq. 'How would you be able to look Leo in the eye in twenty years' time if you are the leader who helped start a war?' Chirac asked him. That infuriated Blair. When Leo was born in May 2000, Chirac was one of the first guests seen cuddling the new baby in his arms. A photograph of that moment, signed by Chirac, hung on Blair's wall.

The following day, at the plenary session, Blair told the other heads of government the deal was invalid. Straw pointed out to Blair, as he was going along, lines in the relevant document, the 'Berlin conclusions' of March 1999. The Foreign Secretary knew by heart what paragraph 22 said about the 'mid-term review' and what paragraph 72 said about the 'abatement', the UK's rebate. Straw told Blair that Chirac's claim that a review of farm subsidies was not necessary before 2006 showed 'basically he was lying'. Blair turned to him and whispered: 'You'd better bloody well be right.' He then read out the paragraphs to the assembled audience. Joschka Fischer piped up and confirmed what Blair had said. Sensing that the room was with him, Blair then told the other leaders that an unreformed CAP was doing irrevocable damage to the Third World.

It was a moral victory for Blair, but it had its consequences. As the meeting broke up and the ministers gathered their papers, Chirac contrived to collide with Blair. His foreign minister, Dominique de Villepin, and other officials stood behind him, as one British witness put it, 'like lads looking for a brawl outside a pub on a Friday night'. Chirac and Blair are tall men. The French President went eyeball to eyeball with him, gesticulating, almost prodding Blair in the chest. He told him: 'You are very rude and I have never been spoken to like this before.' Blair tried the lofty response. 'I've noted what you said, Jacques. I have a different point of view. I'd like to point out that—' He was not allowed to finish. Chirac marched off, beckoning his officials to follow.

Chirac had been looking for an excuse to have a public row with Blair. From 9/11 to the European convention, he had had enough of the Prime Minister upstaging him. As he stormed out of the room, Chirac told Blair, then his own officials, that he was cancelling the annual Franco-British summit. Blair and Campbell were alarmed, partly by the developments on the CAP, but more by the way they feared the news might break. With officials from fifteen member states bearing witness to the argument, they were sure the story would come out. They took the decision to get their story in first, to portray it as a British victory. Godric Smith, one of Blair's official spokesmen, briefed several Sunday broadsheets about the confrontation. But the papers were full of graphic accounts of the siege at the Moscow theatre, and a complicated story about European agriculture did not compete. He had another go on Sunday, for the Monday papers.

The advice from British officials was to keep it quiet. One serving senior ambassador recalls how he first saw the story in the *Financial Times*. He had assumed it came from another capital, not from Number 10. 'I did not imagine they would have done something as crass as that,' he recalls.

This was an example of Blair and Campbell's predilection for short-term news management over long-term strategy. Another serving ambassador says it typified Blair's problems with Europe. He describes Blair's presentations at summits like this.

> Blair's arguments are coherent and persuasive. They are not profound. He reads little. You have the impression some of the time that he's not listening. He is given reams of briefing notes. He hardly reads them. His interventions at European councils are often banal and platitudinous. He often gets frustrated, wondering why things don't happen the way he wants them to. He likes to tickle. His genius is as a presenter, articulator or evangelist. He often fails to engage in the detail. We often got frustrated with him. We would cover up for him all the time, especially his negotiating skills. We've missed serious tricks over the years.

In global terms, 'le row', as it came to be known in Westminster, seemed trivial and avoidable. It was. It may have been more of a symptom than a cause of a big problem, but it played a major role in ensuring that bad blood remained – just at a time when the two countries needed to work together. The rift between London and Paris coincided with growing differences on how UN Resolution 1441 on Iraq was being interpreted. Chirac's distant respect for Bush soon turned to disdain. He could understand why Blair had got on with Clinton, and had made compromises for him. He simply could not comprehend the political or personal rationale behind the Blair–Bush relationship. That relationship damned Blair in Chirac's eyes. Chirac put out feelers to Vladimir Putin, the Russian President. His contacts with Schröder intensified. He calculated that a stronger alliance with Berlin would boost France's diplomatic leverage and lock the traditionally Atlanticist Germany in the anti-war camp. Fischer was more circumspect.

Bush used a visit to Europe at the end of November to give the Germans a ticking off. As had been the case the previous year, the US President again felt more comfortable, more appreciated, in the East than in the West. The main reason for the trip was a Nato summit in Prague, when seven former Communist countries were formally invited to join the alliance. Bush confronted Schröder about the resumption of his anti-war rhetoric. He had been told that again it was part of political campaigning, this time for two regional elections. An exasperated Bush then turned to Joschka Fischer and asked him: 'When are your damned elections over?'

The spat was important for Bush also in his relations with Blair. The Prime Minister had told him he would fix relations between Germany and the US. For all his good intentions, he had failed to do so. Bush would remember that.

All this time Blair believed Chirac's anger was manufactured. He was doing nothing more than protecting French interests in Iraq, playing sides off against each other and posturing. When push came to shove, assuming French oil interests in Iraq were secured, Chirac would fall into line. He had done so in the first Gulf War. This is what French leaders did. Schröder was being awkward, but Germany was not a permanent member of the UN Security Council and did not want to cause trouble. As for Putin, Blair was convinced all the way that the Russian President was too much of a pragmatist to antagonise the Americans. In any case, why would he side with Chirac and Schröder, who had been far more outspoken in their criticism of Russian actions in Chechnya than the British government had been?

Blair got all of the above wrong.

As 2002 drew to a close, there were bigger forces at work than tactics. Javier Solana, the EU's foreign policy chief, pointed to what he called a 'cultural phenomenon' dividing the US and Europe. The US saw foreign policy from a religious point of view, he said. 'It is a kind of binary model. It is all or nothing. For us Europeans it is difficult to deal with because we are secular. We do not see the world in such black and white terms.' He did not mention Blair.

In his own New Year's message, Chirac sent out mixed signals. He told the French people it was 'safe to assume' demands would continue on the French military where it was already involved, adding, 'There may also, unfortunately, be new theatres.' That message was interpreted in the French press as sounding hawkish about Iraq. Blair seized on it to confirm his conviction that Chirac would eventually come round. The Americans were not so sure. They did not like what he said when entertaining Hans Blix in Paris in the middle of January. Any unilateral military action, Chirac declared, would be in breach of international law. He added: 'In life, you know one must not confuse friends with sycophants. It is better to have only a few friends than to have a lot of sycophants.'

The British might have been confused about the French, but the French concluded early in January that the British position had changed. 'Something happened to Blair over Christmas,' one senior official remarked. 'He's lost patience with the whole process. He's moved completely into the American camp.'

Any lingering doubts the British or Americans had about the French position ended on 20 January. This was Martin Luther King Day. Colin Powell had been due to address a number of meetings celebrating the black civil rights campaigner. Instead, he had to go to the UN in New York. The French held the rotating monthly chair of the Security Council. De Villepin, their foreign minister, called an unexpected meeting to discuss 'anti-terrorism'. That was relatively uneventful. Afterwards, however, at a press briefing, De Villepin launched a full-frontal assault on the US approach to Iraq. 'If war is the only way to resolve this problem, we are going down a dead end,' he said. 'Nothing today justifies envisaging military action.' That day was dubbed 'the ambush' and the 'French resistance'. Powell was furious. He had already lost any remaining faith in the Iraqis after their 12,000-page document in December. Now he lost any residual faith in the French. The neocons in the administration had a long time previously lost any remaining faith in him – and Blair. Powell's world was collapsing around him. One of Straw's jobs was to 'track his mood'. They would, according to one official, 'cry telephonically on each other's shoulders'.

On 22 January, in the resplendent surroundings of Versailles, the French and German leaders, their Cabinets and their two parliaments – the Assemblée Nationale and the Bundestag – met in joint session to celebrate forty years of the Elysée Treaty. The pomp and the poignancy was lost on no one. Chirac and Schröder consolidated their newfound friendship and vowed to work together on Iraq. On the eve of that meeting, the Chancellor had told an SPD rally: 'Don't expect Germany to approve a resolution which would give legitimacy to war.' Chirac declared before the joint gathering: 'War is always an admission of failure. Everything must be done to avoid it.'

Blair was faced with two unpalatable realities: the old axis at the heart of Europe was back, and the gap between America and Europe was wider than it had been at any time since Vietnam. He kept his counsel. In Washington, Donald Rumsfeld did not.

'Germany has been a problem and France has been a problem,' he told Washington's foreign press corps the following day. 'If you look at the whole of Europe today, the centre of gravity is shifting to the East. You look at vast numbers of other countries in Europe, they're not with France and Germany . . . they're with the US. You're thinking of Europe as Germany and France. I don't. I think that's old Europe.' Reaction in Berlin and Paris was furious. Reaction in London was mixed. Blair told his aides that the diplomatic wrangling was not helped by Rumsfeld shooting from the hip as he so often did. At the same time, it probably was not a bad thing for someone to tell Chirac some home truths.

Blair's relations with the Germans were becoming equally fraught. Mandelson, who had invested much in maintaining good links, wrote with Blair's authority to Matussek, the German envoy to London, expressing hurt and exasperation. 'I'm at a loss with you,' the letter began. Campbell, Mandelson and Philip Gould, Blair's pollster, all accepted invitations to dinner and told their host in no uncertain terms that the Germans had not played their part. Matters came to a head when John Reid, then Labour Party Chairman, confronted the Germans at – of all places – a reception at the Israeli ambassador's residence. In front of the assembled diplomats, Reid shouted: 'You guys are dishonest and shameful. Your level of argument is lower than that of my constituents.' Matussek responded, ever so demurely, that at least he didn't change his reasons for war every fortnight.

Around this time, Mike Gonzalez, a journalist on the *Wall Street Journal*, had an idea for an opinion piece. The deputy editor of the paper's European edition, who was based in Brussels, wondered whether one or two European governments who did not share the Franco-German worldview might want to offer their thoughts on his pages. He placed a call to a friend in the Italian government, asking whether Silvio Berlusconi, the Prime Minister, might want to write a piece. After that he dialled a Spanish source and put the idea to him as well. Out of those conversations the idea emerged of an article written by the leaders of Spain, Italy and the UK – the three countries most in tune with the US. Gonzalez's London-based colleague e-mailed Campbell. He said he would think about, but suggested it was unlikely Blair would want to do it. Shortly after, Campbell confirmed his original view. 'I regret that due to other media commitments at this stage, the PM won't be able to do this. Sorry to send a disappointing reply.'

Gonzalez *was* disappointed. But on 25 January, out of the blue, he received a call from Madrid. His contact there said the three prime ministers were working on a first draft.

Blair felt comfortable with José María Aznar, Spain's first right-wing leader in two decades of democracy. Blair liked him for his sobriety, austerity and Atlanticism. The two had always got on well. The problems with Chirac and Schröder were bringing them even closer. Aznar was angry that the French and Germans gave the impression at the UN and elsewhere that they represented the views of the EU. He told Blair: 'We cannot let the European view be misrepresented in this way.' Blair's relationship with Berlusconi was more circumspect – after all, the media tycoon's mix of business and politics was not for the squeamish – but it was not so circumspect to prevent Blair from lobbying the Italian premier on behalf of a deal Rupert Murdoch was wanting to strike early in 1998.

In one of their regular phone chats, Aznar and Blair discussed the *Wall Street Journal* idea. They decided it would be good to bring in others. On 29 January Madrid and London produced nearly identical drafts of what would be an open letter. Gonzalez was told there might be six signatures, but one of Blair's conditions for the letter was that it be given, as well as to the *WSJ*, to one newspaper per signatory country. When Václav Havel, the Czech President, agreed at the last minute to join them, they were up to eight. Portugal, Hungary, Poland and Denmark signed as well. The wording was agreed. The letter began by saying Europe shared many values with America, including 'democracy, individual freedom, human rights and the rule of law'. It added: 'The Iraqi regime and its weapons of mass destruction represent a clear threat to world security . . . We must remain united in insisting his regime is disarmed.' Europe, or at least that part of it, was foursquare behind the US. Other former Communist countries were clamouring to show their loyalty to Washington. Ten more leaders would later sign a similar letter of their own, a gesture of defiance that led a furious Chirac to launch a tirade against them at an EU conference. 'They missed a great opportunity to shut up,' he chided the applicant countries. Blair responded by quietly writing to each of the ten leaders a note of support.

On the afternoon of 29 January, Gerard Errera set off from his office in Knightsbridge for a very important meeting. Ambassadors to the Court of St James did not often get the privilege of seeing the Foreign Secretary. They were hardly ever given a one-on-one with the Prime Minister. But the French ambassador was a serious player. Before arriving the previous September he had been Political Director at the Quai d'Orsay – one of the top jobs in the administration. He had been Ambassador to Nato and had served in Washington. The man he replaced in London, Daniel Bernard, was jocular, ebullient and popular. His outspoken manner had got him into trouble when his description of Israel as a 'shitty little country' made it from the dinner party table to the newspapers. He was dispatched without ceremony to Algiers. Chirac wanted a big hitter to keep tabs on Blair. The Prime Minister's office had let it be known in early January that he would like a meeting. The date agreed turned out to be a little awkward for him.

With a warm handshake, Blair welcomed Errera into his Downing Street office, the den. Powell was there, as was Matthew Rycroft, a member of his foreign policy team. They got down to business quickly. Blair had two messages. We, the British, have to be more European. That included the Euro. 'I want to do it before the end of the parliament, so that the British people feel more at ease with Europe,' he told him. But, as for America's relations with Europe, Blair insisted people should be under no illusions. It was not a relationship of equals. He then moved to the specific dynamics of France. 'In France you have to make up your mind, to come to an arrangement with the US, or to lead a crusade against them,' Blair told him. Errera replied that France had no quarrel with the US or Nato, but the Americans did not listen. He harked back to September 11, to the huge reservoir of solidarity the French expressed for America. 'The Americans had the world at their feet. We had a dream of a new beginning,' Errera told him. All that was wasted by Bush's actions in subsequent months. He stressed good transatlantic ties were just as important for the French as they were for the British, but they could not be based around one side deciding the rules. He also agreed that relations between France and the UK had taken a knock. Chirac's re-election had not brought about a new beginning. The two men agreed on that and promised to make greater efforts to improve matters. They ended the meeting as warmly as they had begun.

A few hours later all hell broke loose at the Quai d'Orsay. Television news was reporting that the British and other European leaders had signed an open letter. They were calling it 'the letter of eight'. Not only had Blair not even given Errera so much as a hint, his old friend Peter Ricketts, the Political Director at the FCO, had let on nothing when they met at a reception that evening. France's ambassador had been spectacularly double-crossed.

The letter had been kept so tight that few people in the FCO knew anything about it. That included Blair's envoys to Paris, John Holmes, and to Berlin, Paul Lever. Not only had the French and Germans been kept in the dark. So had Solana. Only three days earlier, he had persuaded EU foreign ministers to agree a common statement on Iraq, allowing inspectors to carry out their work. He heard about the letter first on the radio. The Greeks did not know anything either. They were supposed to be running the EU for these six months but Blair insisted they be kept out because they might blow his cover. One government did see it. Campbell had e-mailed it over to the White House the day before.

Once again, most British diplomats had found out about policy via the media. Many were angry not just at the spin, but also at the strategy. A few cheap headlines had been made, but for what longer-term gain? Britain would have to deal with the French and the Germans long after Iraq was over. Coming two days after Rumsfeld's comments, it looked as if the schism in Europe had been officially approved in Downing Street. Still, Blair and Campbell were pleased with their handiwork. One of Blair's aides said: 'You must admit that as insults go, this one was well judged.'

13

TRUST ME

BY THE MIDDLE OF JANUARY 2003 DOWNING STREET WAS IN A panic. Policy was being run hand to mouth. Sally Morgan, Blair's political adviser, warned of 'drift'. Campbell called a strategy meeting to 'get a grip'. In Cabinet, fears were being expressed with uncharacteristic candour. 'It seemed to us that Tony was making the classic political error,' recalls one senior Cabinet member. 'He had got himself into a situation with no exit strategy. He became subject to forces he could not control.' Gordon Brown told his colleagues of the huge battle ahead for public opinion. He warned of growing anti-Americanism in the UK, putting it down to a 'lack of identification' with the US and particularly the Bush administration. That was diplomatic code for a depiction among many in the Labour Party of the 'Toxic Texan' determined to go to war to find lucrative oil fields for his friends and to complete his father's unfinished business. Blair knew he had to turn that sentiment around. In the State Department, there was increasing anxiety about Blair's power base back home. 'We gotta throw this guy a bone, this guy needs help,' one of Colin Powell's advisers said. They were not sure what bone they could find. They knew that the

Defense Department did not have Blair's interests uppermost in its mind.

Blair fought to suppress his concerns. 'We'll get UN cover under all conceivable circumstances,' he told a Cabinet colleague. He told a meeting of Cabinet colleagues: 'Trust me, I know my way through this.' At Westminster the talk was not *if* war would take place, but when. The mid-February date favoured earlier by the Pentagon had clearly slipped. Dates were being plucked out of the air for different points in March. The first hurdle was 27 January. That was the point when Hans Blix had to give his first formal assessment of the inspections. The French said it was not a deadline, but a process. They agreed with Blix that his inspectors needed 'space and time'.

The hawks in Washington were hopeful they could turn the date into a trigger for war. 'People who are saying that the 27th is not an important day don't know what they are talking about. It is a very important day marking the beginning of a final phase,' Donald Rumsfeld declared. 'What we can't do is let Iraqis turn the inspection regime into a trap for the international community. What we're saying is that with the Iraqi record there is a presumption of guilt and not innocence.' He was convinced that once the war started, America's allies would scramble on board. 'Leadership in the right direction finds followers and supporters.' Even Colin Powell was now talking about a 'coalition of the willing' rather than more formal international structures.

The problem was that Blix did not seem to be getting very far. He had been urging the Americans and British for some time to stop sniping and to help. He urged Bush and Blair: why not provide him with the same intelligence material that had led them both to argue passionately that Saddam was a real and growing danger to the world? At Blix's request, Jeremy Greenstock, the British Ambassador to the UN, phoned London and asked: 'Have we got anything we can give him?' In the end the British did provide him with intelligence, reluctantly, because they suspected the monitoring team was not watertight. No matter how much Unmovic tried to surprise the

Iraqis, they always seemed to get the materials out of the sites before the teams arrived. That, at least, was the British perception. 'There were a lot of frustrations in getting the inspectors to go to places they were supposed to get to,' says one intelligence chief. 'We assumed the inspectors were under surveillance, so what information we did give them we handed them in Cyprus.'

Blix's first discovery had come on 16 January, when a group of inspectors found twelve chemical warheads. They had found them, the British said, thanks to their tip-off. The same happened when documents relating to nuclear plans were found in a scientist's house. None of these amounted to the 'smoking gun' they were all seeking. 'We knew they didn't have a cat's chance in hell of finding anything, but we had to be seen to be trying,' says one Downing Street official. 'We created Blix. The political failure was making so much of him and the process without knowing what he could possibly contribute.'

Blix was as frustrated as the Americans and British. But he was adamant that the failure to come up with compelling evidence was not a fault of the inspectors. 'Evidently, if we had found any smoking gun we would have reported it to the Council,' Blix said. 'Similarly, if we had met a denial of access or other impediment to our inspections we would have reported it to the Council. We have not submitted any such reports.'

When Blix paid a courtesy call on Blair at Chequers, the discussion was polite but to the point. Blair told him he was disappointed with progress. 'We had a sensible conversation with him,' recalls one official who was present. 'We told him he'd never get anything unless he was lucky, they were careless, or people were forced to give us information.' Blix drew an analogy with the IRA: 'You've been crawling around on your bellies in Northern Ireland. How many arms finds have you made?'

After the war, when he found himself in trouble for exactly the same reason – a failure to find WMD – Blair would use the same example.

With each day, the military were getting more agitated. They needed clarity. Their American counterparts had it. Rumsfeld had on 11 January ordered more than 60,000 troops to head for the Gulf, accelerating a build-up designed to enable a full-scale invasion by the end of February. The battle plan was to have more than 150,000 soldiers, sailors and airmen in place. At the Pentagon, military planners were talking of a plan to have US forces in Baghdad within two days of war. Their confidence was boosted by the absence of trenches used by the Republican Guard in the 1991 war.

Finally, on 20 January, the British military received the news they wanted. Hoon told parliament he was committing 26,000 troops, taking the total to 35,000 – a quarter of the British army, a far higher proportion than was sent to the Gulf in 1991. He also despatched more than 100 aircraft – a third of the RAF's front-line force. Hoon admitted that not all the troops had desert kit and it would be several weeks, if not months, before the forces would be 'combat ready'. The figures far exceeded predictions. While Hoon continued to insist that 'none of the steps we are taking represents a commitment of British forces to military action', nobody was under any illusions. Blair had made up his mind. On the same day a *Guardian*/ICM poll showed support among voters for military action had fallen to its lowest level since the question had been first posed in the summer of 2002.

The Americans and British were not expecting much from Blix when he appeared before the Security Council on 27 January. They were pleasantly surprised by what he had to say. 'Iraq appears not to have come to a genuine acceptance – not even today – of the disarmament which was demanded of it and which it needs to carry out to win the confidence of the world.' He spoke of 'disturbing incidents and harassment of inspectors inside Iraq'. El Baradei, the head of the IAEA, took a more conciliatory line, calling for more time for the inspectors to do their work.

Blair seized on Blix's statement. He thought this brought war closer and would make it harder for anyone to oppose it, especially if a second resolution were passed declaring Saddam in material breach. Of the five permanent members, the US and UK would obviously vote in favour. China would probably abstain – Iraq was not enough of an issue for it. Russia might come on board, Blair assumed. That left the French. Although publicly he insisted that a second resolution was not necessary, from the moment 1441 was passed Blair believed he would probably have to get one. The American rhetoric was not helping his cause. Although Bush produced little of the drama of the previous year, he used his State of the Union address to warn Blair and others that he did not need further UN authorisation. 'We will consult. But let there be no misunderstanding. If Saddam Hussein does not fully disarm, for the safety of our people and for the peace of the world, we will lead a coalition to disarm him. The course of this nation does not depend upon the decision of others.'

Blair had to balance several forces. He knew he would have to assure Bush that, whatever his domestic problems, he would back military action. At the same time he had to convince parliament that no decision had been taken. That assertion ran against his instinct. Sometimes, when rattled, he would let his guard slip. During Prime Minister's Questions on the eve of his trip to Washington, Blair was asked by a backbencher, Lynne Jones: 'Who's next?' Raising his voice over heckles, he replied: 'After we deal with Iraq we do, yes, through the UN, have to confront North Korea about its weapons programme. We have to confront those companies and individuals trading in weapons of mass destruction.' To another cry of 'When do we stop?' Blair answered: 'We stop when the threat to our security is properly and fully dealt with.'

Just as he needed to see Bush face-to-face in September to persuade him to go to the UN, he decided he needed to visit him again to persuade him to go for a second resolution. A summit was arranged for 31 January. One of Blair's briefing papers came from Christopher Meyer, the Ambassador to Washington. Meyer told him

Bush 'has not yet bought into our insistence on a second resolution', that an argument was raging within the administration and the President was 'agnostic'. When Blair landed, Meyer took him aside and said: 'You're going to have to clinch the deal.'

Blair and Bush had not spoken for some time. On the eve of their meeting, they talked on the phone and agreed to concentrate not just on Iraq, and what they called a 'constant campaign of persuasion', but also the Middle East. Blair believed that if he could get some form of assurance on the Palestinian issue, he would have less trouble selling Iraq to his party. Bush did not see the link. His people, in any case, did not appreciate what they saw as Blair's unhelpful meddling on the issue.

Blair's sudden proclamation to his party conference of 'final-status talks' by the end of 2002 had not materialised. They had not come anywhere close. Palestinian suicide bombings were met with Israeli reprisals. American frustration with Yasser Arafat had increased. Blair knew he was whistling in the wind, but he took the view that something – even a gesture here and there – was better than nothing. His gambit in October had caught the Foreign Office on the hop. They had the task of turning it into something remotely credible. Straw announced that he would hold a conference in London in January on Palestinian political reform. This would involve the Palestinian Authority, but not Arafat, other Middle Eastern countries and the Quartet – the US, the EU, the UN and Russia. The Israelis, who were not invited, saw it as British grandstanding. Even the usually friendly State Department in Washington was lukewarm. 'You stand a risk if you hold a conference simply to hold a conference,' said one senior official.

By the end of 2002 efforts by the Quartet to produce a road map, leading to the creation of a viable and independent Palestinian state by 2005, had come to a screeching halt. Blair saw two forces at work – elections in Israel and resistance of the hawks in Washington. Their cause was strengthened in December by Bush's appointment of another veteran of the Reagan years, Elliott Abrams, to handle Middle East policy at the National Security Council. That meant Israel and Iraq, among many regional problems. Another neocon had been brought to the heart of policy-making. In 2000 Abrams had written: 'The Palestinian leadership does not want peace with Israel, and there will be no peace.'

That was the mindset the British had to confront. Still, they pressed ahead with their plans for the Palestinian conference. A suicide bomb in Tel Aviv on 5 January gave the Israelis a pretext to ban the entire Palestinian delegation from travelling to London. Straw phoned Powell and asked him to intercede. Powell phoned Netanyahu to ask him to reverse the decision, but he knew he was going through the motions. The Israelis had received a nod and a wink from the NSC, the US Defense Department and the Vice-President's office. That was how it worked.

Ariel Sharon had another reason to be angry with the British. On 9 January Blair met the leader of Israel's Labour Party, Amram Mitzna, for lunch in Downing Street. For a Prime Minister usually keen not to be seen to be taking sides in countries' domestic affairs, it was a deliberate decision. Some around Blair, like Jonathan Powell, counselled against. The British Embassy in Tel Aviv thought it a bad idea. Michael Levy, Blair's special envoy, was adamant it should go ahead. So was Straw. 'We were never naïve enough to think he could win. But we had to do something. We were looking at the complete collapse of the peace camp,' said one minister.

Straw told his officials: 'Sharon loves deciding when to take umbrage and when not.' When Straw said he could understand that people saw double standards in Western policy towards the region, the Israelis were apoplectic. They released the tape of a furious telephone conversation between him and Netanyahu. Straw confided in his team: 'They find it difficult to have a go at Tony, so I'm the one.' There was a reason for that. Straw believed Blair had until that point been too pro-Israeli. He saw Blair's decision to press on with the conference on 14 January as an important sign of a shift. The conference did take place, with the Palestinians taking part by video link. A Middle East peace process that had been to Oslo and Camp David, that had seen the great handshakes of Anwar Sadat and Menachim Begin, of Yitzhak Rabin and Yasser Arafat, was now reduced to a conference call.

Blair believed that he could still change Bush's ways. He needed a letter to take to Washington. On the morning of 23 January he had sent his special envoy on a secret mission to Ramallah. Michael Levy had seen Arafat every few months. Sometimes their meetings would be productive. The Palestinian leader would be well briefed. Other times he would meander, and retreat into a long discourse on historical injustice. Levy let it be known he would only come this time 'if they had something serious'. He wanted a commitment from Arafat that he would agree to the appointment of a Prime Minister, one with real powers. That was an American precondition for any form of engagement in the process. Even Levy, who knew the place well, was shocked by the state of the Mukata, Arafat's compound. The stench of untreated sewage was overpowering. The ground was littered with rubble from fallen masonry. He walked along the shattered entrance area and staircase and into one single committee-type room that was still functioning. Arafat needed some convincing. Levy told him, on behalf of Blair, that this was his final chance.

He got the letter, flew back to London and handed it to Blair. That was influence, proper influence. And on the rare occasions when Blair really did make a difference in Washington, he did not advertise it, for fear of antagonising Bush. That was the nature of their relationship.

The latest Bush summit got off to an inauspicious start. Fog, rain and ice forced it to be switched from the relaxed confines of Camp David to the White House. Unlike the previous meetings at the presidential retreat and the Texan ranch, there was no opportunity for 'down time'. They went straight into meetings, Blair accompanied sometimes only by Manning. At other times Powell, Campbell and

Morgan would join him. Blair needed two things. He needed a commitment to the road map. He needed a commitment to a second resolution. Publicly he got neither. Bush told Blair he suspected the UN process was little more than a delaying tactic. Some of the greyness outside seemed to carry over in the sombre and even tense mood of the joint press conference, which was first delayed, and then abruptly ended by Bush after only fifteen minutes. Both leaders agreed that Saddam must be disarmed 'in weeks not months' and that he was not fully co-operating with the inspectors.

Bush mentioned a second resolution only when pressed by journalists. 'Should the United Nations decide to pass a second resolution, it would be welcomed if it is yet another signal that we're intent upon disarming Saddam Hussein.' That was hardly the ringing endorsement Blair was depending on. Bush's advisers compounded the problem by stressing that a new vote was 'desirable but not necessary'. Campbell was aggrieved. Neither leader had spoken to their agreed scripts. After dinner he briefed Bush and Blair that journalists were writing that they had rowed. They both raised their eyebrows but said nothing more.

Blair believed he did get something. He was sure that Bush had promised him that once Iraq was over, the road map would be published. On the plane back, he and Manning agreed that they might be the only two people on the planet who thought that Bush was sincere. 'Clinton messes you around,' Blair told one of his aides, 'but when Bush promises something, he means it.' Was this self-delusion? One official who watched Blair and Bush together in all their summits describes the process:

Bush listens politely, agrees that the points being made are good. He says things like: 'I'll do what I can.' As soon as Tony is in the air on his way back home Bush forgets the conversation and we know he has forgotten. There have been several moments when Tony really felt Bush had got it. Tony would say things like: 'We really are on the same page. Bush has finally clicked.' Then a few hours later soberness would set in and he would realise he hadn't.

In the run-up to the Washington summit Campbell had been worried that growing differences between the US and UK over the need for a second resolution would dominate press coverage. He needed a diversionary tactic, a different story that would produce a 'top line'. He was exasperated that MPs, journalists and the public had not got the message about just how bad the Iraqi leader was. Campbell would regale visitors to his office about Saddam's crimes. He would tell them of intelligence showing that graffiti was emerging on the streets of Baghdad criticising the regime. On all issues he worked from the assumption that it was only when reporters became bored of a message that it was finally getting through. The Coalition Information Centre (CIC), the ad hoc war press office set up for Afghanistan, had just been reactivated ('It was like an ageing rock band getting back together,' said one of its staffers). Campbell had a quick but important job designed for the CIC, to come up with a new dossier of Saddam's human rights and other abuses. 'We thought it would be good idea to put out a briefing paper,' a senior official recalls. 'It was bothering us that the public kept on asking how come the UN inspectors just couldn't find the stuff. We wanted to try to explain the nature of the regime.'

Journalists travelling to Washington were presented with a new document. 'Iraq: Its Infrastructure of Concealment, Deception and Intimidation' had been prepared hurriedly. But its nineteen pages were graphic and, to an untrained eye, reasonably compelling. It was posted on the Downing Street website immediately, claiming that it was drawing upon 'a number of sources, including intelligence material'.

The CIC, assembled in the Foreign Office, collated all the material they could find. The security services constantly supplied them with raw data that they had cleared for general use. There was also no shortage of open-source information.

As Campbell and the others would later admit, this was absorbed into the FCO system and therefore passed around. In that process attributions were deleted from published articles, notably the one by a 29-year-old Ph.D. student at the Monterey Institute of International Studies in California, Ibrahim al-Marashi, which had appeared in the *Middle East Review of International Affairs* in September. Al-Marashi's words had been changed, to add to the sense of drama: 'monitoring' had become 'spying', 'opposition groups' had become 'terrorist organisations'. One official admitted later: 'It had not been fact-checked. We did not expect it to be treated in the same way as a dossier.' This was a classic New Labour tactic of the 1990s, playing fast and loose with the facts for what it believed to be a greater good.

While the September document had turned inconclusive and hedged intelligence into something more, at least the formal procedures were adhered to. Scarlett did formally sign it off. This time, in their haste and hubris, Campbell and his team ignored the basic protocol of clearing the material with the JIC. The agencies had willingly provided the information, but not for use in the way it was. Then they were asked if they had anything else. 'Alastair's people phoned and asked if there was anything more that we had. They were often doing that,' says one senior official. 'There was nothing new to put it in. We had nothing more to give them. The first dossier had been our best shot. It had all the best bits of our post-1998 intelligence in it already.' This went to the heart of the difficult relationship between the intelligence agencies and the politicians they serve. 'With the first dossier the Prime Minister told the JIC quite formally, through Manning, that it was important for the overall campaign to set out the case. That is quite different from being rung up by someone in the communications cell and being asked to hand over stuff just like that,' says one senior intelligence official.

Blair's senior policy people, including David Manning, said they knew nothing about what came to be known as the 'dodgy dossier'. Campbell told Manning on the plane to Washington that journalists were to be handed a briefing note, but he did not think any more of it. Nor did Jack Straw. The Foreign Office News Department did receive a draft on the morning of Blair's departure, but no particular importance was attached to it. The first ministers, including Straw, knew about it was when they saw it in the Sunday papers. 'I remember reading the newspaper accounts and saying "What the hell is this?" Jack went ballistic,' recalls one senior minister. Scarlett knew nothing either, but for the moment kept his counsel.

Still, Blair was happy enough to draw attention to the document as he reported back to MPs on 3 February on his Washington summit. He spoke in dark terms about the threat posed by Saddam. 'When people ask me why am I willing to risk everything on this politically, I do not want to be the Prime Minister when people point the finger back from history and say: "You knew those two threats were there and you did nothing about it."' He announced that the document had been placed in the House of Commons library, turning this supposedly minor briefing paper into a government document. Two days later Colin Powell, the US Secretary of State, would sing its praises to the UN. On Thursday 6 February, the 'dossier politics' would rebound with catastrophic effects on Blair.

Glen Rangwala, a lecturer in politics at Cambridge University, first spotted the plagiarism. He revealed to Channel Four News that four of the nineteen pages had been copied, with only minor editing and a few insertions, from the Internet. 'The British government's dossier is nineteen pages long and most of pages six to sixteen are copied directly from al-Marashi's document, word for word, even the grammatical errors and typographical mistakes.' He added: 'Apart from passing this off as the work of its intelligence services, it indicates that the UK really does not have any independent sources of information on Iraq's internal policies. It just draws upon publicly available data.' Amid all the welter of comment that followed, this point was largely forgotten. The reason the material was drawn upon was because it provided a more compelling case for war than any of the available intelligence.

When the story broke, Straw and his officials demanded that heads should roll. It was only then that they were told that Campbell had ordered the dossier in the first place, that he signed it off, and that he distributed it. The security services were equally furious. After the row blew up, Scarlett confronted Campbell, calmly, registering his concern at the error and embarrassment. He had been put in the most awkward position of any of them. He was the one who had persuaded the intelligence chiefs, against many of their instincts, to go along with previous dossiers. Now he feared they would refuse all future requests. Throughout the intelligence community there was intense anger that their reputation had been impugned. Campbell apologised, in a manner of speaking, to Scarlett and the intelligence chiefs. In the inner circle they realised immediately that the row had done damage. They did not realise just how much. In one respect it was avoidable. It stemmed from a growing sense of panic. 'We were always up against it, selling the message,' says one insider.

Blair was trying to show that life was going on as normal. He went to Le Touquet for the summit with Chirac that the French President had postponed in his fit of pique over 'le row'. Once again, Campbell had allowed his spin obsession to get the better of him. That morning the British press proclaimed that the French were about to cave in on Iraq. 'There were two problems with that,' said one British official present at the meeting. 'First, it wasn't true. Secondly, it was counter-productive. This was all very unhelpful macho posturing. It was wishful thinking.' Chirac tried to break the tension with a joke. When his Prime Minister, Jean-Pierre Raffarin, made a point about the 'social aspect' of Europe, meaning employment protection, that kind of non-Anglo-Saxon talk, the President declared: 'Here we have a leftist Prime Minister [Raffarin] agreeing with a rightist one [Blair]. You see: cohabitation does work.' The French delegation chortled; Blair smiled one of his awkward smiles.

On the substance they agreed to differ. Chirac praised the inspectors and noted that under Unscom in the 1990s more weapons were destroyed than in the first Gulf War. Blair was relieved that confrontation was avoided and the atmospherics were better. He remained convinced that Chirac would eventually buckle.

The salesman, it seemed, was losing his touch. A meeting was organised to discuss public services. Labour headquarters picked the audience with great care. In front of television cameras, a 21-year-old sociology student slipped through the net. 'Why are you going to war with Iraq? What evidence have we got? Why won't you listen to the people, most of whom are totally against the war?' he shouted. Shortly after, Blair flew to Gateshead for a grilling from Jeremy Paxman. Mixed with the anger came derision. Members of the studio audience taunted him, calling him 'Mr Vice-President' and 'the Right Honourable member for Texas North'. He fell back on a phrase he would use increasingly, as desperation set in. 'I don't feel that I'm doing the wrong thing and I may not be doing the easy thing, but I do believe I'm doing the right thing.'

Blair was receiving frequent assessments from the JIC and its chairman, John Scarlett. The message was the same: Saddam had not accounted for his weapons and therefore must be hiding them. To those around the Prime Minister, no other explanation was conceivable. There were others, though, that did the rounds of the Foreign Office and foreign governments. Perhaps Saddam was addicted to brinkmanship, so even though he had nothing to hide, he felt he could string the world along and he would always get away with it. Perhaps it was national pride: he did not want to be proved to have nothing, since this might, in his view, weaken his standing in the Arab world. Perhaps it was bureaucratic inefficiency: no one in the regime had kept proper documentation.

The credibility of the case for war hinged on the credibility of the intelligence. In Washington, Colin Powell spent three days camped out at the CIA's headquarters in Langley, Virginia. The

Americans had called a special session of the UN Security Council to present what they promised would be the definitive proof of Saddam's guilt. One historical analogy was drawn – delegates were looking for another Adlai Stevenson moment, when the US Secretary of State produced compelling photographic evidence of a Soviet build-up during the 1962 Cuban missile crisis. Powell was under at least as much pressure as Blair. The neoconservatives, Rumsfeld and Cheney in particular, not only disparaged the State Department's diplomatic approach, but were keen to ensure that Powell present the US intelligence to their satisfaction – along the lines of the Office of Special Plans – rather than the CIA's more circumspect approach. The end product was a messy compromise, dressed up with as much conviction as the Secretary of State could muster.

'I cannot tell you everything that we know. But what I can share with you, when combined with what all of us have learned over the years, is deeply troubling,' he began. Using a PowerPoint presentation, his lines finely honed, his intonation fluctuating between a television news presenter and a university lecturer, Powell spent an hour and a half playing tapes of intercepted Iraqi military communications, showing surveillance photographs of military sites, and recounting information received from sources 'who risked their lives to let the world know what Saddam Hussein is really up to'.

Blix was underwhelmed. He told his colleagues it had been 'interesting, but not compelling'. This fell far short of the burden of proof required in any court, he said. The Americans never aspired to that level of proof and were reasonably pleased. The British were cautious. Greenstock, Britain's UN ambassador, told his American opposite number that Powell had made his presentation far too early. The British had persuaded Powell to take out 'reams about a link with terrorism'. They wanted a stronger emphasis on weapons of mass destruction. There was, they said, 'too many bricks with too little straw'. There was some sympathy for Powell. 'Colin went out on a limb. It was the best intelligence he could screw out of the system,' said one British official. MI6 had tried to persuade the CIA to declassify more humint on chemical and biological weapons. They refused. 'I was uneasy about his reliance on satellite intelligence,' said a senior British official. He was particularly disparaging about the allegation that Iraq was harbouring Abu Musab al-Zarqawi, a Jordanian–Palestinian militant and al-Qaeda sympathiser, whom Powell said had been granted 'safe haven' in Baghdad in May 2002, where he established a base of operations with two dozen other extremists. The Americans had tried this and other claims before, back in the autumn of 2001. The British security services had scoffed at them then. Nearly eighteen months on, their reaction was no different. 'This stuff is hopelessly over-egged,' was one British intelligence official's reaction. 'If you do a presentation like that, it's best to have a smoking gun.' And yet, with so much intelligence shared between London and Washington, Blair was drawing his conclusions largely from the same pool. As if emphasising that point, Powell called the Security Council's attention 'to the fine paper that the United Kingdom distributed [in February 2003] . . . which describes in exquisite detail Iraqi deception activities'. He had no idea at the time that this would come to be known as the 'dodgy dossier'.

The next day Bush declared, 'The game is over.' The French replied it wasn't a game and it wasn't over. In case anyone was in any doubt about French opposition to an early war in Iraq, its actions in Nato should have made it abundantly clear. France reinforced its alliance with Germany by enticing Belgium's Prime Minister to join them. Guy Verhofstadt – once fêted by Blair as one of Europe's 'new thinkers' – was facing a difficult election. He knew, just as Schröder had found, that hostility towards US military plans brought in votes. The three European neighbours plunged the alliance into the biggest crisis of its fifty-four-year history by voting to block plans to bolster Turkey's defences in case of war with Iraq. They argued that to begin military planning would undermine diplomatic efforts to avoid a war.

Turkey responded by invoking Nato's Article 4, under which the security of a member state is declared at risk. Rumsfeld called the Franco-German-Belgian action a 'disgrace', but said war would not be delayed as a result. Lord Robertson, the Nato Secretary-General, chose his words carefully, but privately he was furious. Nothing could have been better designed to divorce the US from Europe than a row like this, or to vindicate better the neocons' 'Old Europe' jibe, he told his aides.

With Nato in crisis, on 14 February Blix delivered his second assessment to the UN Security Council. The timing was sensitive, coming on the eve of international demonstrations against the war. His presentation this time was shorn of the single soundbite the Americans and British needed as evidence of Iraqi non-compliance. With the mild manners of meticulous headmasters, Blix and El Baradei reported in effect that Iraq had made some progress but could do better. On the debit side for Saddam, Blix said the potential production of 8,500 litres of anthrax, 1.5 tonnes of VX nerve agent and thousands of chemical shells were still unaccounted for. He said the Iraqis' al-Samoud missile programme had broken the 150-kilometre limit set by the UN and would now be banned. On the credit side, he said three private interviews had been conducted with scientists; Iraq had declared its ballistic missile programme and the ranges reached by rockets in tests; documents about the destruction of chemical agents had been given as well as the names of some witnesses, to back up claims that this material had been destroyed; and inspectors had seen no evidence that Iraq knew which sites would be inspected in advance.

Most damagingly, Blix gently mocked Powell's intelligence presentation of the previous week. The US interpretation of satellite pictures, claiming they denoted chemical weapons activity, could be wrong, he said. Powell and Straw exchanged furious glances across the horseshoe table. The Secretary of State responded to Blix by warning that the world would not be fooled by 'all the tricks that are being played on us'. It was then the turn of Dominique de

Villepin. France's foreign minister produced a *tour de force* that had the Chinese and the Russians leading an unprecedented burst of applause at the end. 'The option of inspections has not been taken to the end,' he said. 'The message comes to you today from an old country,' he added, in a jibe at Rumsfeld. This old country, he added, had 'never ceased to stand upright in the face of history and before mankind'.

Blair was despondent when he watched the Blix performance. He saw malign forces at play. 'Blix was encouraged by the French and others to see himself as having the weight of war on his shoulders,' says one Blair aide. 'They were telling him: "You will have blood on your hands." It seemed to us that Blix then went out of his way to ensure that his information was not seen as a pretext for military action. That wasn't how it was supposed to be. That wasn't his role.'

Just as they despaired of Blix, so Blix had despaired of the Americans and the British – not so much their political positioning as their professionalism. He started to tell colleagues that, after all, perhaps Saddam did not have as much biological and chemical capability as had been feared. For the first few weeks of the process the Iraqis had not taken it seriously. Blix thought they might not be regretting the defiant tone of their 7 December declaration. It was only by the end of February that the Iraqis realised what was at stake. By this point they were frantic and were giving the inspectors a list of people for interviews. But it was too late. As for the British intelligence, Blix remarked: 'My God, if this is the best they have and we find nothing, what about the rest?'

Blix's statement to the Security Council was just what the anti-war lobby had wanted. Nobody could tally the numbers properly. On Saturday 15 February up to 100 million protesters converged on 600 cities in 60 countries. London saw the biggest demonstration in British history – up to 2 million people from all parts of the UK taking part in the 'stop the war rally'. These were not just the usual marchers – left-wingers, single-issue protesters – but the very

Middle Britain families that Blair had assiduously courted for the best part of a decade. Several speakers called, less than convincingly, for Blair to resign. Jesse Jackson, the veteran American civil rights campaigner, drew the biggest applause by linking the war to American arms sales to Saddam in the early 1980s. 'Donald Rumsfeld talks about Saddam's weapons of mass destruction. What Donald Rumsfeld doesn't tell you is that he has the receipts for all of Saddam's weapons of mass destruction,' he declared.

'We all knew people on the demo,' recalls one Blair aide. 'We knew that many were opposed outright, but others might stomach a war with a second resolution.' Blair was in Glasgow for a speech to Labour's spring conference. The timing was unfortunate, but they believed they could make a virtue of it.

They concluded that, on the specifics of Resolution 1441, Blix was winning the battle for indefinite delay. Blair had to broaden his case to justify military action and to confront his opponents. 'The moral case against war has a moral answer: it is the moral case for removing Saddam,' he told the delegates. 'It is not the reason we act. That must be according to the UN mandate on weapons of mass destruction. But it is the reason, frankly, why if we do have to act, we should do so with a clear conscience. I do not seek unpopularity as a badge of honour. But sometimes it is the price of leadership and the cost of conviction.' He had not used the 'moral' argument before.

Blair changed tack partly in desperation, partly out of genuine anger. He was passionate that people should not fall into what he called 'Saddam fatigue'. What mattered most was his integrity. He told friends he could handle people saying he was wrong, but not that he was immoral. He would say of the protesters: 'Those people are not the moral majority.'

He was, however, shocked by the scale of the public hostility. Church leaders were speaking out. Former diplomats were speaking out. Labour MPs were signing motions in parliament, their confidence strengthened by safety in increasing numbers. It was around this time that the US Embassy in London told the State Department that Blair was in considerable danger and needed support. The memos back home were becoming more urgent. At this point, Blair himself was not trying to alert the White House to his predicament. 'The Americans watched this whole process but didn't get it,' said one of his people. 'They didn't understand until very late how difficult his position was. We didn't tell them. Tony doesn't bleat.' The problem was, as one of his inner circle remarked: 'Bush gives the impression that the UN is just a process to get through.'

Bush told Blair he was prepared to help him out, as long as the second resolution was secured quickly. US troops were ready to go within weeks, and he did not want to keep them there in the desert. Both leaders talked of the weather, of the desert heat arriving in April, as a reason not to delay.

Blair's world was closing in on him. The Americans were becoming impatient. Blix was finding nothing. Opposition at home was growing. The second resolution, which had only ever been a desirable option, had now become a matter of political survival. The more he needed it, the less he was likely to get it.

France's Ambassador to Washington, its former UN envoy, Jean-David Levitte, told the number two at the NSC, Stephen Hadley, that the Americans should not back Blair's plans, because they would not get a second resolution. If the Americans were determined to go to war before Blix had exhausted his enquiries, then it should go ahead, assemble its 'coalition of the willing' and not seek further UN legitimacy. From the other side of the argument, the Spanish also counselled against a further vote.

Bush decided, against the will of Rumsfeld and Cheney, to help out his friend, and instructed US negotiators at the UN to press ahead on a draft. It contained no ultimatum and no explicit threat of war. Its long preamble reiterated that the Security Council had 'repeatedly warned Iraq that it would face serious consequences as a result of its continued violations of its obligations'. It concluded: 'Iraq has failed to take the final opportunity afforded to it in

Resolution 1441.' The last line was telling, but still open to different interpretations.

Blair began a four-week diplomatic whirlwind, the likes of which few world leaders have seen. His first audience, on 22 February, was the most poignant. He and Cherie and their children paid homage to Pope John Paul II. He was the first British premier to receive such an honour since Churchill. The immorality argument put forward by opponents of the war was the one Blair found hardest to bear. He was not expecting to convince the pontiff, who had made clear his condemnation of military action. But as a man still wrestling with his religion, Blair did want to talk it through with him. Their discussion was long and intense. Blair had made it clear to his aides he did not want its details divulged. He found all talk of his religiosity, his moves towards Catholicism, his interest in ecumenism, deeply embarrassing. Although the meeting had been billed as 'strictly private', the Vatican later took the unexpected step of issuing a statement, quoting the Pope as urging Blair to avoid 'the tragedy of war' and to 'make every effort to avoid new divisions in the world'.

For all the criticism, for all the *realpolitik*, Blair was convinced that this would be a 'just' war. He had formed his interpretation of justice before any of his military conflicts, in the Christian socialism of his early years when he wrote of Christianity as being 'a very tough religion', of it being 'judgemental', of there being 'right and wrong, good and bad'.

The UN has always been an intriguing mix of the grandiloquent and the grubby. As the US, Britain and France sent ministers from one obscure capital to another, the combination of bribery and intimidation was not hidden. Blair tried to pretend otherwise, to profess moral methods for his moral cause. He began a frantic round of telephone calls to his allies, adversaries and members of the Security Council that by accident of timing would suddenly become the focus of world attention. The ten alternating members, as is the custom, provided a rich mixture of geography and political outlook.

Syria and Germany were just about certain to line up with France. Pakistan's General Musharraf, having taken a huge risk in supporting the Americans against the Taleban, had served notice he would not be open to persuasion again. Spain and Bulgaria – the former Soviet satellite state now known in the White House as the 'quiet American' – were guaranteed to line up behind the Americans and British. Of the five floating votes two came from Latin America – Mexico and Chile – and three from Africa – Guinea, Angola and Cameroon. On 24 February Blair despatched his junior Foreign Office minister, Baroness Amos, to Africa. Hot on her heels in the chase for votes came De Villepin. Blair himself focused on Chile's Ricardo Lagos, the country's first left-wing leader since the CIA-backed overthrow of Salvador Allende, and Mexico's President, Vicente Fox, who had been given such privileged treatment by Bush back in 2001.

Over the next few weeks, the two Latin Americans blew hot and cold. The Africans proved enigmatic. Blair became increasingly frustrated at what was, in spite of all the protestations to the contrary, half-hearted American diplomacy. The moral high ground that Blair sought was being lost amid the unseemly scramble for votes. Bribes and threats from the big powers to smaller ones became the currency. In the Commons, for all his private fears about the state of diplomacy, Blair continued to give commanding performances. It was not too late, he insisted, for Saddam to disarm and for the UN to show resolve. 'This is not a road to peace but folly and weakness that will only mean the conflict when it comes is more bloody, less certain and greater in its devastation.'

Underlying the message all the way through was a deliberate misreading of the second resolution. Blair led his MPs and the country to believe, time and again, that it might provide a route out of war. It was nothing of the sort. He needed the second resolution to provide political, diplomatic and even legal authority for a military conflict to which he was already committed. This resolution would make an almost-certain war certain. It would give Blair the imprimatur he needed. That is why the French and others refused to give it.

On Friday 21 February Labour MPs received pager messages. Out of the blue they were told by Hilary Armstrong, the Chief Whip, that they were required to vote the following Wednesday on a motion concerning Iraq. This would be a 'three-line whip' when support was obligatory. The anti-war backbenchers had begun to organise themselves. One ringleader, Graham Allen, was so incensed by Armstrong's cursory instruction that he tabled a parliamentary motion. It took him less than an hour to gather sixty names for his amendment stating that 'the case for military action is not yet proven'. Worry in Downing Street was tempered by the knowledge that most Labour MPs who threatened to rebel usually fell into line at the last minute. Through the usual mixture of cajoling, coercion, the dangling of patronage – and argument – Sally Morgan, Blair's party fixer, had managed to keep the previous revolt in September 2002 down to fifty-six. She was looking at a figure a little higher, perhaps up to eighty, or ninety at most. That would be awkward but manageable.

On the morning of the vote, 26 February, Morgan, Campbell and Powell went to Blair's flat above 11 Downing Street for breakfast. They agreed the hard message on Saddam should not change. Jack Straw and Mike O'Brien offered meetings with rebels in the Commons. MPs were paged to ask if they 'would like a briefing' from the FCO on any 'outstanding issues'. Blair invited in two groups of six, in his room behind the Speaker's chair. The result that evening exceeded their worst expectations. Some 121 Labour backbenchers voted against the government. The debate was passionate and well informed. Blair's decision to disappear early to do a television discussion in his office with voters increased the determination of some waverers to rebel. When Joschka Fischer, the German foreign minister, had been in to see him the same afternoon, Blair told him there would be fewer than 100 rebels, and he was confident he could cut that down to 50.

The following day's Cabinet was sombre. They did not dwell on the vote. Blair moved the conversation quickly on to plans for the post-war reconstruction of Iraq. By the standards of this government, these meetings had become a little more open. On this occasion, John Prescott was asked to wind up. 'My assessment of the mood of the Cabinet is that we're backing the PM,' he declared. 'Anyone want to say anything to the contrary?' He slowly turned his head around the table twice, eyeballing each member of the Cabinet. There was silence. 'I take it then that everyone's signed up for the policy,' Prescott concluded. That is how decisions were endorsed. The Prime Minister's official spokesman announced that the Cabinet had been 'rock solid'. Technically, he was not wrong. But underlying the public support for Blair by his Cabinet, the unease went well beyond the likes of Cook and Short.

That evening, Blair left for a quick trip to Madrid to see his friend Aznar. The two were working closely. Aznar had just been to see Bush at his ranch in Crawford, the ultimate sign of favour. Before leaving for the US, Aznar had told Blair he wanted to advise the President that whenever the neoconservatives said anything about the war they made life harder for him. Blair agreed with him but was reluctant to criticise Bush in public. He told Aznar it would 'sound better coming from you'. As one aide put it: 'There's always been an annoyance here that the hawks were the ones with the best lines. The devil has the best tunes.' As agreed, the news was leaked to the press at a convenient moment. Aznar confirmed it to reporters: 'I did tell the President that we need a lot of Powell and not much of Rumsfeld. Ministers of defence should talk less, shouldn't they?'

On his plane to Madrid, Blair gave one of his most revealing interviews. His combination of moral fervour, allusions to Chamberlain and Churchill, and justification for the four wars he had already fought proved a heady mix.

People have just got to make up their minds whether they believe me or not, I'm afraid . . . I've never claimed to have a monopoly of wisdom, but one thing I've learned in this job is you should always try to do the right thing, not the easy thing. Let the day-to-day judgments come and go. Be prepared to be judged by history. A majority of decent and well-meaning people said there was no need to confront Hitler and that those who did were warmongers . . . I am proud of what we've done on regime change in Kosovo and Afghanistan, and, in a different way, by supporting the regime in Sierra Leone . . . if you go back now, for all the problems they have got, and you ask if we did the right thing, I believe we did. Those who benefited most from military action had been the people of those countries . . . I believe if we have to do this in Iraq, the people of Iraq will be the main beneficiaries.

He was asked why he was so devotedly following the line set out by George W. Bush. 'It's worse than you think. I believe in it. I am truly committed to dealing with this, irrespective of the position of America. If the Americans were not doing this, I would be pressing for them to be doing so.'

Blair was looking haggard. His aides were worried that he was taking on too much. He was even trying a new initiative in Northern Ireland. Manning was exhausted and frustrated. The close-knit team were getting in before seven in the morning and staying until after midnight, trying to operate on a number of fronts. Diplomatically they were trying to extract what votes they could on the Security Council for a second resolution. They were having to persuade Bush and his principals to give them just a little more time.

On 1 March the Americans suffered a serious reverse. The Turkish parliament rejected the blandishment of $6 billion in aid and refused to endorse the government's decision to deploy 62,000 US troops along its border. Elections the previous November had brought to power for the first time an Islamic party under Recep Tayyip Erdogan. He was initially banned from becoming prime minister following a conviction for religious incitement. As Nato's bulwark to the east, Turkey had been crucial. Its role in this war was seen as vital to determining future relations. Erdogan had to look both ways. He haggled over the economic terms for co-operation and eventually secured them. But Bush and his advisers underestimated the pressures and the antipathy felt towards them. Two months earlier Wolfowitz had proclaimed after a visit to Ankara: 'Turkish support is assured.' The diplomacy was a far cry from the first Gulf War in 1991.

The setback forced a major rethink on military and diplomatic strategy. Having cast aside traditional tenets of diplomacy at the outset of the Bush presidency, the Americans tried belatedly and half-heartedly to relearn them. In Washington, the message was at last beginning to sink in. At his White House press conference on 6 March, Bush was asked: 'What went wrong that so many governments and people around the world now not only disagree with you very strongly, but see the US under your leadership as an arrogant power?' He did not feel the need to answer.

British diplomatic efforts were also getting nowhere. 'We're on tenterhooks. We never thought it would come to this. The French are playing desperately high stakes. We have a very small margin for error, even with a second resolution. Without one we have no room for error at all,' a senior intelligence figure said at the time. On the phone, Russia's Vladimir Putin urged Blair to gain some distance from Bush: 'If you have a relationship that is too close, you lose your room for manoeuvre,' he told him. Over breakfast in Downing Street, Blair urged the Russian foreign minister, Igor Ivanov, to think again. He said the UK would not wait for Blix. Ivanov replied: 'We can't accept your position. Don't make that a hard decision for us.' That was code for saying: withdraw your resolution. Ivanov headed immediately for Paris. Joschka Fischer cancelled his engagements to join. The French, German and Russian ministers signed a joint statement calling for diplomacy and pointing to 'increasingly encouraging results' from Unmovic.

Blair was being caught in a pincer movement. Bush referred to

Saddam as 'this cancer inside of Iraq'. He could not have made his ambivalence towards a UN resolution more obvious. 'We really don't need anyone's permission' to defend US security interests, he declared. 'No matter what the whip count is, we're calling for the vote.' Asked about British efforts to find a consensus on the Security Council, Bush said: 'It makes no sense to allow this issue to continue on and on.'

On 7 March Blix made his third presentation to the Security Council. His report was devastating. Iraq, he said, had accelerated its co-operation since January, although it was still incomplete. In all the inspections so far no evidence had been found of proscribed biological activities. He had investigated in detail US claims of mobile biological labs and underground facilities and had come up with no evidence to support them. He then pointed to Iraq's al-Samoud missiles. Some thirty-four had been destroyed – just under a third of the total. Tests on the missiles had shown their range to be in excess of the 150 kilometres allowed by the UN. This, he said, represented very real disarmament. The British and Americans had dismissed the destruction of the al-Samouds as a 'game'. In his speech, Blix responded with dry fury: 'We are not watching the breaking of toothpicks; lethal weapons are being destroyed.' He concluded by appealing for more time, saying the inspections would take several more months to render meaningful results. By the end, as Blix liked to point out, he had detected sixty-four al-Samouds, which he pointed out was 'no mean feat'.

El Baradei, the head of the IAEA, compounded the annoyance by exposing one of the claims in Blair's September document – the one that said 'Iraq has sought the supply of significant supplies of uranium from Africa' – as a sham. It transpired that the minister from Niger, whose signature was on a document, had been out of office for a decade. A US envoy sent to investigate the claims had reported to the CIA back in February 2002 that they were fakes.

But the White House, influenced by Rumsfeld's Office of Special Plans, ignored the warning. El Baradei's revelation coincided with growing discomfort in parts of the UK intelligence community. At that time a classified intelligence briefing from the Defence Intelligence Service was leaked, warning that not only had there been no link between Iraq and al-Qaeda but that Bin Laden regarded Saddam and his secular regime as 'infidels'.

Within hours of Blix's presentation, Bush had dismissed it out of hand. He urged members of the Security Council to 'show their cards'. Blair invented a new concept, the 'unreasonable veto'. Various deadlines were now being mooted for Saddam to comply or face war. Canada, which was trying to act as a broker behind the scenes, suggested three weeks. That was rejected. Straw began working on a new version of the draft. Day and night he, his Political Director, Peter Ricketts, and Greenstock e-mailed versions to and fro. Some of the language was softened. The demand that Saddam disarm was changed to 'yield possession of weapons'.

The bottom line for Blair was that he needed to show Bush he was making progress on the vote. Britain needed at least nine of the fifteen Security Council members to vote in favour, and to ensure that none of the permanent five cast their veto. Blair despatched Manning and Scarlett on a secret mission to Santiago and Mexico City to try to persuade Lagos and Fox. Lagos told them he needed more time, and he needed Fox's backing. Fox said he was not prepared to give it. He then retired hurt to undergo a back operation. These countries resented being thrust on to the diplomatic front line and being seen as pawns in a nineteenth-century colonial game.

Blair sought solace in the relative seclusion of Chequers, where he secretly received a visit from Bill Clinton. Blair needed his help, and the two men discussed Iraq several times during that period. Most of the weekend Blair spent on the phone. He talked to Lagos several times. He even promised to make the 7,000-mile journey himself. Lagos declined. He said the British deadline of the end of March was too soon. 'That was the point when we realised Chile wasn't going to vote with us,' recalls one of his team. The conversations were so sensitive that the Foreign Office was instructed not to brief about discussions with the Mexicans. In Washington, Colin Powell said the US government was still confident of passing the resolution.

Buoyed by their moral victory last time around, the anti-war lobby in the Parliamentary Labour Party were gearing up for a second vote that Blair, under duress, had promised them. The talk was of a rebellion of up to 200 Labour MPs. Blair would be in the virtually untenable position of having to rely on the Conservatives to get through. Hilary Armstrong, the chief whip, told Blair: 'Without a second UN resolution I cannot guarantee the party vote.'

As the diplomatic efforts ran into the ground, the atmosphere at Westminster was fevered. There was talk of mass resignations from party activists, of meltdown in the local elections, of several resignations from the Cabinet – perhaps even of Blair having to stand down.

On Sunday afternoon, 9 March, Alastair Campbell took a few hours off from the crisis to watch his favourite team, Burnley, play in the FA Cup against Watford. When he got back to his north London home, he received a call on his mobile. He was told that Clare Short had just done a BBC radio interview and had made it clear she would resign if Blair went to war without a new UN mandate. Campbell phoned Blair at Chequers to tell him. He was furious and nervous. If she really did go she might take others with her and galvanise the party into open revolt. He tried to keep his mind on the job of salvaging that UN vote. He talked again to Lagos, the Chilean president.

Had Blair been reckless, the show's host, Andrew Rawnsley, asked Short? 'I think the whole atmosphere of the current crisis is deeply reckless, reckless for the world, reckless for the undermining of the UN in this disorderly world – which is wider than Iraq – which the whole world needs for the future, reckless with our own government, reckless with his own future, position and place in history. It's extraordinarily reckless. I'm very surprised by it.' Blair didn't listen to the programme. But shortly after he did call her. He had always given her privileged treatment, offering her 'bilaterals', as they were grandly called, almost whenever she wanted. Their last had been after the previous Thursday Cabinet meeting. This caused bad feeling among others in the Cabinet. Those who resented the depiction of her as the moral conscience of government called her 'Mother Teresa'. Blair called her again in the morning.

He consulted Morgan, Powell and Campbell about what to do with her. They quickly decided their best interests would be served by keeping her inside the tent. She was, said one of them, a 'busted flush'. There was no point in making her a martyr and giving their opponents a figurehead to rally round. Some interpreted the 'do nothing' approach as a sign of weakness. In fact, it was an inspired piece of crisis management. The next day's headlines had been well spun. But crisis avoided was only crisis deferred.

Adept day-to-day tactics masked a strategy in tatters, however. Blair was chasing shadows. He was still hoping against hope that others would 'see reason' and back a second resolution. He refused to accept that there was nothing in it for other leaders to provide the international endorsement he so desperately needed to fight that war. The great persuader had found himself with precious few friends.

14

HOW LONG IS A MILE?

THEY CHOSE TREVOR McDONALD BECAUSE HE WAS NOT A member of the Rottweiler club. Even so, Blair knew it was not going to be easy. So bad were the polls he felt he had no choice but to get out there and make the case. This formed part of what Campbell called his masochism strategy, but nobody predicted the pain would be so strong. This ITV special was designed around an all-female audience. Each woman had a particular locus. One woman had been in the Bali bombing, in which her boyfriend had been killed. One mother had three sons fighting in the first Gulf War. One woman was an Iraqi victim of Saddam's regime and now exiled in Britain. One mother had lost her only child in the World Trade Center and could not bear any other mother to suffer her agony. They had two questions for Blair. Why? Why now?

Blair went through his paces, gave the stock answers with conviction and passion. This was deeply wounding but compelling TV, culminating in McDonald's devastating put-down: 'What is the going rate for a vote in the Security Council these days?' Five million people had tuned in, much more than the usual current affairs audience, to watch the remarkable spectacle of a jaundiced Blair being hunted by women in fear of war. As the programme ended and the credits rolled, the audience subjected him to a slow hand-clap.

Campbell spent the long hour watching on a monitor behind the set, not saying a word. Unusually for him, he did not complain. He did not send one of what was known in the trade as his 'green ink' letters. But Blair was furious. These ritual public denunciations were getting to him. When he got back to Downing Street he shouted: 'Who the fuck fixed that up? Thanks very much, guys.' They did not have much time for a postmortem. Chirac, they were told, had just done an interview for French TV. Adopting a magisterial pose behind his desk at the Elysée Palace, Chirac gave viewers a lesson in French diplomacy, exulting in his new role as the bulwark against America. Asked if he enjoyed being likened to De Gaulle, Chirac asserted that the General had been 'the first to stand side by side with the US each time it faced a crisis'. He produced a telling statistic: France had wielded the veto eighteen times in the UN's history, compared to Britain's thirty-two and America's seventy-six. He could have but did not mention the fact that the last time the US used its veto was on 20 December, when it refused to back a resolution condemning the killing by the Israeli army of a British UN aid worker in Jenin and the destruction of a World Food Programme warehouse in Gaza. He did not need to. France had over the years incurred the wrath of the rest less often than its partners.

Several times Chirac said France would vote 'no' to the resolution as currently drafted. He went through the scenarios. He insisted that the French position would be academic, as Britain and the US would not muster the nine votes required for a majority. 'There won't, in this scenario, be a majority. So there won't be a veto problem,' he said. He was right. On the eve of Chirac's TV appearance, Greenstock reported back his calculations. They fluctuated daily. On this occasion he said the US and UK could actually be down to four votes, with not a single waverer coming into line.

Sometimes the position improved slightly. But at no point in the whole process did Greenstock report back that he had the necessary nine votes – in other words, whatever the subsequent spin applied by Blair, at no point was it even close to being determined by the French vote.

Chirac was asked to sum up. He then used a phrase that would inadvertently end any hopes of delaying the war. 'My position is that, whatever the circumstances, France will vote "no" because she considers this evening that there are no grounds for waging war in order to achieve the goal we have set ourselves, that is to disarm Iraq.'

When Manning heard what Chirac had said he was spitting nails. 'This really is bloody-mindedness,' he confided to a friend. 'It is a wrecking strategy.' He and Blair concluded the fight had got personal, that Chirac had adopted a strategy designed to bring the Prime Minister down. 'We were defending the Alamo,' one member of the team recalls.

Out of adversity, however, the British spotted an opportunity. They could suggest that Chirac had committed himself to frustrating the US and Britain no matter what evidence was brought forward, or no matter what developments took place. That was not what he said. His use of the phrase 'whatever the circumstances' seemed to mean whatever the voting line-up. He also repeatedly used the word 'tonight', suggesting that while that was France's firm position at that point, it might conceivably change. The French were furious at what they saw as wilful distortion by the British. Factually they may have been correct, but while Chirac might have expressed himself somewhat awkwardly, he was clear that France would use its veto if it had to.

The next day, Errera, the French ambassador, had a scheduled meeting with his old friend, Peter Ricketts, at the Foreign Office. It was a fiery encounter. Errera accused the British government of wilfully distorting Chirac's words, of Soviet-style disinformation to hide the diplomatic fiasco. Ricketts responded: 'It's such a gift, we won't stop there.' He waved the front page of *Le Monde* at him, which hailed the 'nobility' of Chirac's cause. 'If that's the position of your President, then that's it,' he said. He kept it as a memento. Errera phoned Straw complaining that Britain was wilfully distorting Chirac's remarks. Straw then phoned De Villepin, describing Chirac's remarks as 'extraordinary'.

It was now down to political survival and, in Blair's eyes, the ends justified the means. Blair, Campbell and Manning spotted a way out. They conjured a further reason for war, an excuse to explain away weeks of failed diplomacy. 'We needed to show that it was Chirac who scuppered the whole thing, that if it hadn't been for him, we would have got agreement, the UN would not have been torn apart,' says one official. The facts do not bear that out. Certainly, after Chirac's intervention – whether misinterpreted or not – the wavering countries gave up the ghost. These countries, some small and impoverished, never wanted to be under the spotlight, determining the fate of world peace. They wanted the permanent five to sort it out. But, thrust into this uncomfortable role, they proved far more resistant to blandishments than Blair or Bush had predicted.

Campbell orchestrated a campaign of open season against the French. Newspapers, previously exhorted to show Britain at the heart of Europe and to refrain from Eurosceptic xenophobia, were prompted to say whatever they wanted. The *Sun*, Downing Street's favoured organ, featured a series of passport-style shots of Chirac and Saddam merging into one. Blair tried to co-ordinate an anti-French message with his allies in Rome, Madrid and Canberra. The Americans needed no encouragement to denounce the 'axis of weasel'. Ministers were given 'the highest authority' to lay into the French.

Two arguments were put forward. Blair was now on the search for a 'moral majority' if not a legal one. In other words, even if the French vetoed, as long as he had garnered the nine original votes, then that was all that mattered. If that failed, the other line was to argue that, knowing that the French would veto, the wavering countries had concluded that support for the US and UK position had been rendered pointless. The rhetoric against the French was stepped up.

Relations had not been so bad since De Gaulle vetoed Britain's entry to the Common Market in 1963. Whatever the rights and wrongs of the case, how had Blair, his advisers and the whole machine got Chirac so wrong? Many senior figures in the Foreign Office believe the failure of analysis was not confined to France. Blair had exaggerated to himself, as much as to anyone else, his influence on Bush. In those crucial final weeks he underestimated the Americans' willingness to help him. He misread Schröder. He misread Putin. Even on the weekend before Chirac's TV interview, when he was at Chequers, he was still convinced that the French President was bluffing, and would at the very least abstain on a second resolution.

It was in the glow of victory after securing Resolution 1441 that Blair miscalculated. He believed, against the repeated advice of experienced Foreign Office officials, that the French would eventually come on board. 'We may have underestimated Chirac's determination to recast Europe in a Gaullist anti-American mould,' says one member of the Cabinet.

The Germans had been giving out more mixed signals. When Schröder made a private, unannounced visit to Chequers in December he gave Blair the impression that Germany was preparing to go back to its pre-Kosovo position. It would not take part in any military action. But it might give it moral endorsement. That could have been managed. Then Chirac overtook him, and by the time they met at Versailles the position had hardened. At that crucial point, the British took their eye off the ball. 'We weren't looking closely enough at the Elysée anniversary,' says one official. 'We misunderstood the Germans. It suited them to have Chirac as political cover. We have had a consistent problem misreading Franco-German intentions going back through the 1980s.'

If the Monday had been 'turbulent', the Tuesday came to be known as 'wobbly'. With the Commons vote looming and with the second resolution no closer, Hoon called Rumsfeld to talk through the options. Whereas the Powell–Straw and Rice–Manning axes were strong, Hoon had always had trouble making his presence felt on his American opposite number. 'Unless you were making an instrumental phone call – making it clear you were bringing something to the table – Rumsfeld wasn't interested in foreigners,' says one senior military figure. At the Ministry of Defence they collated the 'Rumsfeldisms' with a mix of alarm and amusement. There was the time he was asked how close the US was to catching Bin Laden: 'It's kind of like running round the barnyard chasing a chicken. Until you get it, you don't have it.' There were several quotes he gave for holding Taleban prisoners in Guantanamo Bay, but one stood out: 'Will they be restrained in a way so that they are less likely to be able to kill an American soldier? You bet. Is it inhuman to do that? No. Would it be stupid to do anything else? Yes.' In the middle of February, at a Pentagon gathering of international officials, Rumsfeld proclaimed: 'There are four countries that will never support us. Never. Cuba, Libya and Germany.' What's the fourth, someone asked. 'I forgot the fourth,' he said.

That night Hoon told Rumsfeld: 'We in Britain are having political difficulties, real difficulties, more than you might realise.' He urged him to be careful not to do or say anything that would make matters more difficult than they already were. He urged him not to try to talk down the decision of the House of Commons, or the feelings in the Labour Party. Crucially, he told him that if the vote were lost, contingency plans might have to be made to 'disconnect' British troops entirely from the invasion, demoting their role to later phases and to peacekeeping. Rumsfeld said he understood.

An hour later, the US Defense Secretary held one of his regular briefings. He was asked directly: would the US go to war without Britain?

Their situation is distinctive to their country and they have a government that deals with a parliament in their distinctive way. And what will ultimately be decided is unclear as to their role, that is to say their role in the event a decision is made to use force . . . Until we know what the resolution is [of Blair's problems], we won't know what their role will be. To the extent they're able to participate in the event the President decides to use force, that would obviously be welcomed. To the extent they're not, there are workarounds and they would not be involved, at least in that phase of it.

Rumsfeld's remarks provoked a mixture of panic and fury in Downing Street and the MoD. On one level, he was right. The British role was seen in Washington much more as one of political alliance than military necessity, but it would still involve a recalibration of forces, with more US troops deployed to the southern sector of Iraq, which had been designated for Britain. Given that the Americans no longer had the route through Turkey, a further change to operations would set back the timing. The potential damage to Blair was far greater, reinforcing in the minds of opponents of the war that he was scampering to give the Americans help they did not really need.

The Political Director at the MoD, Simon Webb, got straight on the phone to Rumsfeld's office, trying to point out the potential scale of the disaster. Rumsfeld's team said 'he was only trying to be helpful'. He had to say that the US respected Britain's position as a sovereign nation. They accepted it had come out 'differently to the way he intended'. The two offices quickly worked out a statement in Rumsfeld's name. 'In my press briefing today, I was simply pointing out that obtaining a second UN Security Council resolution is important to the United Kingdom and that we are working to achieve it.' The US Embassy in London, acutely aware of Blair's predicament, was in despair. Senior diplomats called Manning first thing the next day to apologise and to try to sort out the mess. A few days later, Rumsfeld admitted to Hoon that perhaps he had 'messed up'. Hoon did not disagree.

British government, in the normal sense of the word, had

ground to a halt. Blair cancelled many of his meetings. A small
group of Cabinet ministers met several times a day. He and Manning
were rarely off the phone to Greenstock in New York, to the Bush
administration, to other capitals. Hilary Armstrong, the chief whip,
and John Reid, the party chairman, spent their entire time trying to
work out the extent of the forthcoming rebellion in the Commons.
In the Treasury, Gordon Brown kept his head down. He was working on his assessment on whether Britain should join the Euro. He
was preparing his budget. He had always taken the view that whatever he said on foreign policy – on wars such as Kosovo and
Afghanistan – would be misconstrued as interference, so he tried to
say as little as possible. Then he was accused of undermining the
Prime Minister. Once in a while he gave a particular interview to
stress his loyalty and his support for the action against Iraq.

A dinner had been scheduled for that evening, 11 March. Blair,
Brown and Prescott had arranged a long session on general political
strategy at Prescott's flat. Instead, they spent the whole time discussing the war, with Blair setting out the problems. The irony was
not lost on them. In their first years of government, Blair and his
entourage would try to relegate foreign policy to concentrate on
important domestic affairs.

Before that evening Blair had not once asked Brown his advice
or help on the war. Brown did not mind particularly. In any case, his
views did not diverge on any major point of principle towards Iraq.
Brown and Prescott concluded that evening that Blair's position
might be bold, but he didn't have a coherent strategy. They realised
that Blair and his team were operating hour by hour, desperately
trying to salvage something from a process that long before had
gone wrong. They learned that there was no Plan B. The three agreed
to meet again the following morning at 8 A.M. They continued that
pattern, of talking and co-ordinating once or twice a day. Brown was
suddenly told his presence at impromptu war planning meetings
was vital.

At the UN, the British were frantic. Some of the wavering

countries were suggesting a variety of deadlines for Saddam to comply, perhaps up to forty-five days. US forces were now battle-ready. The Americans told Greenstock that they weren't in the mood for delay. Manning told Rice he wanted more time, 'a few more weeks'. The date of 28 March was floated. Manning believed that if a set of tests were set alongside a deadline, that might be acceptable to the US, and it might bring in some of the floating votes on the Security Council, isolating France. Nobody quite believed it, but they thought it was worth one last throw of the dice. Manning e-mailed his five 'benchmarks' to Greenstock – Iraq must surrender its anthrax and other chemical and biological agents; it must surrender all mobile chemical and biological production facilities; it must allow its thirty most important scientists to travel to Cyprus for UN interviews; it must complete the destruction of its remaining al-Samoud missiles, and it must give a full account of its undeclared drone aircraft programmes. Manning and Greenstock then discussed them on a conference call, before Greenstock set off across the road from the British delegation to Blix's office on the thirty-first floor of the UN headquarters.

Blix was enthusiastic about Manning's tests, so much so that he added one himself: Saddam must make a public statement in Arabic, broadcast on television and radio in Iraq and in the government-controlled media, that: Iraq has, in the past, sought to conceal its weapons of mass destruction and other proscribed activities, but has now taken a strategic decision not to produce or retain weapons of mass destruction or other proscribed items or related documentation and data; that Iraq will without delay yield to Unmovic and the IAEA for destruction of all remaining prohibited weapons, proscribed items and related documentation and data; and that it fully co-operates in resolving all outstanding questions. The British were pleased that Blix was pleased. 'We were surprised by his positive response. We didn't want to say no, but we felt we might eventually have to discard the part that he inserted,' says one official. Still, they agreed to table it, with Blix's new test becoming the first on the list.

Immediately, one Latin American delegate described the idea of a confession by Saddam as 'grotesque'. At the time, the British were in too weak a position to make it clear that this was Blix's idea. They still needed the votes, and that meant being polite about him in public.

Labour left-wingers were openly touting the idea of an emergency conference to discuss a motion of no confidence in Blair. More moderate opponents of the war were horrified. They feared that attempts to merge their principled disagreement with the government with the idea of unseating the Prime Minister would deter many MPs from siding with them in the final vote in the Commons Blair had promised. Sally Morgan told Blair the opponents of war might be fracturing. By now, full meetings of the Cabinet were almost incidental. Blair was seeing his key ministers and advisers around the clock. But it was important for the public to know that the government was united. At the weekly meeting on 13 March Clare Short breezed in, making a beeline for Brown, and trying to show that as far as she was concerned it was business as usual. Brown was polite, but not nearly as friendly as he would have been before her 'non-resignation'. Others in the Cabinet recoiled. It was Robin Cook's interventions that were noticed. He raised a series of well-chosen questions about the legal status of the war and the government's planning on a reconstruction of Iraq, post-Saddam. He finished with a carefully worded statement on the importance of securing a second resolution. Whereas the previous week the Cabinet had been described as 'rock solid', this time Downing Street had to construct a phrase that support for Blair's position was 'broad'.

Blair was feeling more isolated than at any point in his premiership. He depended hugely on his inner circle for support. Powell and Campbell told him that, contrary to press speculation, they would stay on through thick and thin. He spoke more frequently to his two former confidants, Peter Mandelson and Anji Hunter. Their job was to shore him up, rather than talk about specifics. Blair preferred these informal relationships to the traditional tools of government. At no point during this period did he produce a formal government paper setting out the options. At no point did the Defence and Overseas Policy Committee, comprising senior ministers, meet in a way that would have been usual in the past.

His reconciliation with Brown was sincere. The battle between the two entourages had in the months before reached a new cycle of intensity. Some of Blair's supporters had been suggesting that Brown might be forced out of the Treasury and into the Foreign Office. These briefings were designed to show who was boss; they were suspended as war loomed. Blair appreciated Brown's private support and his impassioned defence in the media, irrespective of the motive. Brown did have his misgivings about Blair's strategy, but he knew that the mere hint of divergence at this critical point would be devastating. In any case, he preferred to fight his battles on the Euro and on the domestic agenda.

Also on 13 March, Blair phoned Bush. The President told Blair he understood his predicament and sympathised. But he had become increasingly frustrated. The diplomatic timetable was now out of step with the military one. The British approach, which the Americans called 'strategic patience', had run its course. Bush pointed out that it was now six months since he had given the UN a chance to deal with Iraq. That was enough. He regarded the benchmarks as futile. He had long ago given up on the need for a second resolution. He was allowing the Prime Minister to pursue it just to help him get out of a hole that the Americans saw was of Blair's own making. 'This is Blair's cause,' said one US official. Still, favours done in the past meant favours returned. He agreed to give Blair just a few more days. Ari Fleischer said the US would help Blair to go 'the last mile'. A reporter asked: 'Is a mile ten days long?' Fleischer replied: 'I'm not going to define the length of the last mile.'

Blair's last remaining hopes of salvaging anything from the UN process died on Friday 14 March. Chile tabled a proposal giving

Iraq thirty days to complete the six British benchmarks. Within half an hour Fleischer had knocked it down. His words exuded exasperation. 'I was asked several days ago about whether or not the President would be open to extending the deadline thirty to forty-five days – now you could say that's twenty-six to forty-one days. If it was a non-starter then, it's a non-starter now.' The proposal had been killed off even before it had been formally presented to the Security Council. Chile's President Lagos sought solace in humour. He asked Kofi Annan's advisers whether he should apply to the *Guinness Book of Records* for the shortest time in UN history – twenty-one minutes, to be precise – between the tabling of a resolution and its rejection. Blair was upset at Bush's studied disdain of his efforts. The State Department was upset that Blair was being damaged further. But the die was cast. Greenstock then phoned the Prime Minister. He used one of his favourite phrases. The process, he said, had 'no traction'. He could now rely only on the original four votes – Britain, the US, Spain and Bulgaria. The waverers would no longer support them. Britain was close to becoming a figure of fun. Sergei Lavrov, Russia's envoy to the UN, an experienced diplomatic with a laconic turn of phrase, turned to Greenstock and asked in his impeccable English: 'How are those benches? Are they leaving marks?'

At that point Blair told Bush he accepted that war should begin the following week. He agreed that they should meet to present a united front. They agreed to meet halfway, at a US military base on the Portuguese Azores islands, together with the Spanish and Portuguese leaders. Blair asked for one final favour in return, to help him save his skin. Bush had indicated in Washington at the end of January that he would publish the long-awaited road map towards settling the Israeli–Palestinian conflict. It wasn't an absolute promise, but Blair had been led to believe that he would do it. He didn't. Blair was forced to recast his version of events, saying it would be produced once the Palestinians had a new Prime Minister, leaving Arafat as little more than a figurehead. The man Britain and

America invested their hopes in was Abu Mazen, who had been instrumental in negotiating the Oslo accords at Michael Levy's home ten years earlier. Mazen was a pragmatist, and had called for an end to the latest *intifada*. The question was: could he deliver the militant groups such as Hamas and Islamic Jihad? On 8 March the Palestinian Authority approved his nomination. Arafat did not want to transfer most of his powers, but eventually relented.

Blair said that before they got to the Azores, he needed a commitment to the road map. Manning told Rice, and Straw told Powell, that Blair's future depended on it. 'If Bush reneges on the road map, Blair could be finished,' one minister said, urging the President to ignore the co-ordinated opposition of Ariel Sharon and Dick Cheney. On the afternoon of 14 March Bush stepped out on to the lawn of the White House and, flanked by Powell and Rumsfeld, announced his readiness to publish the road map as soon as Abu Mazen was installed as Prime Minister. 'We have reached a hopeful moment for progress,' he said.

For Blair, that was a lifeline. If he could no longer get a UN sanction for the war, at least he could try to present it in a more palatable way. The following day, as Unmovic prepared to leave Baghdad, Blair held an early morning meeting with Prescott, Brown and his inner team to go through the final stages.

It was with some trepidation that Blair and his small circle of confidants – Manning, Powell and Campbell – set off that Sunday morning for the remote islands perched in the mid-Atlantic. The location had been designed to demonstrate that Blair was not running to the White House. Morgan stayed behind to co-ordinate the intensive lobbying of Labour MPs ahead of an imminent debate in parliament. For once Blair did not step down the plane to talk to the press. He knew he was now a hostage to events beyond his control. He had failed to keep the UN united. He had failed to bring France, Germany and Russia on board. He had failed to convince many smaller countries of the merits of his case. He had failed to win around the doubters in his party and in the country. What was left in his armoury was solidarity with the US, the semblance of movement, however belated, in the Middle East, hostility towards France, which played well with some – and a moral argument he put forward with a zeal rarely seen in modern politics.

Not since Nixon had met France's Georges Pompidou and Marcelo Caetano of Portugal in 1971 to discuss monetary policy had the Azores seen such a high-powered gathering. This was a council of war, and pleasantries were kept to a minimum. Blair, Bush and Aznar went straight into a meeting room at the Portuguese military base at Lajes Field. They did not even use up their allocated time. They agreed early on their strategy – one final twenty-four-hour ultimatum to Saddam to disarm. They knew it was meaningless. Blair was distinctly nervous as the three leaders, accompanied by their Portuguese host, came out to the face the world's press. Bush, by contrast, seemed serene. The body language was correct, but the mutual compliments were kept to a minimum. The waiting would soon be over. 'Tomorrow is a moment of truth for the world,' he declared, 'the day that we can determine whether or not diplomacy will work.' After facing the press, the three leaders enjoyed a quiet dinner, washed down with some Portuguese red wine.

By midnight a tired Blair was back in Downing Street, ready for the most dramatic week of his six years in office. That night, teams of US Army sappers were cutting the barbed wire fence along twenty miles of the border between Kuwait and Iraq, leaving just desert between 150,000 troops and Baghdad.

First thing next morning, before the daily meeting of the 'War Cabinet', Robin Cook marched into Downing Street and handed in his resignation. His decision came as no surprise, but it was no less damaging for that. Cook had been preparing to go since the middle of February. He had wanted to wait until the last chances of a UN resolution had been exhausted. He telephoned Jonathan Powell on 12 March to warn him of his intention. The wooing operation – 'suicide watch', they called it – began in earnest. In a matter of hours he was contacted by Blair, Straw, Prescott and others to try to talk him out of it. Back in December, those who knew Cook well realised he was on the brink. Peter Hain once called Cook on the Friday before Christmas from his mobile as he was returning on the Eurostar from a trip to Brussels. Cook told him then he would hang on for a while.

In the first weeks of 2003 John Scarlett gave briefings to Cabinet ministers on the threat posed by Iraq. He ran through the same assessments as he gave Blair. Towards the end of February he received a special request from Cook. A few weeks earlier, during a parliamentary recess, he and his wife Gaynor went walking in the Norfolk Broads to discuss the future. Resignation was a strong option. They decided that before taking that step he should try to get more information about what had really been happening. He asked for a one-to-one with Scarlett. That was accepted. Scarlett went over to Cook's residence at Carlton Gardens to show him the intelligence. That briefing did nothing to allay Cook's fears that Blair's road to war hinged on flimsy evidence.

In his final weekend in the Cabinet Cook had asked to perform one final official function on behalf of the government. On 15 March he flew to Belgrade to represent Blair at the funeral of Serbia's reformist Prime Minister, Zoran Djindjic, who had been gunned down by assassins. Returning for a day as *de facto* Foreign Secretary, especially to the Balkans, was a poignant moment for Cook. He was accompanied there by Michael Williams, his special adviser, who had stayed on to work for Straw. Williams tried to talk him out of quitting, but realised quickly that his mind was made up. As soon as he returned to London, he began working on his resignation speech. That done, he appeared reconciled to life out of government, as he told friends: 'I may not have been able to make peace in the world, but I have made peace with myself.'

The same could also be said for Blair. When the Prime Minister saw Cook on 17 March, he appeared rueful but resilient. Cook then discussed the management of his resignation with Alastair

Campbell, with whom he had, surprisingly, got on quite well. A deal
was done. If Number 10 refrained from briefing against him, he
would avoid gratuitous attacks on Blair. If the spinners reverted to
type, all bets would be off.

Iraq produced possibly Cook's two finest moments in parliament. The first, in 1995, was his speech on the Scott Report into the
illegal sale of arms to Saddam under the Conservative government.
Cook had destroyed what flimsy defence John Major's front bench
had tried to put up. On the evening of 17 March 2003, Cook produced another *tour de force*. At his forensic and laconic best, he
ripped to shreds much of Blair's rationale for war. His points were at
times general: 'Why is it now so urgent that we should take action to
disarm a military capacity that has been there for twenty years and
which we helped to create?' At other times he was specific. He
pointed out that as Foreign Secretary, he had seen the intelligence
over the years. He knew what Blair knew. To gasps, he said: 'Iraq
probably has no weapons of mass destruction in the commonly
understood sense of the term – namely a credible device capable of
being delivered against a strategic city target. It probably still has
biological toxins and battlefield chemical munitions, but it has had
them since the 1980s.' Cook had always insisted that while they
might have some substances, they had not yet been weaponised. He
told Blair's aides time and again that he had been through the
'prodigious paperwork and had found nothing to conclude that
whatever Iraq might still have could be seen to pose an immediate
threat to the region, least of all to Britain'. The very term 'weapons of
mass destruction' was, he said, a misnomer, used deliberately to
enhance the case for war.

Cook was one of three ministers to resign in total on the eve of
war. The other two were John Denham, a Home Office minister
and rising star, and Lord Hunt, a junior health minister. Six parliamentary aides also left the government in protest. The total was
bad, but could have been much worse for Blair. Clare Short, after
being kept on and ruminating for a week, decided after that Cabinet

meeting, to hackles of criticism from left and right alike, to stay on. She argued that at least she could influence the plans for post-war reconstruction.

There was another minister who was deeply unhappy. Jack Straw had spent Christmas with his family mulling over the prospects for war. He was proud of Resolution 1441. He wanted the UN process to run its course. He wanted Blix to have time. He wanted the Labour Party to stay as united as possible.

Although disappointed by the Iraqi declaration of 7 December, although he spoke melodramatically of Saddam's finger on the trigger, he had seen no reason for haste. Straw told colleagues that just as Unscom had proved reasonably successful at containing Saddam in the 1990s, so Blix and Unmovic were trusted with doing the same. Concern grew at the FCO with the speed at which Bush and Blair seemed to be condemning the whole exercise within weeks of the inspectors arriving in Baghdad.

As 1441 was being negotiated, Straw began arguing the case to Blair that parliament needed to be at the heart of decision-making. In previous wars, a debate was held after the action had begun and a vote taken on the technical motion 'on the adjournment', rendering it virtually meaningless. That was the Prime Minister's way. The Foreign Secretary insisted that whatever the risks this time they should hold a debate and substantive vote ahead of time. Resistance in Downing Street was strong, particularly from Powell and Blair.

From September 2002 Blair had been talking openly, albeit intermittently, about regime change. Straw's emphasis was different. When asked by one colleague at that month's Labour conference if he was confident that Blair and Bush would see the UN process through, he replied: 'I'm working on it.' In an interview with the *New Statesman* on 18 November, he said: 'I will regard disarmament by peaceful means as an optimal result. I don't regard Saddam Hussein staying in place as optimal, but it is no part of this resolution to change the regime.' He described the regime as 'distasteful' and 'preposterous', but added: 'We are talking here about the limits of international collective action. It is legitimate for international collective action to deal with flagrant breaches of UN resolutions on disarmament. Regime change *per se* is rarely a lawful objective of international action.' So would he be reconciled to Saddam staying in office? 'Reconciled is the wrong word. Would I put up with the fact that he is there and that it would be inappropriate to use international assistance to remove him from office if he complies with the resolution? Yes.'

He liked to call it the 'Straw paradox'. Talk up the prospect of war with Iraq in order to try to avoid it.

As soon as he got back to work in January, he resolved to try to slow down the rush to war. 'Jack genuinely thought there was a possibility of avoiding conflict, and if it was not avoidable, he was not sure Britain should take part without a second resolution,' says one member of the government.

At the conference for British ambassadors in January 2003 Straw bumped into *The Times*'s political editor, Philip Webster. They got into conversation, and the following day the paper's front page quoted a 'senior minister' as saying that war was not inevitable, that if a bookmakers had before put it at 60:40 on, now it was 60:40 against. Over the weekend the media speculated about the identity of the source. On the Monday morning Straw confessed on the *Today* programme. This was, he said, 'a reasonably accurate description'. The response from Downing Street was tart. 'This is not William Hill's,' said a spokesman. Just to rub it in, Geoff Hoon took to the airwaves to say war was not an issue for betting on, adding, with Blair's authority: 'I don't believe that it helps to make these kinds of comments at this stage.' Straw did not regret it. 'Jack meant to say it,' says one government member. 'It was a matter of conscience for him. He was also much more mindful of the mood in the party than Tony Blair.' Straw privately told one ministerial colleague that Blair was 'obsessed' with the threat of WMD. In the ensuing months Straw would on several occasions express private reservations about the rush to war. His fears would culminate in the final weekend before the conflict.

As Blair returned from the Azores on 16 March, Straw decided to write him a 'personal minute', urging the Prime Minister to think about alternative strategies. He suggested that, without a second UN resolution, Britain might consider offering full political and moral support to the US. It would offer to deploy troops at the end of the war for peace enforcement. But this should stop short of full military engagement. This was not the first time Straw had put this option to Blair. In so doing he was reflecting a body of opinion inside the Foreign Office deeply concerned about the impending war. Straw was in little doubt that Blair had long before made up his mind, but he felt duty bound to say it. Jonathan Powell was shocked when told. Campbell was less cross.

'The reservations some people were expressing by this point were futile,' says one aide to Blair with barely disguised disdain for the professional diplomats. 'The military could not hang about. They were vulnerable to attack and battle-ready. These obvious factors were being overlooked by the FCO. They weren't carrying the responsibilities. They weren't taking any of the decisions.' Blair told Straw his eleventh-hour appeal was out of the question. He asked him to clarify whether or not he would support the war, now that it was definitely going to happen. Straw said he would. They agreed to put the issue behind them.

Having expressed his reservations and seen them rejected, Straw fell firmly into line, arguing the case for war with as much vigour as anyone else. When, after the war, he gave an interview to *The Times*, in which he said he had been ready to resign along with Blair if the government had been defeated in the final vote, it was interpreted as demonstrating how staunchly he had always been behind the policy. 'I was simply conscious of the fact that if it went wrong – if we did not get the support we needed in the Commons – he would almost certainly go and I would go with him. I did give it quite a bit of thought.' It could also be read in a more ambiguous way.

The day after his dignified resignation and his devastating speech, Cook was basking in the congratulations. Wherever he walked, MPs from all parties slapped him on the back and shook his hand. This new show of friendship towards a man often seen as prickly does not suggest he was spoiling for a fight. In fact, he had gone out of his way to avoid it, co-ordinating his decision to step down with Downing Street – so much so that he agreed to give his personal statement on the eve of Blair's speech. Had he made it minutes before Blair stood up, as was his right, he could have turned the Commons menacingly against the Prime Minister.

On the crucial debate, Blair received a vital piece of support from his close friend, the Attorney General, Lord Goldsmith. Lawyers had been debating for some time the legal status of a war in Iraq. Back in November, Matrix Chambers, the legal practice founded by Cherie Blair, prepared a legal opinion for CND. Its findings were unequivocal. The UK, it said, would be in breach of international law if it were to use force against Iraq without a further Security Council resolution. Resolution 1441 had been ambiguous and had not used the phrase 'all necessary means', the customary code for a threat of attack. But it had referred back to the relevant resolutions on the conflict – 678, which condemned the invasion of Kuwait and threatened war; and 687, which, on victory, provided for the deployment of the inspectors under Unscom.

At the Foreign Office, the legal advisers were edgy. The number two, Elizabeth Wilmhurst, a legal adviser for thirty years, showed her disagreement with the government line by resigning on the eve of war. She was not alone in her anxieties. Others kept their heads down. At the Ministry of Defence they were equally worried. 'We needed to know whether this was a legal operation,' recalls one senior official. 'We were all waiting for the Attorney General to give his verdict. We were certainly nervous.'

Later, Admiral Boyce, the Chief of the Defence Staff, would

concede that he too had been concerned about the legality. Boyce had not won over Blair in the way his predecessor, Guthrie, had. He had expressed misgivings about the Americans' approach to the war on terror. He worried about military overstretch, especially the commitment to fill in for striking firefighters. He was never scared to tell politicians the truth. On his retirement, after two years in the job rather than the more customary four, he warned that early British involvement in any new wars could not be achieved without 'serious pain' to the services. He also warned against Britain and America being seen as occupying powers. 'In 1991 we were liberating Kuwait. In the Falklands we relieved the Falkland islanders. I would have some difficulty saying the same thing for Iraq. If you are an Iraqi person, is that how you see it? We do not want to seem arrogant or patronising about the Iraqi people.'

Paradoxically, countries like France, which opposed the rush to war, were more exercised by its legitimacy than its legality. This was a grey area. Many wars deemed just by much of the international community, such as Kosovo, did not have specific UN authorisation.

For days rumours had been rife that Goldsmith himself had reservations about the war. Government ministers and Downing Street spokesmen denied this, saying he saw no legal impediment. Cook's resignation brought matters to a head. Such was the pressure on Blair that he and Goldsmith decided to break precedent and publish a summary of his legal findings. He argued that authority to use force existed from the combined effect of the three resolutions. These resolutions 'were adopted under Chapter VII of the UN Charter which allows the use of force for the express purpose of restoring international peace and security'. In his crucial passage he argued: 'A material breach of Resolution 687 revives the authority to use force under Resolution 678. In Resolution 1441 the Security Council determined that Iraq has been and remains in material breach of Resolution 687, because it has not fully complied with its obligations to disarm under that resolution.' His judgement provided a lifeline.

By the time Blair addressed the House of Commons the diplomatic endgame was over. Bush had gone on television the night before to announce a forty-eight-hour deadline for Saddam to leave Iraq. 'The tyrant will soon be gone. The day of your liberation will be near,' he declared. He called on Iraqi soldiers to give up their weapons.

At the UN, Jeremy Greenstock announced that nothing more would be placed before the Security Council. 'Having held further discussions with council members over the weekend and in the last few hours, we have had to conclude that council consensus will not be possible in line with Resolution 1441,' he said. 'One country in particular' – everyone knew who he meant – 'has underlined its intention to veto any ultimatum "no matter what the circumstance". That country rejected our proposed compromise before even the Iraqi government itself.' Greenstock was close to retiring after an illustrious diplomatic career. He confided to his friends that he had felt 'sick' about having to make that statement. He knew that the UN Security Council had not voted specifically for military action even though one of the justifications put forward for that action was to uphold the UN's credibility. Greenstock knew, as Blair and everyone around him knew, that the preceding months had been one of the most inglorious periods of recent British diplomatic history.

In Downing Street, Blair and his inner circle did not have time for such ruminating. Gordon Brown, Jack Straw, John Prescott, David Blunkett and others spent much of Tuesday 18 March camped out in their private rooms behind the Speaker's chair to meet wavering MPs. Several were 'invited' by Sally Morgan to see Blair himself. 'Tony will be very disappointed,' she told them. 'Now is not the time to undermine the Prime Minister.'

They had worked out a survival strategy for that day. Each wavering MP was put into a particular category. Each category contained a different argument that might appeal to them. Some were told this was about saving the integrity of the UN. Some were given the full moral case against Saddam, emphasising his human rights record. Some had the specific line on WMD. Some were asked if they really wanted to reward the perfidy of the French. Some were reminded of the domestic political implications, that the government could be in peril. Some were told their protest was futile. It was too late to bring the troops back now.

This was a case of different strokes for different dissenters. 'We tried to work out the misgivings of each individual,' says one senior official. 'This was a case of *à la carte* reassurance.' Was it particularly honest? 'It worked.' They left nothing to chance. Even ten minutes before the vote, they were still at it, each and every minister doing what they could, with whatever means were at their disposal.

Everyone was guessing. But the most important part of the Downing Street plan was to talk up their predictions of a possible defeat, to manage expectations for after. There was talk of 160 Labour rebels, 180, even 200. The hope was that any figure that fell short of that could be portrayed as a 'victory' for Blair. The atmosphere became more fevered when the Conservatives suggested that up to fifty of their own could defy their own party and vote against the war. 'We were all affected by a certain madness that night,' one Blair aide recalls.

Blair's speech that day was one of his most accomplished in parliament. He combined principle with determination with just a touch of humility. He repeatedly accused Saddam of failing to disclose full details of his weapons of mass destruction and said Britain must act. The future of the international order and his own leadership were at stake.

> This house wanted this decision. Well, it has it. In this dilemma, no choice is perfect, no cause ideal. But on this decision hangs the fate of many things. I will not be party to such a course. This is not the time to falter. This is the time for this house, not just this government or indeed this Prime Minister, but for this house to give a lead, to show that we will stand up for what we

know to be right, to show that we will confront the tyrannies
and dictatorships and terrorists who put our way of life at risk,
to show at the moment of decision that we have the courage to
do the right thing.

He went headlong into the most controversial aspect of his
road to war – his relationship with George W. Bush. 'Partners are not
servants, but neither are they rivals,' he told MPs. The next passage
was addressed to Europe, but Blair was actually talking about himself.

What Europe should have said last September to the United
States is this: 'We understand your strategic anxiety over
terrorism and weapons of mass destruction and we will help
you meet it. We will mean what we say in any UN resolution we
pass and will back it with action if Saddam fails to disarm
voluntarily.' However, in return Europe should have said: 'We
ask two things of you: that the US should indeed choose the UN
path and you should recognise the fundamental overriding
importance of restarting the Middle East peace process, which
we will hold you to.'

He was admitting that while he had pressed Bush to deal with
the Likudniks in Washington and Jerusalem, he had not pressed
him hard enough. It was a 'tragedy' that this had not happened.

I do not believe that there is any other issue with the same
power to reunite the world community than progress on the
issues of Israel and Palestine. Of course, there is cynicism about
recent announcements, but the United States is now
committed – and, I believe genuinely – to the road map for
peace . . . and that should be part of a larger global agenda: on
poverty and sustainable development; on democracy and
human rights; and on the good governance of nations.

This attempt to re-invent and re-interpret Blair's security doctrine of pre-emption and US primacy into something more palatable for the British centre-left was critical. So was the suggestion, all the way through, that the Prime Minister knew more about Saddam's arsenal than he was able to divulge. The threat, he insisted time and again, was real and growing, and the people would have to trust him. At the end of one of parliament's most highly charged and passionately argued debates for years, just enough Labour MPs gave Blair the benefit of the doubt. A rebel cross-party amendment, insisting the case for war had not yet been made, was defeated by 396 votes to 217. The 139 Labour rebels represented more than half the 264 'non-payroll' vote – those MPs who were not in government service. But in one of the most skilful sleights of hand by Alastair Campbell, this was trumpeted in the media as representing a victory for the Prime Minister. Needs must. He had survived. That was all that mattered.

Bush phoned Blair to congratulate him. To show its approval, the White House Office of Global Communications posted a section of his speech as its 'quote of the day'. In Downing Street the relief was palpable. That fortnight had been an unbearable dénouement to months of fraught politics and diplomacy. Now it was down to the military. With 170,000 coalition troops massed on the Kuwaiti border, all that remained was the command to go in. The following twenty-four hours gave a chance for the players to catch their breath, to leave the office early, to brace themselves for a war – a war that Blair had gone through contortions to justify.

15

LIBERATION NOT
OCCUPATION

IT WAS MID-AFTERNOON, WASHINGTON TIME, ON WED-
nesday 19 March. George Bush had called a meeting of his inner
Cabinet to put the final pieces in place for war. Operation Iraqi
Freedom was due to begin the following night. George Tenet, the
Director of the CIA, told the President they had a window of opportunity. Human intelligence had a rare fix on Saddam Hussein,
reporting that he was holed up in a bunker under a villa compound
in the southern suburbs of Baghdad with his two sons and three
other lieutenants. Bush mulled it over. His father had failed to get
him. It wasn't part of the early war plan, but it was worth a try. 'Let's
do it,' Bush said. The meeting broke up at 7:20 P.M. Forty minutes
later, as the deadline for Saddam to leave the country expired, Bush
gave the order. The first air-raid sirens were heard in Baghdad half
an hour later.

At a quarter past midnight, London time, David Manning
phoned Blair, waking him to tell him that strikes had been launched
to 'decapitate' the Iraqi leadership. Blair had been up, watching the
football highlights and catching up on his red boxes, enjoying the
brief calm. He switched to Sky and watched the sudden American

change of tactics materialise on TV, just like everyone else. Condoleezza Rice had phoned Manning and asked him to pass on the news. Blair had been informed, not consulted. Neither Manning nor Blair remembered to tell the press team. The first thing Tom Kelly knew about it was when a TV reporter woke him to tell him the war had started. His first reaction was that someone had confused the talk of air strikes with the no-fly zones over southern Iraq. He told himself to stay calm, and not to say it was supposed to be the following night. That was a state secret. He got out of bed and exchanged text messages frantically with the other spokesman, Godric Smith, and their boss, Campbell. Kelly and Smith had told the duty press officers it would be a quiet night. They had both briefed journalists that they could go home early that evening, nothing would happen.

Within minutes they cobbled together a statement, a testament to their inability to portray the government as on top of events. 'The Prime Minister was informed shortly after midnight that attacks on a limited number of command and control targets were being brought forward.' Bush, in a televised address, said strikes had been launched against the first 'targets of military opportunity'. Soon after, Iraqi state television broadcast a defiant message from Saddam. He was alive and would repulse the invader.

For all Blair's attempts, the so-called coalition was nothing more than the US and a few loyal allies. It bore little resemblance to the multinational force assembled by George Bush senior in 1991. For the first time since Vietnam, US forces were engaging in a big military conflict without the support of several of America's most important European allies. This time there was Britain, Spain, Italy, Poland and Australia. Counting in the likes of Eritrea, Albania, El Salvador and Ethiopia, the US State Department put the total at thirty. Kofi Annan, the UN Secretary-General, summed up the dismay felt in much of the international community: 'Perhaps if we had persevered a little longer, Iraq could yet have been disarmed peacefully or – if not – the world could have taken action to solve this problem by a collective decision, endowing it with greater legitimacy and therefore commanding wider support than is now the case.'

France and Russia were quick to condemn the air strikes. Blair was due in Brussels for an EU meeting, where he would have to confront Chirac only hours into the war. He considered not going, but decided that would suggest he was ducking a confrontation. Their handshake before the cameras was studiedly frosty. Dominique de Villepin had the previous day complained formally to Straw, saying he was 'shocked and saddened' by the anti-French rhetoric in the Commons debate. Chirac, with European public opinion firmly behind him, refused to commit France to economic aid to rebuild Iraq. He did, however, send a note of condolence about the first British soldiers killed in the conflict.

Before leaving, Blair recorded a TV address, admitting the deep divisions the war had produced, but urging the nation to rally round the troops. He knew how to do it – after all, this was his fifth war. But this one was unlike any other. He knew how many people had opposed it. He knew how much of it would now be out of his hands.

With an empty backdrop save a single lamp, a gaunt and greying Prime Minister announced that he had given orders for British forces to take part in military action. 'Britain has never been a nation to hide at the back,' he said. Then he repeated a message he had employed several times before, that Saddam posed a danger to each and every Briton. 'My judgement as Prime Minister is that this threat is real, growing and of an entirely different nature to any conventional threat to our security that Britain has faced before.' Those words 'real and growing' suggested that not only did Saddam have weapons of mass destruction but that he was on the verge of using them. British soldiers in Kuwait had gone through intensive training in dealing with chemical and biological weapons. The speed with which they donned their special kit would determine life or death.

For most, it was not a question of whether Saddam would deploy his WMD, but when.

The fighting began in earnest that night. Explosions were reported close to some of Saddam's royal palaces, the Ministry of Defence and the military airport. Royal Marines invaded the al-Faw peninsula, a short but important advance. The bombings, while heavy, did not resemble the 'shock and awe' tactics that had been widely predicted. The following day British troops secured key oil installations at al-Faw, meeting only light resistance. They also entered parts of the port of Umm Qasr. As the British set about securing the south, US forces were tasked with moving north. Some 200 Iraqi soldiers surrendered to the Americans only an hour after they had crossed the border. US and British Marines sped into the second city of Basra. The Pentagon said the first sorties had gone well but warned that 'several hundred' targets would be hit from the air the following night.

Blair and Geoff Hoon tried to avoid bullish predictions. Even though Saddam's forces had been considerably weakened since the 1991 war, planners at Central Command anticipated stiff resistance the further north the forces moved, if not from regular army units then from his special Republican Guard and Fedayeen militia. In the early days of the war Blair had to cope with a steady stream of British casualties from US 'friendly fire'.

Day four of the war, Sunday 23 March, saw the first heavy engagements. For the US it marked the worst day for casualties since American Special Forces' failed raid on Mogadishu ten years earlier. In fighting in and around the strategic town of Nasiriyah, a key crossing on the Euphrates river, ten US Marines were killed, fourteen were wounded and fourteen more, including two British soldiers, went missing. Iraqi TV showed five captured American prisoners being paraded, and footage of four American corpses. That was broadcast around the world by al-Jazeera. The station that had given them so much trouble in Afghanistan was doing the same in Iraq. Downing Street appealed to British television networks not to show it. In spite of the setbacks, US Central Command insisted the forces were 'on track' and would soon arrive in the vicinity of Baghdad.

Blair and Campbell knew that, even more than in previous wars, the media campaign was crucial. Campbell had dispatched his most trusted spokesmen from Whitehall to different parts of the world. He had revived the Coalition Information Centre. The twenty-four-hour media day would start in the field, move to London and end in Washington. Everything would be co-ordinated. The trouble was, the Americans concentrated almost exclusively on their own domestic audience – the one that needed the least convincing about the justification and success of the war. Such were the technological advances that broadcasters were now able to give real-time updates from the front. The Pentagon and Ministry of Defence sought to harness that by 'embedding' reporters with particular units. This was a new, high-risk venture. The idea was that the 'embeds' would give the vivid, microscopic accounts. The big picture would be set out in a prefabricated warehouse in the middle of the desert. That was Central Command, Centcom, at the Americans' forward military base at Camp as-Saliyah, Doha. It was from a press centre inside the tent, replete with a multi-million-dollar Hollywood-designed set, that the message was to be co-ordinated.

One of the most important propaganda tasks was to find the weapons of mass destruction that Blair in particular had cited as his main reason for war. On the difficult first Sunday Fox News, Rupert Murdoch's cable network in the US which scored huge ratings successes with its highly patriotic and partial take on events, reported a potential chemical weapons find at a 100-acre site near the town of Najaf. The story took off before the error was put down officially to a 'zealous over-interpretation of a briefing'. Several times in the war journalists at the front were briefed exaggerated versions of events, in order to bolster morale and encourage local forces to surrender. At one point British forces reported an uprising in Basra that turned out to be something far more limited.

Blair was already trying to manage expectations on that front.

At a Downing Street press conference on 25 March, day six of the war, he said he had no doubt Saddam's WMD would be found. But he qualified that by suggesting it might be discovered only after the war was over: 'The idea that we can suddenly discover this stuff is a lot more difficult in a country the size of Iraq, but of course once the regime is out, then there will be all sorts of people that will be willing to give us the information that we seek.'

He was asked whether he had not in recent weeks changed the pretext from disarming Iraq of its WMD to regime change.

> I think it is a good point and it is one we have wrestled with throughout, because we have had to operate within the context of international law and the demands of the UN, which were for the disarmament of Iraq of weapons of mass destruction. And the logic of that position has been somewhat uncomfortable, frankly, for me and for others – that if Saddam had voluntarily disarmed he could have remained in place . . . In one sense I feel more comfortable with the position now, where we are saying quite plainly to people the only way now to disarm him is to remove his regime.

Perhaps inadvertently, perhaps not, Blair had let his true wishes be known. In effect, he was admitting that the WMD allegations had been a device to secure a different aim – getting rid of Saddam. But he knew he could not have got that past his party.

Anti-war Labour MPs abided by the convention not to undermine the forces once the military campaign had begun. Opinion polls, as had been the case in Blair's previous wars, showed that much of the public was rallying behind the government. But among many, anger remained strong. Some 200,000 people took part in an anti-war rally in London. It was the largest wartime demonstration ever in Britain, but still a fraction of those who had taken part in February.

Blair knew that winning the war militarily would not be

enough to salvage his credibility. 'There are bound to be difficult days ahead, but the strategy and its timing are proceeding according to plan,' he told MPs. The mismatch between that message and the gloom-laden observations of armchair generals in the television studios was stark.

The next few days saw the low point in the military campaign. British forces met resistance in Umm Qasr, despite earlier reports that the port town had been taken. The anticipated pictures of grateful Iraqis, especially Shias around Basra, cheering their liberators did not materialise. Fierce sandstorms stopped the US advance north. Thousands of American soldiers were forced to hunker down in their positions around Nasiriyah, Najaf and Karbala, the closest units being about 100 miles south of Baghdad. American generals insisted that it was nothing more than a drawing of breath. They maintained that progress had been much quicker than expected and they needed supply vehicles to catch up.

Having lost patience with the UN ahead of the war, Blair was eager to get the multilateral institutions involved in the reconstruction of Iraq as quickly as possible. Blair had told his aides in January that he favoured a 'Kosovo' option for Iraq. US-led forces would take charge of security, while the UN would handle the civilian side. He had talked about it with Bush before the war, but found it hard to get him to focus.

Blair knew that his exhortations now counted for less. He had convinced the Americans to wait for him while he tried to stitch together a second resolution. They waited, and he failed to deliver. Domestically, however, it was important for him to get some movement from the White House, some gesture, even rhetorical, that it had not given up on the UN. There was a legal problem too. Clare Short had suggested privately and publicly that under international law the occupying powers would have no authority to run Iraq once the war was over. She persuaded Blair to ask Lord Goldsmith, the Attorney General, to pronounce on the matter at the War Cabinet.

Goldsmith had done the business on the eve of war. His advice that military action was lawful, even though a second UN resolution had not been secured, helped save Blair's leadership in those desperate days. The news Goldsmith brought the War Cabinet on the morning of 26 March was not what Blair wanted to hear. He knew it would cause problems. Once the presentation was over Blair did not invite questions. He swiftly moved the agenda on.

Later that day Goldsmith decided he had to put his thoughts into a confidential memorandum addressed to Blair and circulated to a small number of key Whitehall departments. The document made for striking reading. Goldsmith told Blair and his senior ministers that all American and British activity in Iraq from the end of the war, beyond the most essential maintenance of security, would be unlawful without specific authorisation from the UN. 'My view is that a further Security Council resolution is needed to authorise imposing reform and restructuring of Iraq and its government,' Goldsmith wrote.

He warned that the US-led organisation that was supposed to take over the temporary running of the country, the Office of Reconstruction and Humanitarian Aid (ORHA) would be unable to operate legally without formal UN endorsement. That meant everything from forming an interim Iraqi administration to the control of oil and the award of reconstruction contracts to US corporations would, under a British reading of the law, be invalid.

Citing the two main pillars of international law, the Geneva Convention of 1949 and The Hague Regulations of 1907, Goldsmith listed specifically the 'limitations placed on the authority of an Occupying Power'. These included attempts at 'wide-ranging reforms of governmental and administrative structures', 'any alterations in the status of public officials or judges' except in exceptional cases, changes to the penal laws and 'the imposition of major structural economic reforms'. Goldsmith went further. In his conclusion, he referred back to 678, the resolution that authorised the use of force against Saddam in 1990 – the one he maintained provided a legal mandate for both the first Gulf War and this year's war on

Iraq. Any military action must, the Attorney General said, therefore
be limited to what is necessary to achieve the objectives of that resolution, 'namely Iraqi disarmament'. He went on: 'The government
has concluded that the removal of the current Iraqi regime from
power is necessary to secure disarmament, but the longer the occupation of Iraq continues, and the more the tasks undertaken by an
interim administration depart from the main objective, the more
difficult it will be to justify the lawfulness of the occupation.'

Blair did not receive the advice at the last minute. This was at
the beginning of hostilities. Time and again at the War Cabinet and
in other meetings he was challenged by Short to tackle the issues
contained in Goldsmith's briefing. So concerned did senior officials
at the Foreign Office and Ministry of Defence become about the
legality of the reconstruction plans that they asked the Attorney
General to obtain some form of memorandum of understanding
with the Americans. Goldsmith tried, but was unable to convince the
office of his US counterpart to commit to any form of undertaking.

So highly charged was this judgement that Blair and Goldsmith
agreed to keep it confidential. As Blair left for Camp David later
that day, with the Attorney General's warning ringing in his ears, he
was determined to get Bush to focus on the reconstruction effort.
Only ten days earlier the two men had met in the Azores. That was
their final council of war. Blair now needed to move the discussion
on, to talk about reconstruction.

His problem was that everyone was talking about the 'week
one wobble', of 'quagmire', of a war that might last until Christmas.
On the plane to Washington, one journalist asked Kelly how they
were going to prepare for Armageddon in Baghdad. Pundits suggested Saddam had ordered his elite forces to retreat to the outskirts
of the capital, and then engage American forces in street combat, in
the hope that bloody images of dead soldiers, and the harvest of
Western bombs that had gone astray, would turn public opinion so
violently against the war that it had to be halted. Blair scoffed at
these predictions. He and his aides spoke of war symmetry. 'We'd

been through it before, in Kosovo, Afghanistan, when people said we'd got into trouble, only to have to eat their words a few days later,' recalls one of his entourage. 'We knew we'd just have to live through it.'

Bush welcomed Blair back to Camp David, a place more conducive to their intimate chats than the White House. 'America has learned a lot about Tony Blair over the last weeks. We've learned that he's a man of his word. We've learned that he's a man of courage, that he's a man of vision. And we're proud to have him as a friend,' the President said. Blair responded: 'I believe the alliance between the US and Britain has never been in better or stronger shape.' Blair was asked how long he was prepared to keep his forces in theatre, given that resistance appeared to be strengthening. In the split-second Blair had to prepare his answer, Bush interjected, 'However long it takes.' He added: 'Slowly but surely the grip of terror around the throats of the Iraqi people is being loosened.' The TV footage of dead, captured and executed troops might make the leaders angrier, but it would not make them flinch. Blair then accused Iraq of executing two British soldiers, whose bodies had been shown on al-Jazeera. 'If anyone needed any further evidence of the depravity of Saddam's regime, this atrocity provides it,' he said. So keen was he to use all available information to prove his case that Blair did not wait for military officials to check their original reports. The Ministry of Defence had to backtrack later on his behalf and apologise to the families.

The real business of that summit was done in their private sessions. Taking up their now customary seats on the veranda of Laurel Cabin, President and Prime Minister discussed reconstruction and the Middle East. They continued their chat over a four-mile walk on the mountain trails inside the security ring, deep inside the Catoctin mountains, accompanied only by their bodyguards. Blair later told his team he believed the conversation had had a profound effect. He had always believed Bush was more prepared to engage with multilateral institutions than he was given credit for. In all his meetings with Bush, Blair seized on any nugget of evidence to back up his claim. He felt the Americans would now agree to some form of UN presence in Iraq, although it fell far short of the prominent role he was under pressure to negotiate. For Blair, early and deep UN involvement would help bind the wounds caused by the road to war. He wanted a central role for the UN, partly on principle, partly as a political counterweight for failing to get a second resolution on the eve of war – and for legal reasons. For all the attempts to finesse the language with the Americans, he did not get very far.

They agreed to meet again later on in the war. As a show of solidarity, the Americans would come to the UK. Blair appreciated the seclusion that Camp David afforded. The most likely British alternative was Chequers, but that was small and also quite visible from the road. On the journey home Blair turned to Tom Kelly and asked him: 'Would Hillsborough be mad?' The Queen's official residence in County Down, with its manicured gardens and its opulent rooms, was also home to the Northern Ireland Secretary when in the province and increasingly was the venue for negotiations. Kelly, who had been brought to Downing Street after being head of media in Belfast, had to think on his feet and replied: 'Why not?' The decision was kept quiet until the agreement of the White House had been secured.

Later that day, Blair dropped in at the UN to see Kofi Annan, to talk about the role the UN could play, post-war. The first steps in a *rapprochement* were being made, with the Security Council preparing to pass a resolution restarting the oil-for-food programme, linking oil exports with humanitarian assistance. The real test would come with the endorsement of the American-led office for reconstruction, and that remained far off. The meeting with the Secretary-General was courteous but frosty. Annan said pointedly to Blair that the failure to gain a second resolution had not been the fault of Jeremy Greenstock. Britain's ambassador, he said, had 'played a weak hand well'.

*

At Centcom in Doha, the British minders were increasingly agitated by the Americans' media approach. For several days they had refused to give out any information at all. For the rest it was carefully choreographed with the US networks in mind. Before the war, the US Defense Department had co-operated closely with Hollywood. In 2001 Jerry Bruckheimer, the man behind *Black Hawk Down*, the blockbusting patriotic account of US soldiers rescuing their own in Somalia, had visited the Pentagon. Bruckheimer and fellow producer Bertram van Munster suggested *Profiles from the Front Line*, a primetime television series following US forces in Afghanistan. That aired just before the start of Operation Iraqi Freedom, ushering in a new genre of television 'faction'. So pleased was the Pentagon with this experiment that it tried to replicate it in the Iraqi war.

In the early hours of 2 April, correspondents in Doha were summoned from their beds to Centcom. They rushed in, thinking Saddam Hussein had been captured. The story they were told instead has entered American folklore. Private First Class Jessica Lynch, a nineteen-year-old clerk from West Virginia, was a member of a maintenance company that took a wrong turning just outside Nasiriyah and was ambushed. Nine of her comrades were killed. Iraqi soldiers took Lynch to the local hospital. She was held there for eight days. Releasing its five-minute film to the networks, the Pentagon claimed Lynch had stab and bullet wounds, that she had been slapped about on her hospital bed and interrogated. Just after midnight US Special Forces stormed the Nasiriyah hospital. Their 'daring' assault on enemy territory was captured by the military's own cameraman. They were said to have come under fire from inside and outside the building, but they made it to Lynch and whisked her away by helicopter. That was the message beamed back to viewers within hours of the rescue. That is what most Americans remember about it, or want to remember about it.

Doctors said she had no recollection of the episode and probably never would. 'Researchers' were called in to fill in the gaps. The doctors in Nasiriyah disputed vast chunks of the story. They said they provided the best treatment they could for Lynch in the midst of war. There was no sign of shooting, no bullets inside her body, no stab wounds, they say. At the same time the US forces knew that Saddam's Fedayeen had already left, so the show of helicopters and US military might was purely for domestic consumption. There was one more twist. Two days before the snatch squad arrived, the doctors had arranged to deliver Lynch to the Americans in an ambulance. The driver was instructed to go to the American checkpoint. When he approached it, the Americans opened fire. They fled just in time back to the hospital. The Americans had almost killed their prize catch. The Pentagon furiously denied those claims but refuse to hand over the unedited film.

The Lynch story entered the iconography of American war coverage. To some around Blair it was embarrassing to watch. The Americans' approach – to skim over the details, focusing instead on the broad message – was too much even for Campbell. The government's press chief in Doha, Simon Wren, sent Campbell a confidential five-page note to him complaining about the US media operation. Group Captain Al Lockwood, the British forces spokesman, was publicly scathing: 'In reality we had two different styles of news media management,' he said. 'I feel fortunate to have been part of the UK one.'

Part of the problem was American reluctance to acknowledge errors – civilian casualties caused by bombs falling on the wrong targets, the so-called collateral damage. In the second week of the war two bombs hit markets in Baghdad, killing dozens of people. Those events provided a propaganda coup for the Iraqis. They also pointed to an intensification of the bombing campaign, with B-52s increasingly in action from their base at RAF Fairford in Gloucestershire, bombing Republican Guard bunkers encircling the capital. Slowly but surely, as the weather improved again, coalition forces moved towards Baghdad. Resistance was sporadic. In a fierce battle outside Najaf, US forces killed as many as 700 Iraqi troops.

As March ended, the talk of quagmire had turned to showdown. On 3 April US troops from the 3rd Infantry Division – the spine of the operation – reached Saddam International airport, ten miles from Baghdad's city centre, after heavy overnight bombardment. US armour made a brief foray into a Baghdad suburb, with tanks crossing into the city limits for the first time. Two days later, forces loyal to Saddam appeared to lose control of much of Basra after columns of British troops poured in, destroying the Ba'ath party headquarters.

When Bush flew into Northern Ireland on 7 April, the atmosphere was entirely different from their previous meeting only ten days earlier. US forces were making their strongest push into Baghdad, capturing two presidential palaces. US Marines were pictured relaxing in the opulent surroundings. Resistance was surprisingly low. British troops walked into Basra and did not fire a single shot. There was no sign of militia loyal to Saddam. Colin Powell declared Washington would send a team to Iraq within days to begin looking at the establishment of an interim authority. 'By the time we got to Hillsborough the war had fast-forwarded,' recalls one of Blair's team. 'We were worrying about whether we could put people in quickly enough.'

These were two wartime leaders, modelling themselves on Winston Churchill and Franklin Roosevelt, planning the peace while prosecuting the war. They promised that their 'war of liberation, not of conquest' would restore Iraqi self-government as soon as possible. The three-stage approach they set out had the imprimatur of the Pentagon. Blair did manage to squeeze in the odd change, a reference to the 'vital' but unspecified role of the UN in the rebuilding of Iraq. In stage one, day-to-day life – utilities, infrastructure, medical care and so on – would be run by ORHA, while the US military would retain security control. The Pentagon was planning for a short military occupation, lasting around three months. Iraq would be divided into three regions. Stage two would see the formation of an Interim Iraqi Administration. This was the one area where the

Pentagon had thought ahead. In memoranda to the White House a week into the war, Rumsfeld had proposed that an interim government composed of Iraqi exiles under US tutelage should be installed in areas of the country under US control even before the war was won. Stage three would see a hand-over to representative government after elections. No timeframe was set. Blair suggested six months. Many thought that unnecessarily pessimistic.

Blair had his concerns about the Americans' post-war strategy, but as ever he trod gently with Bush. He told members of his inner circle his worries about the military doing post-conflict reconstruction. The idea of generals running countries, Blair suggested to one of his aides, was 'a bit dubious'. He was told by his military chiefs to be particularly concerned about the man Rumsfeld had appointed to be in charge of the show. Retired General Jay Garner was a Vietnam veteran who specialised in missile systems and during the first Gulf War supervised the deployment of Patriot missile batteries. He was closely associated with the neoconservatives, had close ties with conservative Israeli groups and was involved in formulating the National Missile Defence system. The Pentagon believed those provided him with the credentials to bring order and democracy to Iraq. The State Department was furious not only with the choice but with its exclusion from almost all of the important decisions about the reconstruction. The rivalry between State and the Pentagon had been so bitter for so long that Garner considered resigning even before the war had begun.

Another aspect of the reconstruction plans was particularly unsettling for Blair. Bush was showing no compunction in rewarding US firms close to his administration with contracts to rebuild Iraqi infrastructure. Top of the list were Halliburton, the world's largest oilfield services company, which Dick Cheney had once run and in which he continued to hold millions of shares in a blind trust, and Bechtel, which was close to the Pentagon. It was one thing for the Americans to freeze out the French and the Germans, but the supportive British were getting very small pickings. In the midst of the war UK companies lobbied Patricia Hewitt, the Trade and Industry Secretary, to ask her to ask the Americans at least for some sub-contracting. She tried, but the results were very limited. Where was the much-vaunted influence? No matter how much Blair argued to the contrary, it was hard for him to counter accusations made by many in the anti-war campaign that oil and money were major reasons for going to war.

The American planners portrayed a mixture of supreme confidence and woeful lack of preparation. Garner had gone to Kuwait awaiting his formal deployment to Iraq. He was joined there by about 200 experts in finance, media, government and law. These clean-cut eager young Americans, waiting in their beachside villas south of Kuwait City, were adherents of the Wolfowitz–Rumsfeld school of 'revolutionary transformation'. They believed that, with goodwill, they could resurrect Iraq in a matter of months. On his first venture into Iraq, a lightning visit just over the border to Umm Qasr, Garner declared: 'We're here to do a job of liberating them . . . We will do it as fast as we can, and once we've done it, we will turn everything over to them.' Rumsfeld, Wolfowitz and Cheney had also invested considerable hopes in Ahmed Chalabi and his Iraqi National Congress. Even before US forces had got close to Baghdad, the Pentagon had secretly airlifted Chalabi and 700 of his supporters into Nasiriyah.

Blair and Bush were convinced that, apart from a hard core of Ba'ath party loyalists and others who had done well by the regime, the establishment of order would lead to an outpouring of celebration and confidence among ordinary Iraqis. To press home their message, they broadcast speeches on a TV station, Towards Freedom, which was beamed into the country from a specially equipped Hercules aircraft. Blair's address began by seeking to reassure the Iraqi people that what had happened to them in 1991 – when those who rose up against Saddam were brutalised and tortured – would not happen again. 'I want to tell you that Saddam Hussein's regime is collapsing and that the years of brutality, repression and fear are coming to an end, that a new and better future beckons for the people of Iraq,' he said.

Even before the war was over, even as the reconstruction of Iraq was in its most rudimentary planning, the Bush administration was looking further afield. In a co-ordinated set of warnings, Colin Powell joined the hawks in opening a new front. Syria and Iran were in their sights. On successive days, Powell, Rumsfeld and Condoleezza Rice accused Syria of 'hostile acts' and of 'associating with the wrong people'. They were said variously to be developing their own weapons of mass destruction, delivering military equipment to Iraq, recruiting volunteers to fight there and possibly offering a secret escape group to members of Saddam's regime. The axis of evil, which had been dropped for a few months for a slightly more sophisticated approach, was back with a vengeance. Washington was speaking with one voice, and that voice was alien to a British government that laid so much emphasis, in the months after 9/11, on creating a new dialogue with Iran and Syria.

Only the previous December, Blair had ensured that Syria's President Bashar al-Assad was received by the Queen. It was the latest attempt at a charm offensive. Despite the haranguing he had received in Damascus in 2001, Blair had kept plugging away, convinced that engagement was more productive than confrontation. That approach appeared vindicated when the Syrians did what few thought possible and backed Resolution 1441, giving the US and Britain a unanimous vote in the Security Council. That was then. As soon as the Americans changed their rhetoric, the British started to talk of a 'new reality'. The war in Iraq meant the world had changed and the Americans' already low tolerance of regimes that defied their will had got even lower. Blair hurriedly despatched Mike O'Brien, Straw's junior minister, to Tehran and Damascus to deliver personally the message to behave. Just before the Iraqi war started, O'Brien had visited Damascus and told Assad: 'When the music stops don't be in the wrong place. The Americans will win. So will we. Saddam Hussein will be gone. It will be over relatively quickly.'

When O'Brien returned he reminded his host, who had publicly expressed his hope that the coalition forces would be defeated, that he 'was in the wrong place'.

Privately, Straw and O'Brien were distinctly uncomfortable with the language the US was using. The Foreign Office had been concerned about Syria possibly providing exile to Saddam and his people, but they had no indication that it had any chemical or biological weapons plans. They needed to check the status of the American threats. Straw phoned Colin Powell and told him, or rather asked him, 'There isn't going to be war.' One official recalls: 'The American military had their tails in the air. We needed to make sure that this was just rhetoric.' Blair would later tell MPs there were 'no plans whatsoever to invade Syria'. That was intended as reassurance.

As American forces made further inroads into Baghdad, as the expected street battles failed to materialise, and the apparatus of Saddam's dictatorship seemed to melt away overnight, Blair felt for the first time a sense of relief. But nagging away at the back of his mind was the realisation that, after twenty days of war, not a single trace of Saddam's chemical or biological weapons arsenal had been found. There had been several sightings, but these had turned out to be false alarms. The Prime Minister had begun each morning's meeting of the War Cabinet by asking John Scarlett for a verbal briefing. As the war progressed, Blair became more agitated at the lack of weapons hauls, and by the end would hurry that presentation along. Still, that frustration was more than offset by the news that was developing hour by hour.

In the afternoon of 9 April, one spot on al-Fardus Square would assume its place in history. US forces were greeted with cries of support and bunches of flowers as they moved in towards the Palestine hotel. In front of them a group of men scaled the statue of Saddam Hussein which dominates the square. They secured a noose around its neck in an attempt to pull it down. The Americans offered to help. It happened slowly at first, with the armoured vehicle pulling back gingerly. Then, as the crowd screamed its approval, the vehicle's engines roared and pulled the edifice down. The regime had broken, and this was the symbolic moment broadcast around the world. In his office, Blair watched transfixed. 'This is the moment,' he told his team. 'This is what it was all about.'

16

REPAIRING THE DAMAGE

EVERYONE WAS TALKING OF THE 'BAGHDAD BOUNCE'. TONY Blair had proved his doubters wrong. Saddam had been overthrown. Iraq was free. Now the Prime Minister was master of all he surveyed. His poll ratings shot up. His supporters urged him to use the surge in popularity to impose his will on his party and country, to introduce more radical reform of the public services and push Britain into the Euro.

As US forces consolidated their grip on Baghdad, other units mopped up remaining pockets of resistance to the north. First came Kirkuk, then Mosul, and finally, on 14 April, Saddam's home town of Tikrit. The coalition did not actually declare victory, but victory, it seemed, was theirs.

Blair tried to capitalise on his success. He needed to portray this as a victory for the forces of good. He needed to show that, for all the carping of his critics, he had 'done the right thing'. He chose his favourite outlet, the *Sun*, for an interview that he hoped would dictate the tone of the post-war assessments. He said he had reconciled himself to resigning if the vote had gone against him on 18 March. 'It was always possible that you could be in that situation.

But the point is that some people are going to die as a result of your decision. In the end, if you lose your premiership, well, you lose it. But at least you lose it on the basis of something that you believe in.' Such was the febrile nature of much media coverage that yesterday's horror stories about his grip on power became today's hagiographies. Other members of the Cabinet rushed on to the 'I would have resigned in solidarity' bandwagon. Yet nobody present at Cabinet meetings could subsequently recall any of the protagonists actually saying that to their colleagues.

Blair's entourage knew the bounce would not last, but they were determined to prolong it as much as they could. Their caution proved well founded. Media focus switched quickly from 'liberation' to 'anarchy'. Television pictures showed armed men roaming the streets, looting shops, presidential palaces and even hospitals. They then turned on private homes. Exhausted and battle-weary coalition forces appeared unwilling or unable to intervene. These were combat soldiers, not peacekeepers. Then came news that treasures from the Iraqi National Museum had been carted off in wheelbarrows.

Blair's earlier concerns about American planning of Iraq's reconstruction turned into alarm within days of the fall of Baghdad. ORHA struggled to organise the restoration of basic services such as water and electricity. Baghdad's streets were awash with sewage. Medical care collapsed. The Americans tried to redeploy some of Saddam's former police, but the weeding out of enforcers of the old regime from those who had just done their jobs – de-Ba'athification – was proving difficult. Tens of thousands of former state workers were not being paid. Anxiety grew in Washington and London that Jay Garner was not up to the job, nor were many of the officials working under him.

The problems demonstrated the fundamental flaw at the heart of Rumsfeld's strategy. It demonstrated America's prowess at winning wars and its ineptitude at securing the peace. Three weeks of so-called 'shock and awe', characterised by textbook performances of

high-tech weaponry, clever military strategy and soldierly professionalism, were followed by months in which America's civilian
administrators and hapless soldiers stumbled from one crisis to
another. Was it a matter of tactics? Had the US committed too light
a force, one that advanced more quickly than anyone had imagined
to Baghdad, but was too small to consolidate its position over such
a large country? Or was it something more basic? Where was the evidence, for all the interventions overseas, of American success at
creating democracies out of theocracies or dictatorships? What was
the source of the Pentagon's confidence in its plans for 'revolutionary transformation'?

The American forces were experiencing some success in one
area. While the whereabouts of Saddam himself were unknown,
others who featured on the Americans' most-wanted list of fifty-five
top officials were being picked up. The most high-profile was the
former Deputy Prime Minister, Tariq Aziz. Potentially more important were key figures behind Iraq's WMD programme.

Blair and his entourage were confident that at least one of these
would soon tell all. On 28 April, in his first post-war Downing Street
press conference, Blair warned his critics not to 'crow' about the
failure to find chemical or biological weapons: 'I would counsel
people not to be jumping around gleefully a little too early on this.
We have in place a very deliberate process where we are interviewing
people. We are assessing sites. We have looked at many of those, but
nothing like a majority of them. As I say every time I am asked, I
remain confident that they will be found.'

The war had left gaping wounds in the international institutions and
European alliances Blair had earlier nurtured so fastidiously. He
made overtures to France, Germany and Russia, but there was no
sense of contrition in the countries that had opposed war. Far from
it – Presidents Chirac and Putin and Chancellor Schröder believed
their opposition to Blair and Bush's 'rush to war' had been
vindicated.

On 29 April Blair received two rebuffs. In Brussels, France, Germany, Belgium and Luxembourg, the heart of 'old Europe', held a mini-summit in which they announced plans for a new European Security and Defence Union. Britain was pointedly not invited. That afternoon Blair was in Moscow, at the private residence of President Putin, urging Russia to bury its differences with the UK and US. Putin did nothing of the sort. Instead, he gave Blair a public dressing-down, not dissimilar to the one the Syrian president had given him eighteen months earlier. Putin said that with the war over, 'the role of the UN should be not only restored but strengthened'. With his guest standing at his side, he poured scorn on Blair's assertion that WMD would be found. 'We do not know whether perhaps Saddam is still hiding somewhere underground in a bunker sitting on cases containing weapons of mass destruction, and is preparing to blow the whole thing up, bringing down with him the lives of hundreds of thousands of people.'

A month after the war, with civil disturbances on the rise, political progress negligible and public services still in a desperate state, Blair became increasingly agitated about American maladministration in Iraq. He sent Mike O'Brien, his junior foreign minister, to Baghdad to provide a report from the ground. On his return, O'Brien recommended to Blair that Britain put in a big-hitting diplomat to try to help sort out the mess. It was decided to send John Sawers, formerly Blair's principal private secretary. Sawers was one of Blair's most seasoned diplomats and behind-the-scenes fixers. At the same time, Colin Powell was finally getting the message across to Bush that more needed to be done and that Garner was not the man to do it. They also agreed to send in a diplomat – something that in previous reconstruction operations would have been deemed obvious. Paul Bremer, a counter-terrorism expert with little on-the-ground experience of the Middle East, was an improvement on his predecessor. Water and electricity supplies did get better, only to be hampered by acts of sabotage by increasingly organised gangs, attacking power stations and other strategic points. Early in June

ORHA became the Coalition Provisional Authority. The rebranding was intended to signal a transition in the way the country would be run. But progress remained slow, and over the hot summer months the frustration of Iraqis grew.

Critics of the war, who had been on the back foot after such a speedy victory, became more vocal again. WMD had not been found. The international community remained fractured. The UN was sidelined. The Americans' reconstruction efforts had been found out. Blair was struggling to justify the reasons for war and the management of its aftermath.

On the morning of 12 May, Clare Short finally did what she failed to do two months earlier and resigned. She told MPs she had stayed in the government because she thought she could influence the reconstruction of Iraq. She concluded she could not, that Blair had stopped listening to her. She was not wrong. In those two months he had treated her with the usual courtesies, but he had in his mind already dismissed her. Downing Street did not seek to damp down speculation that in the impending reshuffle she would be cast out. Many on the left were equally dismissive of her. That afternoon, in a devastatingly personal speech, Short recovered part of the ground she had lost. 'The errors we are making over Iraq and other recent initiatives flow not from Labour's values but from the style and organisation of our government, which is undermining trust and straining party loyalty in a way that is completely unnecessary,' she said. While Blair's first term was characterised by spin, 'in the second term the problem is centralisation of power into the hands of a Prime Minister and an increasingly small number of advisers who make decisions in private without proper discussion'. She concluded: 'To the Prime Minister I would say that he has achieved great things since 1997 but paradoxically he is in danger of destroying his legacy as he becomes increasingly obsessed by his place in history.'

The damage to Blair was not as serious as it could have been. If Short had co-ordinated her departure with Cook before the war,

Blair would have been in some trouble. In any case, one of Short's main concerns, the legitimacy of the US-led reconstruction efforts, was on the point of being dealt with at the UN. The Security Council was finally preparing, after weeks of difficult negotiation, to pass a resolution endorsing the terms for an eventual transition back to a new era of Iraqi government.

Blair had sought three assurances from Bush during the war: that the reconstruction would be efficiently handled, something that did not transpire; that it would involve the UN to a degree, something that transpired only in a very small way after some time; and that he would finally address the Israeli–Palestinian issue. On this third point, he was successful.

During a lull in the Camp David summit in the first week of the war, Bush had sat down on his own with Jack Straw. The Foreign Secretary took a less generous view than the Prime Minister of the US administration's intentions towards the Middle East. After their brief chat, Straw told his aides that for the first time he believed Bush was serious. He said the President had made clear his anger at Palestinian suicide bombings and his contempt for Yasser Arafat. He said everyone liked getting votes, but the truth was that the Jewish vote traditionally went to the Democrats. 'In any event, I'm committed to it,' he said, referring to the road map. Ten days later, over dinner at Hillsborough with Blair, Condoleezza Rice and David Manning, Bush gave an unequivocal pledge. 'He told us, in a way we had not heard before from him, that he was deadly serious about the Middle East peace process,' recalls one official.

Three weeks after the capture of Baghdad, the road map was formally presented to Israeli and Palestinian delegations. The aim of the 2,000-page document was bold: 'A settlement, negotiated between the parties, will result in the emergence of an independent, democratic and viable Palestinian state living side by side in peace and security with Israel and its other neighbours.' This was to be achieved in three stages: an immediate end to Palestinian violence, including a statement affirming Israel's right to exist and a clampdown on all potential suicide bombers. That would be followed by comprehensive political reform of Palestinian institutions ahead of statehood. Israel would withdraw from Palestinian areas occupied since the start of the second *intifada* in September 2000, and would freeze all settlement activity. Officials from the quartet – the US, UN, EU and Russia – would monitor the process. By 2004 moves would be taken to create a Palestinian state with provisional borders. A permanent status agreement would be sought by 2005, dealing with the particularly sensitive questions of borders, the status of Jerusalem, refugees, and settlements.

After lobbying at each of his summits, Blair, it seemed, had played a major part in convincing Bush to do what he had vowed not to do – to get involved. Early in June Bush demonstrated his new-found commitment with two summits in two days, culminating in a meeting in the Jordanian resort of Aqaba with Ariel Sharon and Abu Mazen, the new Palestinian Prime Minister. For Bush this was a new departure, but now he had committed himself he was eager to ensure no backtracking. 'All here today now share a goal: the Holy Land must be shared between the state of Palestine and the state of Israel, living at peace with each other and with every nation of the Middle East,' he declared.

This was Bush's moment, but in Downing Street there was a mixture of elation and relief. Nobody was naïve enough to assume the process would go smoothly and that violence would cease. But still, Bush's approach to the Israeli–Palestinian problem – at the heart of so many grievances in the Middle East – went a little way to repairing the damage with Europe and the rest of the world.

The failure to find weapons of mass destruction in Iraq was raising ever more questions about the reasons for war. US intelligence identified 150 sites worth investigating. Within a fortnight of the end of the war they had searched half, and not one had produced a smoking gun. In early May, the US flew 2,000 more experts to Iraq. The Iraq Survey Group joined 600 scientists already there. Another forty sites were checked, and still there was nothing. After the false dawns during the war, when stories of WMD finds turned out to be illusory, it was with some caution that the Pentagon announced it had found a mobile biological weapons laboratory. Both Rumsfeld and Wolfowitz took cover, leaving it to an under-secretary to announce the find of a large trailer. But the official conceded there was no proof that it had actually been used to make biological weapons. His caution seemed justified.

The Joint Intelligence Committee gave regular updates to Blair on how that investigation was progressing, but the news was unhelpful. Not one of the Saddam loyalists on the Americans' deck of cards had yet cut a deal. They had all argued that Iraq had hidden nothing because it had nothing to hide. Blair would not, could not – did not – believe that. He became increasingly frustrated at the Americans' tactics, at their refusal to work out 'a proper system of incentives and immunities' for some of the captives in return for information.

The Conservatives, having staunchly supported the war, began to question Blair's good faith. They started tentatively. The more resonance their attacks had with the public, the sharper they became. They homed in on the question of trust. Iain Duncan Smith, the Tory leader, used the refrain: 'You can't believe a word he says.'

Blair was still convinced that WMD would be found. He repeated that message on 22 May, in his monthly press conference. After all the controversy, he was eager to give his foreign policy a more positive message. Campbell and Powell were working on Blair's first major multi-destination foreign trip since the war. The aim was to show him back in his old guise as the bridge between Europe and America, and as a liberator of grateful Iraqis. The five-country, six-day-long visit, reminiscent of his epic voyages in the autumn of 2001, was to take in Kuwait, Basra, Warsaw, St Petersburg and the French spa town of Evian, the venue for the annual G8 meeting. It would be a diplomatic tightrope, but Blair was looking forward to it.

No sooner had the Prime Minister arrived in Kuwait on 28

May than the rumblings about WMD burst to the fore. The first to revive the problem was Donald Rumsfeld. The debate in the US, while less highly charged, was also taking place. Congress had agreed to hold formal hearings into the quality and use of intelligence ahead of the war. Responding to the accusations, Rumsfeld tried to play down expectations that any chemical or biological weapons would ever be found. 'It's hard to find things in a country that's determined not to have you find them,' he said. Then, in one single devastating line, Rumsfeld seriously undermined Blair's case. 'It's also possible that they [the Iraqis] decided to destroy them prior to the conflict.' To compound Blair's difficulties, Wolfowitz also tried to make light of the problem. 'For bureaucratic reasons, we settled on one issue, weapons of mass destruction, because it was the one reason everyone could agree on,' he said. His remarks were not particularly different from Blair's admission at his press conference at the end of March that he had settled on WMD as a means, even though regime change had been his end. But the atmosphere had now changed.

On 29 May the *Today* programme's defence correspondent, Andrew Gilligan, broadcast a story that would have devastating consequences. Recruited from Sunday newspapers, Gilligan was an atypical BBC reporter – to his supporters, a risk-taker; to his detractors, someone who was driving down the corporation's reputation for careful impartiality. Gilligan told the programme that the government had 'sexed up' the dossier of September 2002 that had set out Saddam's WMD. 'I have spoken to a British official involved in the preparation of the dossier. He told me that, until the week before it was published, the draft produced by the intelligence services added little to what was already publicly known,' Gilligan reported. Using a voiceover, he then quoted what he said was a senior intelligence source who had been involved in the dossier's creation as saying: 'It was transformed in the week before it was published, to make it sexier.' The classic example was the suggestion in the document that Iraq was able to deploy chemical or biological weapons within forty-five minutes of an order to do so. This, the source claimed, 'was included in the dossier against our wishes, because it wasn't reliable'.

The report caused panic and fury among Blair's entourage. They were on the second leg of their trip. Blair was uncharacteristically quiet during his twenty-minute journey on an army Chinook helicopter as he flew over Iraq. Less than an hour earlier he had told British soldiers they had achieved a 'momentous and mighty' act of which the country could be proud. This was supposed to be the perfect picture opportunity, the perfect story – the Prime Minister meeting British troops in Basra to thank them for liberating Iraq from an evil dictator. As Blair was smiling for the cameras, Campbell was trying to manage a news story that was spiralling out of control. When they landed, Blair ignored reporters who asked him about it. By the time, however, they had moved on to Poland, after a five-hour flight, Campbell assessed that the damage was becoming so great they should go on the counter-attack. With an embarrassed Polish Prime Minister, Leszek Miller, standing by his side, Blair said angrily: 'The idea that we authorised or made our intelligence agencies invent some piece of evidence is completely absurd, and what is happening here is that people who have opposed this action throughout are now trying to find a fresh reason for saying why it wasn't the right thing to do.'

The story dogged them for the rest of the trip. Campbell and Tom Kelly worked the phones to try to kill the idea that the security services were at loggerheads with the government. The trouble was, as they were doing this, journalists were being briefed by those very agencies about their unhappiness at having to turn suppositions, the lifeblood of intelligence material, into facts that happened to support the government's position. Matters were not helped when John Reid, Blair's most pugnacious Cabinet minister, blamed the BBC story on 'rogue elements' within the intelligence services.

In the run-up to war, Blair had stressed Saddam's WMD at every turn. After the war, he tried desperately to will them away.

Gradually, Blair's inner circle revised their expectations. They remained confident that they would find something, but perhaps not very much – some missile parts, or some chemical agent – certainly not the amounts nor the delivery systems that were portrayed in the dossiers as presenting a real and growing threat. They claimed the search was no longer the top priority. But what about the fear that these weapons would get into the hands of terrorists, the post-9/11 link Bush, and to a lesser degree Blair, had made when talking up the danger?

'I thought they had the intelligence on WMD, but it was never conclusive,' one senior aide to Blair admitted in May. 'There was always an element of hope involved. In the end we sought support on the basis of the nature of the regime and what it had.' Another senior Downing Street official offered the following: 'The Prime Minister always knew it would be very difficult to find biological weapons. We were never looking for bulk. On chemical weapons we thought we would find munitions. We now know that the destruction and concealment had been better than anticipated. We're prepared for months of embarrassment. But gradually we will unwrap the onion.' He then added, with an intriguing first hint of doubt: 'Our intelligence was absolutely clear. I don't think it was an invention.' Then came this from a senior figure in the Foreign Office: 'When you're dealing with intelligence, you can't pretend to be a lawyer, to prove something beyond reasonable doubt. You have to rely on these people, who have seen all the pictures in the jigsaw. We listened to the advice. We are told now it is going to take more time to find WMD. We were sure he had WMD all the way through. We are still sure. Saddam Hussein's whole behaviour led us inexorably to the fact that he had WMD.' His *behaviour* led them to believe . . . the supposedly rock-solid intelligence had been reduced to cod-psychology, to an analysis of Saddam's past.

Blair bowed to the growing pressure and announced that the Intelligence and Security Committee would investigate the whole issue. That committee operates in secret. In its annual report, issued on 10 June, it said Cabinet ministers had been badly informed and 'not sufficiently engaged' in intelligence matters. It criticised Campbell and his role in February's 'dodgy dossier', saying that 'although the document did contain some intelligence-derived material it was not clearly attributed or highlighted among the other material, nor was it checked with the agency providing the intelligence or cleared by the JIC prior to publication'. In other words, Downing Street had played fast and loose. The report, which made it clear that its criticisms were based on evidence it had taken from Richard Dearlove, the head of the SIS, said it supported the 'responsible use of intelligence to inform the public', but added: 'It is imperative that the agencies are consulted before any of their material is published.' It was evident from those findings that the intelligence services would in future not allow Downing Street to use their material in such a cavalier and haphazard way.

At the same time as that report came out, the Foreign Affairs Committee of the House of Commons began an inquiry of its own. Devoid of statutory authority to summon witnesses or order intelligence papers, this investigation was always going to be rushed, selective and incomplete. Blair had refused a full public inquiry.

The committee heard from Gilligan, the journalist, from various academics and former civil servants, from Straw, and then, on the same day, 17 June, from Cook and Short. The former ministers offered a searing indictment of the government. Cook provided the forensic analysis of the strength of the intelligence. Short gave a telling insight into the workings of Blair's inner circle.

Cook said it was a 'grievous error' to go to war on the basis that Iraq posed a 'current and serious threat', as that judgement had proved to be untrue. Iraq, he noted, was an 'appallingly difficult intelligence target' as there was no hope of putting in any Western agents and there were few leaks from Saddam's regime. He said he was 'disappointed' by the quality of the information in the September document as it did not provide 'any recent and alarming' intelligence to suggest that Iraq was a current and serious threat. He did not reveal that his one-to-one briefing from Scarlett in February had reinforced his view. As Foreign Secretary for four years, including Operation Desert Fox, Cook had seen all the intelligence Blair saw.

Cook restated the argument he made during his resignation speech in March that had so galvanised the House of Commons, that Iraq probably had no weapons of mass destruction.

> Such weapons require substantial industrial plant and a large workforce. It is inconceivable that both could have been kept concealed for the two months we have been in occupation of Iraq. I have never ruled out the possibility that we may unearth some old stock of biological toxins or chemical agents, and it is possible that we may yet find some battlefield shells. Nevertheless, this would not constitute weapons of mass destruction and would not justify the claim before the war that Iraq posed what the Prime Minister described as a 'current and serious threat'.

Cook then delivered this assessment of Blair's motivation for talking up WMD. He did not doubt Blair's 'good faith' in arguing his case over Iraq: 'If anything, I think the problem was the burning sincerity and firm conviction of those involved in the exercise.' Such was the ardour with which they were fighting their corner that they saw no reason to allow detail to hinder them.

Short was more blunt. She accused Blair of a series of 'half-truths, exaggerations and reassurances that weren't the case'. She had reached the 'sad conclusion' that Blair had misled parliament. Had he deceived parliament and the country? She preferred to call it 'honourable deception'.

A week later it was the turn of Campbell. He had initially refused to appear, but decided that at the risk of turning himself into the story he had to rebut each and every charge. His cause was not helped by Straw, who the day before had told the committee that the dodgy dossier had been an embarrassment, a 'complete Horlicks'. In an attempt to insert humour and a touch of menace, the committee chairman, Donald Anderson, welcomed him 'to what some might see as the lions' den'. He noted that one newspaper headline spoke of 'Campbell in the soup'. Campbell was not amused. He began defensively, giving an almost-apology for the dodgy dossier. He gave details of the meetings he had chaired with the JIC ahead of publication of the September document, but denied that he had applied any pressure to intelligence chiefs. 'The idea that you do that glibly or that you try and sex up a dossier as a way of trying to persuade the public that we should do it . . . I know scepticism is fine . . . but are we really so cynical that we think the Prime Minister, any Prime Minister, is going to make prior decisions to send British forces into conflict and wouldn't rather avoid doing that.' He went from defence to attack, denouncing Gilligan's story and turning it into a full-scale condemnation of standards at the BBC. 'If that is BBC journalism, then, you know, God help them.'

This was the culmination of years of pent-up fury from Campbell towards political journalism in general, and the BBC in particular. The feeling was mutual, with executives at the corporation attacking him for what they said was a long pattern of bullying and intimidation. The rest of the media revelled in the battle.

The mood in Downing Street had turned to frustration and righteous indignation. Blair was convinced that his actions were being traduced by a cynical media, and that permeated throughout his team. He insisted he had done 'the right thing'. It was a phrase he used time and again.

The security situation in Iraq deteriorated over the summer. Guerrilla operations by pro-Ba'athist elements against American forces in Sunni areas to the north and west of Baghdad were becoming more brazen and more successful. The individual hit-and-run attacks of the first weeks after the war turned into daylight ambushes on heavily armoured convoys. The British, controlling the mainly

Shia areas to the south, prided themselves on their non-confrontational approach. Instead of helmets, they wore berets. They were not using full combat gear or body armour. They chose where possible to patrol on foot. On 24 June six soldiers were killed in the village of Majar-al-Kabir – the heaviest combat casualties on one day since the Gulf War twelve years earlier.

The appetite in Downing Street for intervention was disappearing fast. In Washington, Congress was also investigating the riddle of the missing WMD, but Bush was gearing up for his re-election campaign and saw no reason to be bashful. The debate, driven by the neoconservatives, was: where next? Having threatened Syria towards the end of the war, the administration turned its sights towards Iran, officially still part of the 'axis of evil'. At one point the State Department was contemplating restoring diplomatic links twenty years after the Islamic revolution and the hostage crisis that destroyed Jimmy Carter. Colin Powell said policy had not hardened, but again it seemed he had been wrong-footed by the Pentagon. Rumsfeld said it was 'a fact' that al-Qaeda terrorists were living in Iran and were being allowed to operate there. Iranian sponsorship of extreme Shi'ite clerics in the new Iraq was another problem. The main cause for concern, and pretext for possible action, was Iran's alleged nuclear weapons programme. The US claimed it had evidence that the Iranians were working on plans to produce their own nuclear deterrent. They treated with great scepticism Iranian assertions that construction of a reactor in the port of Bushehr constituted nothing more than a civil energy programme.

Blair strongly backed the idea of tough monitoring of Iran's nuclear potential. Bush was eager to support anti-government protests in Tehran, calling them 'the beginnings of people expressing themselves toward a free Iran'. Blair followed suit. But at the Foreign Office, there was growing unease. Straw was so alarmed that he felt emboldened to criticise the American position: 'Given the long history of Iran, they have to be allowed to sort out their opposition internally. The thing that would most derail the establishment of better democracy in Iran would be suggestions that the opposition there was being orchestrated from the outside, which happily so far it has not been.'

On 7 July, the Foreign Affairs Committee delivered its report. Its investigation had been haphazard, incomplete and at times unprofessional. The findings were either hedged or contested among its members. Anderson concluded that 'the jury is out' on the main question of whether the government had exaggerated Saddam's chemical and biological threat. Anderson used his casting vote to exonerate Campbell, noting that he 'did not exert or seek to exert improper influence on the drafting of the September dossier'. On several other areas he was forced to intervene, with the committee split broadly along party lines. It did, however, unanimously denounce Campbell for the dodgy February dossier, calling it 'badly handled and counter-productive'. The MPs criticised the government for not putting senior intelligence officials forward. It gave ministers two months to answer a series of further questions on the thrust of the September document, the forty-five-minute claim, the Niger assertion, and the status of Iraqi missiles.

Both sides – the government and the BBC – found enough in the report to support their position. Hopes that both sides would draw a line under the row quickly disappeared, however, as both Gilligan's original report and Campbell's response were dissected. Campbell and Blair were desperate to expose Gilligan's source and discredit the story. Inside the Ministry of Defence all contacts with journalists were probed by intelligence officers. On 9 July Geoff Hoon wrote to Gavyn Davies, the BBC Chairman, naming the source as Dr David Kelly, a microbiologist who had been scientific adviser to the MoD's proliferation and arms control secretariat for more than three years. Kelly had been a UN weapons inspector in Iraq throughout the 1990s, visiting it thirty-seven times. He was sufficiently well-respected to have been nominated for a Nobel Peace Prize by the head of Unscom, Rolf Ekeus. Kelly was at Straw's side when the Foreign Secretary had appeared before the committee the previous September. He was due to return to Iraq to help the government in its increasingly desperate task of finding WMD. This was no rebel, no loose cannon. This was no low-grade spin-doctor.

On 10 July, Dr Kelly was summoned to appear before the Foreign Affairs Committee, which had taken the unprecedented decision to continue its report on an ad hoc basis. He had volunteered to his line managers that he had met Gilligan – he had seen nothing untoward in briefing journalists on largely technical issues. On 15 July, Kelly appeared before the MPs. His voice at times inaudible, he seemed to struggle with the questions. He confirmed the general impression of discomfort at the politicisation of intelligence and scientific advice to ministers. He estimated the probability that Iraq had chemical or biological weapons to be no more than '30 per cent'. But he suggested it was unlikely that he had been Gilligan's sole source. His inquisitors put his reticence down to the natural reserve of a civil servant.

The BBC still refused to confirm that Kelly was the source. The recriminations grew more intense. Campbell was a man possessed. Senior BBC executives fought back, leaving many in the corporation worried about the whole strategy. On 17 July, on the last day of the parliamentary year, Gilligan was recalled to a private hearing of the committee. The MPs wanted to know that if Kelly was not the source, who was? Anderson emerged from the meeting calling Gilligan an 'unsatisfactory witness'. As they were meeting, Kelly left his Oxfordshire home telling his wife that he was going for a walk.

The more pressure he was under, the more Blair relied on his inner circle. But he was about to lose his most steadying influence. David Manning, his demure foreign policy adviser, was leaving for Washington to become British ambassador. That was the pinnacle of the diplomatic career, but it would take him away from the heart of power. In July the great and the good of the diplomatic, military and

political world assembled in Downing Street for Manning's farewell.
He praised his Prime Minister for his resolve and steadfastness. He
was the first among world leaders, he said, to understand the signif-
icance of 9/11 and its effect on the US and the world order. Blair said
simply that he was 'desperately, terribly grateful'. This was, he said, a
'master–pupil relationship'. The diplomat had taught the Prime
Minister.

Manning had one more task – to accompany Blair on a week-
long trip that would take in Washington and a tour of the Far East.
This had been planned for some weeks, but there was less enthusiasm for it now. Relations with Washington had soured. The Bush
administration, which had cited British intelligence claims when it
needed them, was rapidly dissociating itself from the nuclear assertions. A former US ambassador, Joseph Wilson, who had been sent
to Niger by Cheney's office in February 2002 to investigate them,
made it clear he had reported back at the time that none of the evidence stood up. His warnings were ignored. The White House
declared it should not have relied on the British. George Tenet, the
Director of the CIA, agreed to take the flak. But, far from exaggerat-
ing any threat, the CIA had fought a lonely battle in Washington –
and often with London – to tone down some of the claims. One
senior official, Gregory Thielman, a former director in the State
Department's bureau of intelligence, said the Bush administration
had a 'faith-based intelligence attitude – we know the answers, give
us the intelligence to support those answers'.

The same could have been said of Blair's entourage in its rush
to war.

The irony about the BBC row was that Gilligan's allegation
was largely peripheral to the real problem. This had been an insti-
tutional failure, from the intelligence chiefs to Downing Street. This
was not about one or two dossiers, or the orders of particular spin-
doctors. It was about the case for war as presented from the very
beginning by Blair. The most telling comment from the Foreign
Affairs Committee came from its most experienced member, the

former Conservative defence minister, Sir John Stanley. He recalled that never before had a British government gone to war 'specifically on the strength of intelligence assessments' – assessments which, as is now clear, were fundamentally flawed.

Of the nine main conclusions in the September document – the document cited as the most comprehensive guide to the Iraqi threat – by August 2003 not one had been proven. These were that:

1) Iraq has a usable chemical and biological weapons capability which has included recent production of chemical and biological agents.
2) Saddam continues to attach great importance to the possession of weapons of mass destruction and ballistic missiles [and] is determined to retain these capabilities.
3) Iraq can deliver chemical and biological agents using an extensive range of shells, bombs, sprayers and missiles.
4) Iraq continues to work on developing nuclear weapons . . . Uranium has been sought from Africa.
5) Iraq possesses extended-range versions of the Scud ballistic missile.
6) Iraq's current military planning specifically envisages the use of chemical and biological weapons.
7) The Iraqi military are able to deploy these weapons (chemical and biological) within forty-five minutes of a decision to do so.
8) Iraq . . . is already taking steps to conceal and disperse sensitive equipment.
9) Iraq's chemical, biological, nuclear and ballistic missile programmes are well funded.

*

For all the sniping about intelligence, Blair received the kind of welcome in Congress that had long since deserted him back home. This was only the fourth British Prime Minister to be given the honour of addressing both houses. After the first of nineteen standing ovations, he joked: 'This is more than I deserve and more than I'm used to, frankly.' He had a message for Bush and for the American people. The US really was the beacon for the rest of the world to follow, but it should take heed of others just a little more. 'There never has been a time when the power of America was so necessary or so misunderstood,' he declared. 'Even in all our might, we are taught humility. In the end it is not our power alone that will defeat this evil. Our ultimate weapon is not our guns, but our beliefs.'

Then came the closest to a *mea culpa* that he could muster. Blair had in previous days been laying the ground for an admission that chemical and biological weapons might never been found. He had taken to talking only of evidence of WMD 'programmes' rather than the weapons themselves. He told Congress: 'Can we be sure that terrorism and WMD will join together? Let us say one thing. If we are wrong, we will have destroyed a threat that, at its least, is responsible for inhuman carnage and suffering. That is something I am confident history will forgive.'

As the Prime Minister was luxuriating in the praise that only America could afford him, the body of Dr David Kelly was lying in an Oxfordshire ditch.

Dr Kelly had told his wife he was going out for a walk. He would not return. The police concluded he had taken his own life. Friends and family said they knew how upset he was about the controversy, particularly the tone of his questioning by the Foreign Affairs Committee, but nobody had any idea it would come to this. Blair was told of Kelly's apparent suicide as he was flying from the US to the Far East. He knew from that moment the fate of his premiership was in the balance. He called for a period of reflection, to allow the official inquiry he had set up under Lord Hutton, an eminent law lord, to take its course. Nobody was listening, including his own officials.

Attention turned to the future of Alastair Campbell. He let it be known that this time he wanted out, but not before he had won his battle with the BBC. Geoff Hoon appeared the most vulnerable as the Ministry of Defence was forced to admit that it had encouraged selected journalists to focus on Dr Kelly as the source of Gilligan's story. Two days after the body was formally identified, the BBC acknowledged that Kelly had indeed been the person Gilligan had spoken to. As the two sides engaged prominent lawyers to put their case to Hutton, Blair made it clear he wanted the inquiry to confine itself to the specific circumstances of Dr Kelly's death and not to look at the bigger question of how he took Britain to a war against Iraq on the basis of intelligence that was flawed from the start.

How had it all gone so wrong? The missionary Blair, the man who had travelled light in opposition, who had known little of the world, had convinced himself that he, the Prime Minister, could change that world. Blair had acquired a passion for military intervention without precedent in modern British political history and without parallel internationally. Five wars in six years was a remarkable record.

Each had its own dynamic and justification. Desert Fox, Blair's first tentative foray into military action, was a brief but sharp warning to Saddam Hussein not to impede the work of UN weapons inspectors. Blair had shown his credentials as a tough leader, but the air strikes achieved little. In fact, by ensuring that the inspectors could not return, the action had set back the disarmament process. But it was over so quickly that it had little political or diplomatic impact. Kosovo, while militarily flawed, did see the end of Serb ethnic cleansing and started the process that led to the removal and trial of Slobodan Milošević. This was the high point of Blair's humanitarian intervention. Sierra Leone started out as a small mission to rescue captured peacekeepers and turned into a longer operation to rout brutal rebels. It evoked some fears of a British colonial burden, but was widely endorsed internationally. Afghanistan did not bring about peace and stability in that troubled country. It did not see the capture of Osama bin Laden or Mullah Omar, but the medieval Taleban regime was routed and, after the terrible events of September 11 in the US, al-Qaeda was dealt a setback.

Each of those actions had its critics at home and abroad. But with each war, Blair's confidence grew. He tried to build around them a worldview, harnessing the debate that was going on about using force for moral ends.

It was only when George W. Bush and the neoconservatives around him saw in the new global dangers the need to assert a doctrine of pre-emption and US primacy that Blair's troubles began, and his philosophy started to unravel.

From that point, for all the confident rhetoric, he was always on the defensive. Each time he saw Bush he hoped he had left a mark. Sometimes he did. Much of the time he did not. He would call the Americans 'Britain's best friends but most difficult allies'. His self-styled role as a bridge between Europe and America turned into an attempt to reconcile two seemingly irreconcilable approaches – the need to preserve multilateralism, consensus and the rule of law versus the need to impose a world order dictated by Washington and driven by a simple but ardently held view of right and wrong. The incompatibility of the two outlooks was provocatively argued by the conservative academic Robert Kagan, who said from the start of the Iraq crisis that it was time to stop pretending that Europeans and Americans shared a common view of the world.

The British Prime Minister refused to accept this, but when forced to, he chose one position over the other. 'Tony's default position is to go with the Americans,' says a senior adviser who has worked with him closely. 'To get him to do otherwise you have to make a special case.' Even some in Washington recognised the flaws in the approach. Sidney Blumenthal, Bill Clinton's close adviser, warned in April 2002: 'Blair's influence elsewhere is at risk if he lets an unrealistic idea of his relationship with Bush take hold.' From the day power changed at the White House, Blair was determined to show that he could work with a Republican President. He locked himself on to a course from which he could not deviate.

He thought he could handle all the intricacies of diplomacy, but he could not. He thought his powers of persuasion could overcome all obstacles, but they could not. He was both optimist, about his ability to change the world, and pessimist, about his ability to forge a new order that was not in the shadow of the Americans.

Blair paid the price for a failure of diplomacy. It was Britain's failure, but not Britain's alone. Iraq damaged him deeply. He had cultivated a position at the heart of Europe, only to see it undermined. He had dominated his party for a decade, his authority allowing him to push through foreign and domestic policies even when they were at odds with his MPs and activists – even members of his own Cabinet. For the first time, opinion polls were showing that his personal popularity had dropped below that of his party.

So why did he do it? His was a combination of self-confidence and fear, of Atlanticism, evangelism, Gladstonian idealism, pursued when necessary through murky means. His was a combination of naïvety and hubris. These were not his government's wars, least of all his party's wars. These were Blair's wars.

BIBLIOGRAPHY

Ashdown, Paddy, *The Ashdown Diaries: Volume Two, 1997–99* (London: Penguin, 2002)

Clark, Wesley, *Waging Modern War* (New York: Public Affairs, 2001)

Corbin, Jane, *The Base: Al-Qaeda and the Changing Face of Global Terror* (London: Simon & Schuster, 2002)

Frum, David, *The Right Man: The Surprise Presidency of George W. Bush* (New York: Random House, 2003)

Hutton, Will, *The World We're In* (London: Abacus, 2003)

Ignatieff, Michael, *Empire Lite: Nation-building in Bosnia, Kosovo and Afghanistan* (London: Vintage, 2003)

Judah, Tim, *Kosovo: War and Revenge* (New Haven, CT: Yale Nota Bene, 2002)

Kagan, Robert, *Paradise and Power: America and Europe in the New World Order* (London: Atlantic, 2003)

Kampfner, John, *Robin Cook: The Biography* (London: Phoenix, 1999)

Kaplan, Robert, *Warrior Politics* (London: Vintage, 2003)

Lind, Michael, *Made in Texas: George W. Bush and the Southern Takeover of American Politics* (New York: Basic, 2003)

Little, Richard and Mark Wickham-Jones (eds), *New Labour's Foreign Policy* (Manchester: MUP, 2000)

Ramesh, Randeep (ed.), *The War We Could Not Stop* (London: Faber & Faber, 2003)

Rawnsley, Andrew, *Servants of the People: The Inside Story of New Labour* (London: Hamish Hamilton, 2000)

Rentoul, John, *Tony Blair: Prime Minister* (London: Time Warner, 2001)

Seldon, Anthony, *The Blair Effect* (London: Little, Brown, 2001)

Simms, Brendan, *Unfinest Hour* (London: Penguin, 2002)

Woodward, Bob, *Bush at War* (London: Simon & Schuster, 2002)

Young, Hugo, *Supping With the Devils: Political Journalism* (London: Atlantic, 2003)

INDEX